The Task of Theology

The Task of Theology

*Leading Theologians
on the Most Compelling Questions
for Today*

Edited by
ANSELM K. MIN

ORBIS BOOKS

Maryknoll, New York 10545

ORBIS BOOKS
Maryknoll, New York 10545

Fathers and Brothers
MARYKNOLL™

Founded in 1970, Orbis Books endeavors to publish works that enlighten the mind, nourish the spirit, and challenge the conscience. The publishing arm of the Maryknoll Fathers and Brothers, Orbis seeks to explore the global dimensions of the Christian faith and mission, to invite dialogue with diverse cultures and religious traditions, and to serve the cause of reconciliation and peace. The books published reflect the views of their authors and do not represent the official position of the Maryknoll Society. To learn more about Maryknoll and Orbis Books, please visit our website at www.maryknollsociety.org.

Library of Congress Cataloging-in-Publication Data

The task of theology : leading theologians on the most compelling questions for today / edited by Anselm K. Min.
    pages cm
  Includes bibliographical references and index.
  ISBN 978-1-62698-105-8 (pbk.)
  1. Theology. 2. Christianity—21st century. I. Min, Anselm Kyongsuk, 1940– editor.
BR118.T37 2014
230.01—dc23

                           2014017031

Contents

Introduction

Whither Contemporary Theology?

Anselm K. Min

Contemporary Christian theology, like contemporary Christianity, is very much in disarray. It is fragmented, confused, unsure of itself, and certainly greatly challenged by the crises of the contemporary world. It cries out for some kind of sorting out, some kind of self-clarification, some kind of radical thinking through itself. As a way of bringing clarity, vitality, and urgency to the situation of contemporary theology, I organized a national conference at Claremont Graduate University, Claremont, California, held on April 20–21, 2012. We invited eight outstanding theologians representing a broad spectrum of Christianity to address the question, What is the most compelling theological issue today? This topic was deliberately framed in the form of an open question, leaving it up to each participant not only to answer the question in his or her own way but also to define the criteria by which each considers a certain issue to be the most compelling issue facing Christianity.

The question prompted eight very different answers, eight different perspectives on the challenges to which contemporary Christian theology is struggling to respond. This book is a collection of those answers, as well as a response to each. It shows something of the state and trends of contemporary theology, the diversity of the issues it struggles with, and its hopes and anxieties for contemporary humanity. It does not claim to be exhaustive either in the listing or in the treatment of compelling issues facing Christianity, but it does indicate, I hope, certain dominant issues and trends in contemporary theology. It may also pose another question: What next?

I would like to introduce the eight responses with a very brief summary of each. As Robert Schreiter points out in his essay, any discussion of compelling theological issues is shaped by and inseparable from one's conception of the church or Christianity, its identity and mission, and one's assessment of the challenges of the world in which Christianity fulfills its identity and mission. It goes without saying that one's conception of Christianity and one's assessment of the challenges of the world determine and interpret each other. Within this correlativity some may consider issues facing the church more compelling than the issues facing humanity in the world, while others may think the reverse, with a third group occupying the middle in the spectrum. I begin with essays that are more concerned with the challenges facing Christianity as such, move on to the essays that see compelling issues precisely in the way Christianity relates to the world, and end with essays more concerned with problems facing contemporary humanity as such.

Anyone looking at contemporary theology cannot but be struck by its sheer fragmentation: theology has been fragmented into various subdisciplines, each working with its own assumptions and methodologies and no longer relating to or capable of understanding one another. This is especially true of the separation between the study of scripture and dogmatic/systematic theology. Biblical studies concentrate on the historical-critical approach to the texts oblivious of their theological implications, and systematic theologians reciprocate by ignoring the scriptural context of Christian doctrines. Is it possible to overcome this scandal of fragmentation in contemporary theology?

In "'Let Us Return to the Word Delivered in the Beginning': Reflections on the Nature and Task of Christian Theology Today," **John Behr,** dean and professor of theology at St. Vladimir's Orthodox Theological Seminary, advocates a return to the model of Irenaeus, in whom theology was integrated into the context of the reading of the word with the passion, death, and resurrection of Christ at its center. He first provides a critique of the thoroughgoing historicism of modern critical scholarship, the source of so much fragmentation of contemporary theology. Modern scholarship has been preoccupied with the discovery of the "essence" of Christianity, the "real Jesus," or the original apostolic teaching, operating with a very reified conception of the essence and with certain crippling false assumptions that identify truth and chronology, regard truth as pure, and locate orthodoxy in unity and uniformity.

Over against these assumptions Behr retrieves the complexity and hybridity of the identity formation of early Christianity from contemporary scholars and judiciously applies them to the case of Irenaeus. Irenaeus regarded diversity as part of catholicity itself and looked upon orthodoxy not so much in terms of strict unity and consensus as in terms of a "symphony" of different voices throughout time with its own rhythm and rules. Instead of seeking a historically pure essence of the Christian faith or the "real historical Jesus," Irenaeus was more interested in the "coherence" of interpretations of scripture as a mosaic of Christ in the context of a community that celebrates the Eucharist together. Scripture provides the terms, images, and context for the meaning of Christ, the Word of God. Theology would be unthinkable except as the work of interpretation of scripture for the worshiping community with its memory and hope centered on its Lord. Returning to "the Word delivered in the beginning" (Polycarp) is a way of integrating theology and scripture as well as promoting the identity formation of the community. Furthermore, it contributes to the solution of a perennial problem that is peculiarly ours: the denial of death so widespread in contemporary Western society. Christ shows us the face of God precisely in the way he dies as a human being. To remove the face of death from society is also to remove the face of God, of which death is the most potent reminder because it is the radical sign of our contingency and neediness.

In the next essay I, **Anselm Min,** Maguire Distinguished Professor of Religion at Claremont Graduate University, express my own concerns about the fragmentation of contemporary theology, but I am more pessimistic. I think that the most compelling theological issue today is the deconstruction and reconstruction of Christian identity itself. The crisis of Christian identity is a crisis affecting Christianity in its totality and depth, a most radical and comprehensive crisis because Christianity is uncertain about what it believes, what it hopes for, and what it loves; it has been radically contaminated by uncertainty, skepticism, and confusion about itself. The fragmentation of theology is itself a symptom of this crisis. In my essay I attribute this crisis to four causes: certain problems peculiar to the nature and history of each communion; the global popularization of the Enlightenment critique of the content of Christian faith; the relativization of the role of the churches as institutions; and most important, the globalization of a culture of nihilism that indiscriminately pluralizes, relativizes, commercializes, trivializes, and nihilates, reducing all things to the dialectic of desire and power, and leading ultimately to the "death of the subject" who can think coherently and will do so steadily. Identity presupposes a subject with the capacity to form judgments and commit to them, but it is this capacity itself that has been eroded under the merciless attack of nihilism now dominating the Internet.

I then present certain contemporary theological reflections on Christian identity, as well as my own characterization of Christian identity as a collective identity that is possible only as a living tradition. The crisis of Christian identity poses the challenge of revitalizing Christianity as a living tradition, for which there is no mechanical solution. As a way of at least catalyzing a discussion of the crisis that is appropriate to the gravity of the crisis, not as a solution to the crisis, I propose the convocation of an ecumenical council, Vatican III, for Roman Catholicism.

In "The Repositioning of a Theology of the World in the Face of Globalization and Post-Secularity: Prophecy and Crisis," **Robert Schreiter**, Vatican II Professor of Theology at Catholic Theological Union, Chicago, argues that the most compelling theological issues today is how the church should relate to the world. After a brief analysis of the world in terms of four global changes — the growing gap between rich and poor, the demographic imbalances of old and young, women and men, global warming, and the reemergence of religion in a post-secular society — Schreiter singles out the Roman Catholic Church as uniquely positioned to have an impact on that world because it is, of all Christian denominations, the most widely spread, the most internally integrated, and diplomatically connected with the most nations and international agencies. Given the magnitude of the global crises, how Catholicism responds to them becomes crucial, which makes the rethinking of the theology of the world and its correlative, the theology of the church, for Schreiter, the most compelling theological issue today. Such theologies will shape both the analysis of the challenges of the world and the church's response to them.

There are three parts to Schreiter's argument. In the first part, the "pre-history" of his perspective, Schreiter recounts how the category of "catholicity" helped him with his theological analysis of globalization in his earlier engagement with the issue in his *The New Catholicity*, and how the raging debate on the interpretation of Vatican II made him rethink that category. Liberals advocated a hermeneutics of rupture and saw the council as departing from the tradition of the church, while conservatives advocated a hermeneutics of continuity and saw the council as defending the tradition. Schreiter saw these two divergent approaches as two different interpretations of catholicity. Liberals construe catholicity in terms of going out to the whole world through solidarity, justice, and inculturation, regarding the world as the site of prophecy where God speaks to us and carries on God's mission by planting the seeds of the Word. Conservatives construe catholicity in terms of extending the message of divine revelation and confronting the world as the site of sin and crisis. These approaches are based on different conceptions of how sinful and redeemable the world is as well as of what should be the identity and mission of the church.

Schreiter goes on to discuss the history and implications of "reading the signs of the times" so often appealed to since Vatican II. Can we identify the signs of our times as the voice of God? Is atheism a sign or rather an ideology? Does history yield any sign of God's action at all? Is the ordination of women a sign of the times? By what criteria can we legitimately interpret the signs of the times as signs of God's purposes? Should the church's interpretation be the sole criterion, as conservatives tend to think, or should the church also learn to hear the voice of God speaking through secular history, as liberals do? How important is the social location ("where") for discerning the signs of the times? Which is more important, the threat to the dignity of the poor or the threat to faith in terms of atheism and secularism? What about the church that does the reading of the signs of the times? Is it possible to read the signs of the times without a clear and consistent identity of its own on the part of the church?

In the third, concluding part of his essay, Schreiter discusses the question of how to look at the world. Is the world better construed as the site of prophecy where God speaks to the church or as the site of crisis needing the message of Christ and his church? Where are the signs of God speaking in the many challenges of the globalizing world? What are the signs of the crises demanding the attention of the church today? Schreiter's conclusion is that neither the conservative nor the liberal position on reading the signs of the times within the framework of catholicity is adequate by itself: we need both, each learning from the strengths and weaknesses of the other.

The "world" that Schreiter talks about is, at least in part, an increasingly "pluralistic" world consisting not only of the plurality of religions but also of the plurality of fundamental and comprehensive perspectives in metaphysics and ethics, especially regarding the common good of society. How is this "world," this "public space" or "public sphere" to be understood and engaged theologically? Is it to be demonized as the space of "idols" or to be constructively engaged as the space of the public discussion of the common good of society? How, then, do we avoid the imposition of particular religious views on the rest of a society increasingly pluralistic in its composition? Is there an alternative approach to the public space of society, the realm of politics, other than the traditional separation of church and state as institutions and other than the complete banishment of religious sources of insights and opinions from the public sphere? Is it possible to engage the public sphere without demonizing it but also without imposing religious particularity?

In "Faith and Political Engagement in a Pluralistic World: Beyond the Idols of Public Space," **Francis Schüssler Fiorenza,** Charles Chauncey Stillman Professor of Roman Catholic Theological Studies at Harvard Divinity School, argues for a way out of this dilemma. He begins with the recognition that the issue of political engagement from a faith perspective is "fundamental because it is not merely a question of social or political application but rather one that involves the very claims of faith and assertions of theological reflection in the face of contrasting faiths and conflicting viewpoints. It is as much an issue of fundamental or foundational theology as it is of social or political ethics." There is necessarily a public and political dimension to a faith that contains a view of what society should be in its comprehensive vision of the world. How, then, does one go about affirming the political implications of one's faith in a world that is not only empirically but also normatively pluralistic in the comprehensive sense mentioned above?

Against an informative background of theological responses to the problem of faith and politics (German political theology and Latin American liberation theology), an empirical assessment of religions with respect to their attitudes toward civic participation, some recent criticisms of John F. Kennedy as justifying the privatization of religion, and some views of liberalism as putting undue restraint on the role of religion in the public sphere, Fiorenza argues for a positive engagement of public space as the locus of public reason where issues of the common good of society are analyzed, assessed, defended, or at least clarified according to the model of Habermasian discourse ethics based on universalizability and reciprocity.

For Fiorenza, several things are necessary for the integrity of this public space. We must dismiss the prevalent idea that liberalism is an enemy to the public role of religion. At least Rawls and Habermas are open to the role of religious resources and insights in promoting democratic values; the only thing they oppose is the judicial and legislative decisions explicitly and formally based on particular religious beliefs. We must also abandon the simple distinction between religious and nonreligious arguments as though the latter are more accessible and more certain; the latter often derive from the former, and both have complicating background theories to disentangle. Nor do we have to fear that acceptance of pluralism, religious or political, necessarily leads to the reduction of religions to the same. We can avoid this reduction with the practical pluralism that leaves all religious differences alone as long as they do not endanger public order and peace, and with the theoretical pluralism that allows all religions to enter into the public space of discourse with all their normative claims and encourages them to contribute insights and resources for human solidarity from their own tradition, subject to the proviso that they are also willing to learn from others in a genuine dialogue that requires mutual respect and reciprocity.

The integrity of public space also requires that there be no a priori conditions for its entrance that would exclude some from participation; it is in the public space itself that differences will emerge and be argued about. The focus of public debate is not any particular religious belief as such but its implications for the common good of society, the historical conditions of coexistence for all, which does not, therefore, affect the integrity of a religion in itself. The religions contribute to this public space not only by rational arguments but also, it should not be forgotten, by the symbolic actions they take, such as the hospice movement and the celebration of the Eucharist. The public space in this sense, then, is something to be invigorated, not to be demonized as the locus of "idols" such as market capitalism, secularization, individualism, and privatization.

Many people have noted in recent decades that the United States is the most incarcerated country in the world. Since the 1970s the prison population has increased sevenfold to 2.3 million in 2005, compared to 1.5 million in China with a population almost four times as large. America has the highest percentage of its population behind bars of all the nations in the world. Shouldn't this human tragedy be a compelling theological issue today? Why is it that even today prisons receive attention only in terms of "prison ministry" and "pastoral care" and only from prison chaplains? In his essay "'The Prisons Fill Up,' the Specter of Mass Incarceration as Compelling Theological Issue," **Mark L. Taylor**, Maxwell M. Upson Professor of Theology and Culture at Princeton Theological Seminary, addresses the issue with wide-ranging analyses, critical insights, and theological passion.

Based on Aime Cesaire's insight from his *Discourse on Colonialism* that the violence of colonizers in the colonies circles back and boomerangs into the world of the colonizers themselves, Taylor asks about the nature of the vicious cycle of which mass incarceration in the United States may be a part. He mentions three historical lineages as the contexts in which prisons must be understood. The first is the legacy of slavery and Jim Crow that continues into the ghetto and the contemporary prison system as ways of controlling socially stigmatized groups on the part of the white overclass. The second is the history of Western and US colonialism, which is the context of slavery itself and which has been perpetuated in the incarceration of the American Indians, the Chinese, Japanese, and Italian Americans domestically and honed the art of the colonial carceral in Korea and Vietnam overseas. The third is the integration of the production and marketing of confinement and surveillance strategies into the defense industries.

For Taylor, these three lineages are the major forces driving US history, and they exercise their power over American society and culture through the two destructive "specters" of American Romanticism and Contractual Liberalism. American Romanticism produced the myth of American exceptionalism and greatness and the ideology of the United States as "a light to the nations" and the vanguard of Western "civilization," justifying American expansionism and imperialism. The mass incarceration of nonwhite peoples at home serves as an internal reminder of the nonwhite peoples overseas over which the United States seeks to exercise its imperial control. Contractual Liberalism in reality "contracts out" opportunities to the few and "contracts" or "constricts" them for the rest of society and masks the class structure of American society and the workings of its white overclass. The prisons that are filling up are sedimentations of this specter. The corporate interests have managed to couch their economic insecurity and the threat posed by the working class as "criminal" insecurity against the public good. By desocializing wage labor, curtailing the rights and protections of labor unions, and withdrawing the social safety net, economic liberalism drives the poor to despair and to social transgressions.

How do we turn this destructive specter of negativity into the positive one of emancipatory transformation? The objective conditions for the emergence of a positive specter of emancipation are there in the "boomerang" effect mentioned earlier. US mass incarceration is a result of its colonial carceral, the domestic expression of its brutalities abroad. The ruling class will increase its domestic brutality as incarceration increases, but its attempt to purchase social peace through incarceration will not ultimately work because there is a revolving door between prison and society and because the pathologies of social distortion (racism, sexism, class exploitation) cannot be contained within the walls. Children of the imprisoned will swell the ranks of the poor, the communities of color will be stigmatized and locked into caste exclusion, and the law and its force will be eroded, the net effect of all of these being the creation of the "underdeveloped" nations within the United States. This, for Taylor, will generate a positive specter of its own, "critical movements of resistance," built on the history of various movements for liberation at home and resistance against Western colonialism abroad. Such critical movements consist of three impulses, a consciousness of social antagonism, a cultivation of an artistic and imaginative vision of an emancipated future, and a fomenting of resistant and emancipatory practices.

Can Christianity contribute to these critical movements of resistance? This will require the full activation of the liberating potential already there in the early Christian movement around the figure of Jesus. There are three dimensions of early Christian spirituality corresponding to the three impulses of critical movements of resistance. First, Jesus' way of living and dying embodied a politically adversarial stance and practices against the religious and political systems of domination. Second, Jesus' death on the cross as an imperial execution and in its subsequent dramaturgical effect was mimetic and theatrical, capable of generating a full range of artistic representations from creative storytelling to dramatic events, as illustrated in the parables and street theater of Jesus. Third, Jesus' crucifixion is socially kinetic, embedding adversarial and mimetic strategies for concrete social practices and movements for historical change, toward the reign of God based on love and justice.

How, then, can mass incarceration become a theologically "compelling" issue? In an insightful analysis of what constitutes a "compelling" issue, Taylor distinguishes compelling issues from the risking of some interpretation of the human situation or the daring of some new interpretation of a Christian symbol, the two main interpretive tasks for the theologian, according to David Tracy. Nor is a compelling issue to be identified with a particular agenda. A compelling issue arises from crises that offer both challenge and opportunity, and "charges" a theologian's entire theological project and usually throws him or her into a solidarity of struggle with other thinkers and actors.

Feminist theology is a good example of such a compelling issue. Gender injustice and patriarchy are more than an agenda item; they touch practically all levels of our social existence and become galvanizing concerns leading to a rethinking of much of theology, thoroughly pervading the fabric of a theologian's social location and discourse. For Taylor, mass incarceration is another such compelling issue. There is a sense of urgency and crisis about mass incarceration, constraining us to rethink our theological discourse and reexamine our communal praxis. As such, compelling issues ride the force of the "specter." It is the specter of critical movements of resistance sparked by mass incarceration that makes mass incarceration a compelling theological issue. Taylor uses the example of Mothers Reclaiming Our Children, a group working in California against the neoliberal penal system.

Postcolonialism has been pointing out for some time now that colonialism is not finished with the achievement of political independence in former colonies; the colonial habits of thinking and acting tend to endure as colonialism and imperialism continue in different forms even in the postmodern world. Theology constitutes the intellectual core of Christianity, and decolonizing theology and theological concepts remains a most compelling task for a Christianity that seeks to purify itself of all remnants of colonialism and imperialism. In "Decolonizing Christianity," **Susan Abraham**, assistant professor of ministry studies and associate director of the Center for the Study of World Religions at Harvard Divinity School, addresses precisely that issue. Postcolonial theory aims to decolonize Western knowledge, and postcolonial theology seeks to decolonize Western theology and disclose how theology functions to perpetuate imperial systems of domination; both use a variety of methods, notably Marxism and poststructuralism. In this regard postcolonial theology has been both learning from and challenging postcolonial theory.

Culture, experience, and identity were shown to be radically historical, particular, and pluralist, a challenge to the universalist assumptions of Western knowledge and theology, which meant a turn of third-world theologies to their own culture, identity, and experience as matrix of their own theologies. However, in their earlier phase, third-world theologies tended to operate with a relatively fixed notion of identity, to use "experience" in opposition to "reason," simplistically correlating experience and theology, and to fall into the theological equivalent of "identity politics." They were unaware of the immense pluralism of such categories as "Asian," reinscribed the highly problematic relation between "center" and "margin" by presenting themselves as "marginal," and failed to acknowledge the surviving colonialism in the cultural names of "Asia," "Middle East," and "Latin America." Postcolonial theology has tried to overcome these pitfalls by complicating the notions of identity and experience in conversation with postcolonial theory and by grappling with postcolonial writing and reading as ethical practices.

No identity, whether of gender, class, race, or sexuality, is simple and homogeneous. All identities are complicated by power differentials inherent in the cultural matrix as well as by their mutual reinforcements. It is important, as Sugirtharajah points out, to understand decolonization itself in developmental terms and note the moments of ambivalence in all attempts to decolonize Christianity. One's indigenous heritage may contain the liberating moments of critical resistance to colonialism, but also oppressive moments of its own such as untouchability, caste distinctions, polygamy, female circumcision, and widow burning, as in the Indian case. The intrinsic diversity of indigenous culture gives rise to a diversity of hermeneutical theologies such as feminist and Dalit theologies. Postcolonial theology encapsulates the social, political, and cultural conditions of the current order and reflects the ambiguities of decolonization and neocolonization. It not only unmasks colonial domination but also uncovers suppressed voices, oppositional readings of texts, and viable alternatives. It implies the political and ideological stance against neocolonialism and globalization. Applied to biblical interpretation, it seeks to uncover colonial designs in biblical texts and their interpretations while also endeavoring to read the text from the postcolonial perspective of identity, hybridity, and diaspora, best developed in Homi Bhabha's complication and deconstruction of the reified categories of "nation" and "culture."

Postcolonial theologian Marion Grau has shown that there is much ambivalence today about the Christian mission. There is more to the mission than the exercise of power of the colonizer over the colonized. The colonized too are "converted," and conversion means conversion to a hybrid reality always negotiated and reconstructed. There is an economic, cultural dimension to conversion to Christianity, which has appealed more to the socially disenfranchised women and persons of lower class. Colonial encounters meant not only the activities of the missionaries on the indigenous peoples but also the latter's resistance and negotiation, using missionary institutions to challenge patriarchal, social, cultural, and theological norms. Mission and subversion occurred on multiple levels, and all had to be converted in one way or another. Translating the Bible into indigenous tongues relativized the grip of the missionaries over the Bible. Grau demonstrates a twofold task for a postcolonial theology of mission. It means resisting the demand to capitulate to the prevailing idea that mission theology was only a tool of Christian imperialism, and rethinking colonial encounters with special sensitivity to the surprising and novel ways in which agency was enacted. It also means rethinking mission theology in terms of the relationality of mutual conversion and mutual transformation.

Postcolonial theory has contributed to postcolonial theology not only by complicating the notions of identity and experience but also by its poststructuralist critiques of texts and discourses as carriers of colonial and imperialist ideology. In a theological response David Tracy agrees that language is indeed a site of complex negotiations but also argues that it need not be merely a site of power negotiation. He has been concerned with the hermeneutical relationship of the presence-oriented category of word to scripture as written text or writing. For him, Christian scripture can only be analyzed in terms of its referent, and therefore only in terms of an event, the gratuitous event of divine self-manifestation in the Word, beyond the control of the human subject. Scriptural language is the site of an interpersonal encounter between God and human beings, in which Word is both Logos and Kerygma, both disclosure of Jesus Christ and the proclamation, distance, and disruption of our attempts to speak, write, and think of faith in Jesus Christ, both self-presencing *Logos* and self-distancing *Kerygma*. Gospels unite disclosive word and Word as proclamation. The Gospels as writing demonstrate that self-presence is never full, simple, or whole because it operates in a dialectic of disclosure and distance.

Abraham discusses Sharon Ringe as another example of postcolonial reading and writing, following the model of Trinh Minh-ha. For Ringe, feminists in the United States have failed to adequately theorize the category of woman and as a result ignored the fundamental differences of race, culture, class, marital status, sexual orientation, and other factors. They failed to think beyond the "caricature of Everywoman," unaware of the fact that they can be both colonizer and colonized. Furthermore, for Ringe reading scripture is akin to the spiritual practice of unselving. As the opposite of the "heroic" reading or writing that reads or writes oneself into the text, postcolonial reading is a way to read body into the text, not to identify self in the text, but for transformation, to examine relative privilege. The postcolonial feminist stance is to examine their relative positions of privilege and power in relation to the text, a process of self-transformation, "an exercise in undoing privilege to make the space for surprising divine and human revelations."

Not many today will deny the gravity of the situation facing both women and nature, women in their exclusion and marginalization, nature in its pollution and destruction. The inferiorization of women has been a fact of life throughout history, and it is only during the second half of the twentieth century that women's issues were systematically addressed. The exploitation of nature likewise began receiving attention only during the last several decades. Christian theology has been involved in the ideological legitimation of both the inferiorization of women and the destruction of nature, and it faces the challenge of purifying itself of those elements responsible for these evils. How should Christian theology change? In "Faith and Ecofeminism: Religion and the Liberation of Women and the Earth from Oppression," **Rosemary Radford Ruether,** visiting professor of religion at Claremont Graduate University and Claremont School of Theology, traces the roots of the problem to the Hebrew and Greek origins of Christian theology and its historical development, and proposes a radical reconstruction of its traditional content.

As an ecological feminist or ecofeminist, Radford Ruether attributes both the domination of women and the exploitation of nature to the system of patriarchy that seeks to monopolize wealth, power, and knowledge. To ratify this system various religious and philosophical ideologies — myths and systems — were constructed and laws enacted to justify men's domination of women, slaves, and animals. Chief among such ideologies was the Platonic dualism of mind and matter, soul and body, by which men are equated with the mind and soul, and women with the body, matter, and its attendant passions. Just as it is the role of the mind to order the body and its passions, so it is the role of men to order women and their passions, and as it is the role of the body to obey the mind, so it is the role of women to obey men. Furthermore, the soul is regarded as an independent substance separable from the body and living in an alienated state on earth. Likewise, in the Genesis account Adam, the male, is considered the normative human, from whom Eve, the female, is derived as his auxiliary, and it is this woman who is described as disobeying God and spelling the loss of original paradise for all humanity. These Greek and Hebrew assumptions reinforced each other and generated patriarchal patterns that have dominated Christian cosmology, anthropology, Christology, and soteriology ever since.

The first task of ecofeminism is to overcome the dualism of soul and body and the priority of the male-identified mind over the female-identified body, which Radford Ruether considers to be at the heart of the Western distortion of our relations to ourselves, to one another, to our fellow creatures on earth, and to the cosmos as a whole. Humans must learn to accept themselves as integral parts of nature and as creatures of years of its long evolution, not as beings set apart from nature and somehow ordained to dominate it. Our destiny is of this earth and for this earth, our only true home. We must develop a spirituality and ethic of mutual limitation and nurture of reciprocal life giving, not of separation and domination.

For Radford Ruether, who relies on the insights of Ivone Gebara, the Brazilian ecofeminist, our primal sin does not lie in disobedience to God that resulted in death but in the effort to escape from death, finitude, and vulnerability so well enshrined in the myth of original paradise. The desire to escape from death had been part of the fear of death, but such desire took organized, pernicious forms when powerful males rose to organize power over others, land, and animals, seeking the ultimate power over others by rising superior to death itself and ensuring themselves of an invulnerability against finitude as such to which all others are subject. It is this search for salvation from death and vulnerability that underlies all the male attempts to amass power over others and construct systems of abuse and exploitation of other humans and nature. To conquer and flee from finitude meant in particular to rule over and flee from women, who represent the body and the earth, reminders of men's finite origins.

This explanation of the origin of evil also dictates a new concept of salvation. We must give up the notion of salvation as salvation from death and vulnerability, which is only the projection of the desire to escape from vulnerability, the root cause of our sin and that which falsifies our real possibilities here on earth. We need a much more modest concept of salvation, something available here on earth, the establishment of conditions of life for all free from domination and exploitation although not free from death and tragedy, a community of mutual life giving where joys and sorrows are shared, with enough food for all, a clean sky, peace and no armed conflict, no prisoners, no borders, no separated families, with medical care for all, no children neglected.

The dismantling of the escapist self and the escapist conception of salvation also entails the dismantling of the reigning concepts of God and Christ. God is no longer modeled after a male ruler over nature but reconceived as the immanent source of life and the renewal of life in a world of co-dependent origination. The Trinity is understood as the sustaining matrix of immanent relationality, a symbolic expression of the fundamental movement of life itself as a process of interrelational creativity, not a separate, self-enclosed relation of two divine males mediated by the Spirit. God is Sophia, Holy

Wisdom, the sustaining and redeeming matrix of cosmic, planetary, social, and personal life.

Likewise, we need a new Christology. We have to give up the messianic myth, the myth of a heroic warrior who liberates victims from oppression, punishes the oppressors, and creates an ideal earth freed from sin and want. This myth only adds the thirst for revenge to the desire to escape from finitude, only recreating the cycle of violence and new victims. The original vision of the historical Jesus was that of peace, but his followers betrayed him by turning his call to a community of shared love into a new messianism and making him into a warrior savior who would justify the Christian system of imperial domination. Rather, Jesus must be understood as an anti-messiah calling us to rediscover the community of equals beyond the cycle of victimizers and victims, of rich and poor, of oppressors and oppressed. The God he reveals is not the dominating *Logos* of immortalized male sovereignty but the Holy Wisdom that creates and renews the creation. Jesus does this not as a unique and exclusive representative but as one paradigm among others, calling us to our true selves in a life freed from the madness of escapism and domination. Thus transformed, Christian theology must embody the ethic of sustainability with regard to nature and the ethic of the preferential option for the poor with regard to fellow human beings.

For **Mark Wallace**, professor of religion at Swarthmore College, the ecological crisis induced by our indiscriminate exploitation of nature constitutes a *status confessionis*, a situation so grievously contradictory to the gospel as to require a collective declaration and prophetic witness by the whole church. Historically, the Nazi period in the 1930s and the apartheid period in the 1980s constituted situations of such gravity. Today, when global warming is destroying the very ecosystem that makes life possible and rendering meaningless the Christian hope for a new heaven and a new earth, we are faced with another *status confessionis*. It rings hollow to speak of the *mirabilia dei* or wonders of God or of the goodness and beauty of creation in a world where death, degradation, and disasters reign, where the Spirit can no longer renew the face of the earth because the earth can no longer bear the weight of human sin. The ecological crisis is a profoundly spiritual crisis, and saving the planet is the most compelling theological issue, an imperative than which there is none greater. What is at stake is the fate of creation itself. In the last essay of this volume, "The Song of the Thrush: Christian Animism and the Global Crisis Today," Wallace offers the vision of Christian animism as the theological and moral foundation for a radically new way of envisioning the world as God's creation we dare not profane and exploit.

Wallace defines Christian animism as "the biblically inflected conviction that all of creation is infused with and animated by God's presence." Animism is generally used to describe the belief systems of indigenous peoples who attribute life, soul, or spirit to all things, and distinguished from Christianity that tended to look down on the material world as unworthy of the soul. Wallace, however, finds profound bases for Christian animism in the doctrine of the incarnation of God in Jesus and the indwelling of the Holy Spirit in all things that exist. God continually incarnates Godself through the embodied reality of life on earth. It is a thoroughly biblical doctrine that human beings are obligated to care for creation because all creation is the bearer of the Holy Spirit. Nature is a living web of gifted relationships, a self-organizing field of living, dynamic relationships among a marvelous diversity of creatures, all of them made alive and moving by the energizing presence of the Holy Spirit. This is not pantheism that simply equates God and the world without remainder. It is closer to panentheism in which God is fully and completely embodied in the natural world: God becomes one of us in Jesus and gifts the Holy Spirit to all things to infuse them with divine energy and love. God's Spirit "ensouls" all things with sacred purpose, which makes all things the enfleshments of divine power and compassion.

In an ecological biblical hermeneutic Wallace retrieves the biblical heritage of the work of the Holy Spirit as the "green" face of God in the world, highlighting the ministry of the Spirit as the celebration of the good creation God has made for the joy and sustenance of all things. Most significantly, Wallace seeks to retrieve the biblical identification of the Holy Spirit with the four elements, earth, air, water, and fire, and bring out their full ecological power and meaning. As earth, the Spirit is a fleshy, avian life form, a dove, God's nurturing, inspiring, and birthing presence in creation, hovering over all creation at its genesis and present at Jesus' baptism to signal God's approval on his public work. God is not only human flesh in Jesus but also animal flesh in the person of the Spirit, the bird God. As air, *ruach, pneuma*, the Spirit is both the animating breath for all living things and the wind of prophecy and judgment. We inhale God at the moment of our birth and exhale God with our last breath. As water, the Spirit brings life, healing, and refreshment to all creatures, infusing all liquids with sacred energy, the water of baptism, the wine of the Eucharist, the vital fluids of blood, mucus, tears, semen, sweat, urine, rain, rivers, and waterfalls. As fire, the Spirit is the blaze of God that both condemns human arrogance for its injustice and exploitation and ignites and unifies the multilingual and interracial community of the early church. To be true to the biblical legacy is to recognize the continuing presence of the divine Spirit not only in Jesus or in the Eucharist but also in the very elements that constitute existence in nature. It is perhaps time for what Ellen Armour calls an "elemental" theology.

Wallace applies the Chalcedonian formula to clarify the relation between the Holy Spirit and earth: it is one of union, not separation, but also of distinction, not confusion. The Spirit and earth are inseparably united but not in simple identity, and they are distinct but also internally conditioning and permeating the other in a cosmic festival of love and harmony. The Spirit is the "soul" of the earth empowering all life forms to enter into a dynamic relationship with the greater whole, while the earth is the "flesh" of the Spirit making God palpable and viscous in all the changes of nature. The Spirit is the hidden, inner life of the world, while the earth is the outward manifestation of the Spirit's sustaining energy. In this view God is no longer the immutable God of the classical tradition, separated and aloof from the passions and vagaries of this transient world. God is a living being that "subsists in and through the natural world." God is a living, suffering coparticipant in the pain of the world, a tragic figure, and suffers all the afflictions and degradations we inflict on nature. "*God is at risk in the world today* . . . The threat of ecocide brings in its wake the specter of deicide."

Back, then, to our original question: What is the most compelling theological issue today? Collected here are eight different answers based on eight different perspectives. What does this suggest about the state of contemporary Christian theology? Perhaps two things. On the one hand, it suggests that there are indeed eight compelling problems facing Christianity and humanity as a whole, each not quite reducible to the others, although all of them should remain the concern of Christian theology directly or indirectly. Christian theology cannot remain indifferent to any of them because at stake in them is the divine, theological significance of the church, history, and nature. On the other hand, the essays also suggest the fragmentation of contemporary Christian theology: there are eight different perspectives and eight different answers to the question, What is the most compelling theological issue today? They do not agree in their basic concerns, assumptions, and perspectives. Some of these differences are not so radical as to divide them into different religions. Others are indeed so radical and may provoke a discussion about whether they can qualify as *Christian* theology. Both the plurality of questions facing Christianity and the fragmentation of contemporary Christian theology are provocative enough to bear witness to the impossible seriousness of the tasks and challenges Christian theologians have to struggle with in the beginning of the twenty-first century.

I want to thank all the participants in this project from the bottom of my heart. I owe a special word of thanks to Bruce Paolozzi, my always dependable research assistant, for a superb job in taking care of the logistics of the conference that invited these essays and for his preliminary editing of the essays themselves. I now invite readers to participate in the ongoing discussion of contemporary theology by reading not only these essays but also the very perceptive, often critical responses, each with its own concern, insight, and perspective.

1

"Let Us Return to the Word Delivered in the Beginning"

Reflections on the Nature and Task of Christian Theology Today

JOHN BEHR

Looking back at the last century, it is hard not to be struck by the impression that, despite all the great fruits produced by several centuries of intense and diligent scholarly, historical, and critical work, the discipline of theology itself has fragmented into various subdisciplines, fields working with such different presuppositions and methodologies that they no longer relate to each other and hardly even comprehend each other.[1] Not to mention the fields of liturgy, iconology, canon law, asceticism, and many others, this fragmentation is especially true, and most grievous, in the case of the rupture between the study of scripture, on the one hand, and systematic or dogmatic theology, on the other, with "patristics" included in the latter, at least when it was practiced, until the mid to late twentieth-century, as the history of dogmatic theology.

A rather glaring example of this incomprehension is given by Richard Hanson, who, after concluding his mammoth landmark tome *The Search for the Christian Doctrine of God* (1988), notes, on the one hand, that through all the various debates: "The shape of Trinitarian doctrine finally achieved in the fourth century, then,

[1] See E. Farley, *Theologia: The Fragmentation and Unity of Theological Education* (Philadelphia: Fortress Press, 1983).

was necessary, indeed we may say permanent. It was a solution, *the* solution, to the intellectual problem which had for so long vexed the church."[2] The problem to be solved is an intellectual one, that of establishing the doctrine of the Trinity. Yet, on the other hand, this is, for Hanson at least, a task separable from the exegetical practices of those whom he studied. For, as he puts it in the conclusion to his tome: "The expounders of the text of the Bible are incompetent and ill-prepared to expound it. This applies as much to the wooden and unimaginative approach of the Arians as it does to the fixed determination of their opponents to read their doctrine into the Bible by hook or crook."[3] He clearly has no time for the exegetical practices of the theologians of this period (reading the scriptures — the Law, the Psalms, and the Prophets — as speaking of Christ), by which they reached their conclusions. He then continues with this rather perplexing statement:

It was much more the presuppositions with which they approach the Biblical text that clouded their perceptions, the tendency to treat the Bible in an "atomic" way as if each verse or set of verses was capable of giving direct information about Christian doctrine apart from its context, the "oracular" concept of the nature of the Bible, the incapacity with a few exceptions to take serious account of the background and circumstances of the writers. The very reverence with which they honoured the Bible as a sacred book stood in the way of their understanding it. In this matter they were of course only reproducing the presuppositions of all Christians before them, of the writers of the New Testament itself, of the tradition of Jewish rabbinic piety and scholarship.[4]

Their exegetical practice is simply wrong, even if it is a practice going back to the apostles themselves and their proclamation of the gospel, a manner of exegesis moreover shared with the rabbis, and which was, in fact, the common approach to sacred texts in

---

[2] Richard P. C. Hanson, "Achievement of Orthodoxy," in *The Making of Orthodoxy: Essays in Honour of Henry Chadwick*, ed. R. Williams, 142–56 (Cambridge, MA: Cambridge University Press, 1989), 156.

[3] Richard P. C. Hanson, *The Search for the Christian Doctrine of God: The Arian Controversy, 318–381* (Edinburgh: T & T Clark, 1988), 848.

[4] Ibid., 848–49.

antiquity.[5] The doctrine of the Trinity was an "intellectual problem" that was resolved in the fourth century, and it can now simply be called upon as a given of Christian theology. And dividing up the controversies of the early centuries by following the chapters in modern dogmatic textbooks, with the fourth century having established trinitarian theology, it remained for the following centuries to do the same for the incarnation, another given of Christian theology. Hanson never, as far as I am aware, addressed the question of what happens when one takes these supposed core theological elements out of the context in which they were composed, the practice of reading scripture within which they had meaning, and places them in another context, in this case that of systematic theology and a historical reading of scripture.

Although Hanson's words are rather stark, the attitude they present is rather typical, and examples could easily be multiplied. It would not be a difficult task to present the case the other way around as well, to show an increasing disenfranchisement of modern scriptural scholars from dogmatic theology. Features of this will be mentioned later, but a clear example is the collection of essays by scriptural scholars that caused such a storm several decades ago, *The Myth of God Incarnate,* edited by John Hick.[6] *Myth* was apparently the most appropriate term to refer to that for which for other theologians was a fundamental given of theology.

This fragmentation of the (singular) discipline of theology is a challenge. If there is to be Christian theology today, it needs to be reintegrated, and to do this we need to understand the nature of this particular and peculiar discipline. Although, as any dictionary will note, the word *theology* is formed from the words *theos* and *logos*, it cannot simply mean speaking *about* God, in an analogous manner to the way in which, for instance, those who study geology speak about the world and those who study "biology" speak about the phenomenon of life and living creatures, if for no other reason than God is not subject to our scrutiny, to be merely spoken *about,* described in abstract, uninvolved terms.[7] We are usually happy,

[5] See J. L. Kugel, *Traditions of the Bible: A Guide to the Bible as It Was at the Start of the Common Era* (Cambridge, MA: Harvard University Press, 1998), 14–19.

[6] John Hick, *The Myth of God Incarnate* (London: SCM, 1977).

[7] See John Behr, "What Are We Doing Speaking About God: The Discipline of Theology," in *Thinking Through Faith: New Perspectives from Orthodox Christian Scholars,* ed. Aristotle Papanikolaou and Elizabeth H. Prodromou (Crestwood, NY: SVS Press, 2008), 67–86.

as theologians, to speak about God—but which God, and how are we speaking of God? As Rowan Williams notes, "Theology . . . is perennially tempted to be seduced by the prospect of bypassing the question of how it *learns* its own language."[8]

The particular contours of our contemporary predicament are, of course, shaped by our modern times and recent history, about which I will say more, but the predicament itself is not new. Already at the beginning of the second century Polycarp of Smyrna felt the need to exhort his readers to "return to the Word delivered in the beginning" (*Ep. Phil.* 7). Polycarp, of course, stood in a period before the establishment, largely through his disciple Irenaeus of Lyons, of a clearly articulated normative, catholic or orthodox, theological position; moreover, the battles of these early centuries are not the same as the problematics of our own times. And yet, if we want to learn how Christian theology "*learns* its own language," there are lessons to be learned from this period. This does not mean that all we need to do is return to an idealized past; emphatically not! But our contemporary task of reintegration, of learning the language of *theology*—what it is we are speaking and how; how, for instance, scriptural exegesis holds together with systematic theology—requires that we work from the ground up, from the basic elements, and so from the earliest beginnings.

It is, perhaps, then, not surprising that the earliest centuries of Christianity have become such an important battlefield for *modern* Christian identity, for claims to normativity and challenges to any such claims. The books on this topic are legion: among many by Bart Ehrman, the title of his book *Lost Christianities: The Battles for Scripture and the Faiths We Never Knew*, speaks volumes; there are, of course, any number of studies reappropriating *Gnosticism*, with all the qualifications now needed for that term; there are ever new presentations of the "real historical Jesus"; and, on the other side, the recent book by Andreas Köstenberger and Michael Kruger titled *The Heresy of Orthodoxy: How Contemporary Culture's Fascination with Diversity Has Reshaped Our Understanding of Early Christianity*, or Charles Hill's *Who Chose the Gospels: Probing the Great Gospel Conspiracy*; and the list continues, for there is no end of books.

But, I would argue, while the task of dismantling early claims to orthodoxy, and its understanding of the nature and task of theology, have been vigorously pursued, equal scrutiny has yet to be given to the presuppositions of modern scholarship, resulting in a certain

---

[8] Rowan Williams, *On Christian Theology* (Oxford: Blackwell, 2000), 131.

tone-deafness toward the early exponents of orthodoxy, much like Hanson's incomprehension of the exegetical practices of those whose theology nevertheless satisfied his own "intellectual problem." So, by returning to the "Word delivered in the beginning," especially as developed by Polycarp's disciple Irenaeus of Lyons, I would like to address specific contemporary issues regarding the possibility of normativity—a "hypothesis" and "canon"—within Christian theology, the fragmentary nature of theological scholarship today, and, finally, to point to what is perhaps the biggest problem in modern Western culture more generally, which Christian theology is uniquely positioned to address, that of the place and role of death.

Modern Scholarship:
From Historicism to Identity Formation

This task, as alluded to earlier, is made more complex today because of the trajectory of scholarship since the Enlightenment.[9] The establishment of a normative, orthodox or catholic, Christianity in the early centuries was controversial in its own times, and that controversy has only become much more complex today, with a particularly modern character. Bart Ehrman rightly points out that the source of our modern controversies lies with the debates about the historical reliability of scripture that emerged during the Enlightenment, together with a developing secular discourse of science and renewed reflection on the nature of truth.[10] Of particular importance here was the attempt to rediscover, behind the claims of the apostles, the real Jesus, beginning with Herman Reimarus (1694–1768), whose literary "Fragments" was published posthumously by Gotthold Lessing (1729–81),[11] and then followed by many other notable scholars, in a project that was given a new boost in the twentieth century by the discovery of previously hidden caches of material, resulting in repeated new quests for the historical Jesus.

It was also Lessing, ever the controversialist, who more than anyone else recast what was understood by the phrase "the canon

---

[9] The following paragraphs are drawn from my *Irenaeus of Lyons: Identifying Christianity* (Oxford: Oxford University Press, 2013).

[10] Bart D. Ehrman, *Lost Christianities: The Battles for Scripture and the Faiths We Never Knew* (Oxford: Oxford University Press, 2003), 168–80.

[11] See especially his "The Intention of Jesus and His Disciples," in *Reimarus: Fragments*, ed. Charles H. Talbert, trans. Ralph S. Fraser (Eugene, OR: Wipf and Stock, 2009).

of truth" or the "rule of faith."[12] For Lessing, the "*regula fidei*" was "not drawn from the writings of the New Testament," but "was in existence before a single book of the New Testament existed," and so "is even older than the *Church*," and therefore it was "this *regula fidei*, and *not the Scriptures* [that] is the rock on which the Church of Christ was built."[13] The "canon" or "*regula*" is here understood in terms of particular teachings—on God, Christ, and his work—and is detached from scripture, by which Lessing seems only to have understood the writings of the New Testament, for the "Old Testament," now read merely historically, plays no other role for him. Subsequent elaboration of this original teaching is, correspondingly, understood either positively, as Newman's "development of doctrine," or negatively, as Harnack's "Hellenization of Christianity" or "acute Hellenization" in the case of "Gnosticism." The task of theology thus bifurcated into two separate tracks: on the one hand, to recover, through historical critical scholarship, the "real Jesus" behind the layers of interpretation given to him by the apostles and subsequent generations of Christians, that is, to distinguish the Jesus of history from the Christ of faith, as it is sometimes put; and on the other hand, to discern the original apostolic teaching, either as "the essence of Christianity," as Harnack would put it, or as perhaps the resolutions to the "intellectual problem" of God, as with Hanson: the pure Semitic gospel or the trinitarian and christological consensus of the age of the councils.

In both cases the quest is to identify the original essence of Christianity, understood as a reified, pure, bounded, and unchanging identity. But as Karen King points out in *What Is Gnosticism?*, there are certain assumptions at play in much of this scholarship that need to be called into question.[14] First, "the association of truth and chronology," that is, the assumption that what is earlier is necessarily truer. This is combined with, second, "the notion that truth is pure; mixing is contamination," and third, "the assumption that truth ('orthodoxy') is characterized by unity, uniformity, and unanimity; falsehood ('heresy') by division, multiformity, and diversity."

[12] See especially his "Necessary Answer to a Very Unnecessary Question of Herr Hauptpastor Goeze of Hamburg," in *Lessing: Philosophical and Theological Writings*, ed. H. B. Nisbet, Cambridge Texts in the History of Philosophy (Cambridge, MA: Cambridge University Press, 2005), 172–77.

[13] Gotthold Lessing, "Necessary Answer to a Very Unnecessary Question of Herr Hauptpastor Goeze of Hamburg," nos. 2–5.

[14] Karen King, *What Is Gnosticism?* (Cambridge, MA: Belknap Press of Harvard University Press, 2003), 228–29.

King would see these assumptions as deriving from early Christian writers themselves, in their anti-heretical rhetoric, uncritically appropriated by modern scholars, and so she describes the purpose of her book as being

> to consider the ways in which early Christian polemicists' discourse of orthodoxy and heresy has been intertwined with twentieth-century scholarship on Gnosticism in order to show where and how that involvement has distorted our analysis of ancient texts. At stake is not only the capacity to write a more accurate history of ancient Christianity in all its multiformity, but also our capacity to engage critically the ancient politics of religious difference rather than unwittingly reproduce its strategies and results.[15]

And this is not merely a historical exercise, though it is that as well, for as King notes, with respect to the problem of describing "Gnosticism," the difficulty "has been and continues to be primarily an aspect of the ongoing project of defining and maintaining a normative Christianity."[16]

Such assumptions are certainly at work in much modern scholarship, with its quest to uncover the original historical Jesus and his unadulterated message or the original doctrinal core of Christianity. In both cases a pure original essence is sought that can then be used as a criterion to demonstrate the distortions or falsifications of what happens later, so opening a horizon on which other ways of thinking Christian identity, *today,* can legitimately be carried through. But it is a striking and significant fact that if parallels are to be found in the first two centuries, they lie with protest figures such as Marcion, whom Harnack famously compared to Luther standing before the Roman Church. He it was who claimed to have preserved, or critically determined, the original message of the apostle Paul before it was distorted by false apostles, who upheld a single gospel account expurgated of all error rather than a diversity of witnesses, and who established his own church of like-minded believers, separating himself from the broader community. It might well be the case that the assumptions of modern scholarship derive from the narratives of orthodoxy and heresy elaborated in the fourth century, together with the exercise of power and authority that came to be deployed

---

[15] Ibid., 19.
[16] Ibid., 18.

thereafter in imperial Christianity with all the political resources at its disposal. But this does not hold for the first two or three centuries, nor does it help us understand the dynamics of orthodoxy as it was articulated during this period. It is necessary to be sensitive to the different discourses on orthodoxy and heresy elaborated by different figures in different epochs, and a first step toward this would be to turn King's project around, as it were, and to disentangle the early discourse on orthodoxy and heresy from the assumptions operative within twentieth-century scholarship and their roots in the historicizing perspective of recent centuries, so that we can hear how second-century figures, such as Irenaeus, construed the debate on their own terms, for it was not as the quest for a pure, reified essence.

The idea that there was a single origin of the Christian faith, a single essential core, was put decisively to rest by Walter Bauer in his claim that Christianity was a diverse phenomenon from the beginning, that "varieties of Christianity" arose around the Mediterranean, and that in some places what would later be called "heretical" was initially normative.[17] In his reconstruction, through the various struggles among these diverse groups, one form eventually came to dominate as "orthodox," enabling us to speak of its predecessors as "proto-orthodox," while others lost and became "lost Christianities," to use the title of Ehrman's book, until the rediscovery of their own texts. Although some of Bauer's reconstructions are inaccurate and have been dropped, the idea that Christianity was originally a diverse phenomenon has now been generally accepted. While Bauer himself still utilized fairly static notions of orthodoxy and heresy, others developed the "varieties" model in a more historically dynamic fashion into a "trajectories" model of early Christianity, tracing the movement of different trends over time.[18] And yet, in a sense, the "varieties" and "trajectories" models still operate on the basis of some of the assumptions outlined by King; they construe these different groups as defined and fixed entities, in varying degrees independent, and suppose that we can view them as different horses in a rerun of a race, keeping our eye all the time on the one we know to be the eventual winner and so define the race itself in

[17] Walter Bauer, *Rechtgläubigkeit und Ketzerei im ältesten Christentum* (Tübingen: Mohr, 1934); in English (from the 2nd ed., ed. G. Strecker, 1964), *Orthodoxy and Heresy in Earliest Christianity*, ed. R. Kraft et al. (Philadelphia: Fortress Press, 1971).

[18] See James M. Robinson and Helmut Koester, *Trajectories Through Early Christianity* (Philadelphia: Fortress Press, 1971).

the terms given by the winner.[19] Determining the reason why one group eventually came to dominate is no longer sought, as in early modern times, on the basis of a pure originating source, but rather, yet in equally modern terms, through the interaction of historical and sociopolitical forces.

One very concrete benefit of this work has been to recognize that the study of early Christianity needs to be attuned to the different geographical settings of the figures and texts studied, recognizing the differences among them, and, more recently, the differences even within particular local regions, especially large urban centers such as Rome.[20] Another distinct advantage is that it shifts historical study away from a quest for a single origin, in a (modern) reconstruction of either the real Jesus or a single apostolic deposit, to focus instead on *responses* to Christ in their unsurprising diversity. Apart from Christ's writing in the sand (Jn 8:6), which no one is said to have read anyway and has long since been smoothed over, we only have reports, accounts, and interpretations of Christ's life and actions, death and resurrection, the earliest of which, the letters of Paul, are already a response to conflicting interpretations. The history of Christianity can only be written as a history of these different interpretations, and an account of the identity of the Christian church, in theological as well as sociological terms, must reflect its historical reality as a community of interpretation.[21]

The voices in this dialogue are necessarily personal and particular, but it is also of the nature of dialogue that each voice will contribute to the shaping of other voices. In this way more recent historical and critical work, including King and others, such as Rebecca Lyman, Judith Lieu, and David Brakke, has not been concerned simply to point out the original diversity of voices, each expressing distinct claims with one eventual winner, but rather to understand the concrete rhetorical and social practices involved in these conversations

---

[19] See the discussion in David Brakke, *The Gnostics: Myth, Ritual, and Diversity in Early Christianity* (Cambridge, MA: Harvard University Press, 2010), 5–18. Brakke adapts the analogy of a horse race from Philip Rousseau, *Pachomius: The Making of a Community in Fourth Century Egypt*, The Transformations of the Classical Heritage (Los Angeles and Berkeley: University of California Press, 1985), 19.

[20] See in particular Peter Lampe, *From Paul to Valentinus: Christians at Rome in the First Two Centuries* (Minneapolis: Fortress Press, 2003).

[21] For Paul's letters as part of the history of interpretation and reinterpretation, fashioning the basis of a Christian hermeneutics, see Margaret M. Mitchell, *Paul, the Corinthians, and the Birth of Christian Hermeneutics* (Cambridge: Cambridge University Press, 2010).

and the various identities being fashioned through them.[22] It is not merely that the typologies of the varieties of early Christianity used by twentieth-century scholarship to reify distinct theological systems or social groups are not adequate maps of historical reality, needing simply to be refined. It is rather that such an approach does not do justice to the complexity of the means by which concrete early Christian figures developed understandings of themselves as Christian and their relations to others doing the same but differently. Focusing on the analysis of identity formation, King argues, requires being

> oriented toward the critical analysis of practices, such as producing texts; constructing shared history through memory, selective appropriation, negotiation, and invention of tradition; developing ritual performances such as baptism and meals; writing and selectively privileging certain theological forms (e.g. creeds) and canons; forming bodies and gender; making places and marking time; assigning nomenclature and establishing categories, defining "others" and so on.[23]

In other words, the task is precisely one of reintegrating all the various currently divided fields of theology, to see them working together in formation of identity.

A key feature of this approach is that it recognizes the hybrid nature of any identity thus established. "Hybridity," as David Brakke points out, is somewhat akin to the older notion of "syncretism." But whereas *syncretism* expressed a negative view toward what it saw as the mixing of extraneous elements to a pure original essence, *hybridity* emphasizes the inescapably fluid nature of human existence and interaction, the way in which different voices mutually influence one another and the rhetorical dimension in which this happens and boundaries are drawn. Rather than seeing the "Gnostics" or other "heretical" groups as syncretistic representatives of early Christianity, drawing in elements that do not belong to an original essence, attention is focused instead on the way in which all figures

---

[22] See Rebecca Lyman, "Hellenism and Heresy," *Journal of Early Christian Studies* 11 (2003): 209–22; Judith M. Lieu, *Christian Identity in the Jewish and Graeco-Roman World* (Oxford: Oxford University Press, 2004); Karen King, "Which Early Christianity?" in *The Oxford Handbook of Early Christian Studies*, ed. Susan Ashbrook Harvey and David G. Hunters, 66–84 (Oxford: Oxford University Press, 2008).

[23] King, "Which Early Christianity?" 73.

in early Christianity draw creatively upon the diverse cultural elements available to them, as indeed do any historical figures in any age. As Brakke puts it, "The boundedness, continuity, and natural evolution of incipient beliefs and doctrines that we have attributed to early Christians groups were not in fact there in social life, but were invoked rhetorically in the multilateral process of identity formation and boundary setting in which all early Christians were engaged."[24] Within this dynamic, and fluid, situation, one can see claims to "orthodoxy" and "heresy" as being rhetorical constructs attempting to set boundaries and establish identity. The goal, as Brakke puts it, "should be to see neither how a single Christianity expressed itself in diverse ways, nor how one group of Christians emerged as the winner in a struggle, but how multiple Christian identities and communities were continually created and transformed."[25]

Yet this does not mean dissolving all early Christianity into "a soup of hybridity," to use Brakke's delicious image,[26] for it is nevertheless still possible to make distinctions among forms of Christianity and to identify concrete historical social groupings that did occur on the ground. Although interpretative categories or scholarly constructs, such as apocalyptic Judaism, are not social categories, corresponding to historical groups with which particular figures would identify, social categories, on the other hand, while always also being interpretative ones, involving the kind of practices mentioned above, do and did, Brakke rightly insists, actually exist.[27] The modern category "Gnosticism," which was never used by Irenaeus but introduced in 1669 by Henry More, has proved to be untenable and seeking to define its "essence" impossible.[28] Yet there neverless was, Brakke convincingly argues, a specific group that did identify itself as "Gnostic," whose existence can be discerned on the basis

---

[24] Brakke, *The Gnostics*, 12.

[25] Ibid., 15.

[26] Ibid.

[27] Ibid., 16–18.

[28] See Bentley Layton, "Prolegomena to the Study of Ancient Gnosticism," in *The Social World of the First Christians: Essays in Honor of Wayne A. Meeks*, ed. L. Michael White and O. Larry Yarbrough, 334–50 (Minneapolis: Fortress Press, 1995), 348–49. As Brakke notes: "When modern scholars depict many different ancient groups as belonging to the same category—Gnosticism—they replicate Irenaeus's notion of false gnosis but neglect his careful delineation of its diversity" (*The Gnostics*, 4); see also Michael Allen Williams, *Rethinking "Gnosticism": An Argument for Dismantling a Dubious Category* (Princeton, NJ: Princeton University Press, 1999); and King, *What Is Gnosticism?*

of Irenaeus's report, its own texts, and the various ritual and social practices described therein.

Irenaeus and Second-Century Orthodoxy

Likewise, in second-century Rome, a microcosm of Christianity throughout the empire, and the crucible in which "orthodoxy" was forged in the second century, here clearly were communities of Christians that were perceived, even by non-Christians, as belonging together, as "the great church," and that identified themselves, together, in various ways and through various practices, as orthodox in distinction to the heretics, those, that is, who had separated from them. Intriguingly, given the new directions of contemporary scholarship, it was this "great church" that was precisely the place in which diversity was recognized as an integral element of its catholicity. Certainly some, such as Marcion, departed from this broad body rather than being cast out after his attempts at reformation along his own lines were not received, and others, such as Valentinus and his disciples, gradually drifted away, considering themselves possessors of higher knowledge, spiritually superior to other, lower, "psychic" Christians. When Irenaeus intervened in affairs in Rome at the end of the second century, it was not to demand that the Valentinians be excommunicated and their books burned, in the name of an increasingly intolerant patriarchal orthodoxy intent on preserving its purity for its own purposes, as is often supposed. Rather, when Irenaeus did intervene in affairs in Rome, it was to urge that the great church should acknowledge the degree to which the Valentinians had already separated themselves from this community, and to promote toleration of diversity among those who remained together; as Irenaeus reminded Victor in the controversy over Quartodeciman practice, "Our divergence in the fast confirms our agreement in the faith."[29] This fact is important, for it means that the establishment of "orthodoxy" in this period is not the result of power games but has a properly theological grounding.

Certainly such splits and tensions helped the great church clarify its identity and its shared basis for conversation as a communal body of interpretation and ecclesial practice. But rather than imagining this, as much twentieth-century scholarship has done by taking its cue from fourth-century narratives interpreted through the assumptions of the historicism of recent centuries, in terms of static and

---

[29] Irenaeus, "Letter to Victor," in Eusebius, *Historia Ecclesiastica*, 5.24.12–17.

bounded reified identities needing to be preserved or retrieved, it would be better to adapt one of the key themes of Irenaeus's theology: that of a symphony, comprised of different voices throughout time, each lending itself to the melody being played, with different timbres and tonalities, inflections and themes, and each in turn being shaped by the symphony. Speaking theologically, moreover, this symphony is not, therefore, constructed by any individual voice or all the voices together but is governed by its own rhythm and rules, so that, to use Irenaeus's words, it is God who "harmonizes the human race to the symphony of salvation" (4.14.2). Rather than thinking of orthodoxy as being a matter of consensus — the *consensus patrum* as it came to be expressed — it would be better to understand it, as it understood itself during this pivotal period, as a symphony.

In an intriguing manner, then, it seems that after its quest for a historically pure original essence of Christianity, modern scholarship is seeking to recover a concern for catholicity in the manner of none other than Irenaeus (the bogeyman of much modern scholarship)! Through a careful historical analysis, in a modern spirit, of his writings it is clear that Irenaeus's concerns are emphatically not those of recent centuries. He does not attempt to retrieve the "real historical Jesus," understood as the life and teaching of Jesus prior to his passion, but rather to understand this same Jesus on the basis of his passion through the interpretation of the scriptures, that is, what we now call the Old Testament or the Hebrew scriptures, following the apostles in an ongoing reflection and dialogue. This scripture is not read merely historically but as a thesaurus, a treasury of words and images, that fit together as a mosaic depicting Christ; so his concern is for the coherence of this interpretation with scripture, rather than the historicity of the accounts of the evangelists or the "real history" behind those accounts.[30] This does not mean that he dismisses history, but that he recognizes, as we noted above, that in all this we are always already dealing with interpretations, and, in a

---

[30] His concern is so much with the scriptural nature of the apostolic preaching, rather than its historicity, that he doesn't really raise the question of the historical accuracy or reliability of the Gospels, or when he does, obliquely, he comes to rather surprising conclusions, such as his claim that at the time of his public teaching Jesus was over forty years old (*Against Heresies* 2.22.5–6); it is the coherence of scripture and the rhetorical coherence resulting from understanding Christ through the scriptures that are of primary importance for Irenaeus. Facing the question of conflicting details in different Gospels a generation later, Origen made the notorious claim, but one that highlights the point being made here, that "spiritual truth is often preserved in material falsehood, so to speak" (*Commentary on John*, 10.20).

sense, his own theology is therefore more historically grounded than those quests for the "historical Jesus" in that it doesn't presume to get behind the passion or bracket the cross, as if it had never happened, but accepts it as the defining moment.

In a similar manner, when, at the beginning of the third book of *Against Heresies*, Irenaeus lists the succession of teachers in Rome, all of whom, he claims, have consistently taught the same, this is not cast in terms of maintaining, statically, an original deposit of teachings separate from the scriptures, as those following in Lessing's wake would do, but that in their preaching, bound up as this is with the interpretation of scripture, these figures were all part of the same symphony, with all the diachronic and synchronic diversity that this entails. This symphony moreover is both public and continuously unfolding, in contrast to those who, from time to time, prefer to play their own tunes. Such discordant voices certainly continue, nevertheless, to influence voices sharing in the symphony. But as ones who have separated themselves from that symphony of the one body of Christ, their similar but separate tunes can be described as "demonically inspired" mimicry after the model of Simon Magus and can be correlated in various ways, in the case of Irenaeus, at least, with a fair degree of respect for their own diversity. And having argued briefly, in the first five chapters of the third book of *Against Heresies*, for this continuous symphony, Irenaeus's real concern is shown in the remaining three volumes: "since the tradition from the apostles does thus exist in the Church, let us revert to the scriptural demonstration given by the apostles who did also write the gospel" (*Against Heresies* 3.5.1). The task of theology, as Irenaeus understood it, was specifically this "scriptural demonstration."

This image of a symphony does not mean that any and every voice was, or is to be, accepted as singing the same melody; though, at least in this period, it is the discordant voices that leave the broader community of their own accord, not willing to harmonize themselves with others. For Irenaeus, there is certainly a single "hypothesis" underpinning the edifice of "orthodoxy," a unity undergirding the polyphonous symphony that is being played, a basis that Irenaeus referred to as its hypothesis. As Hellenistic philosophy well knew, building upon Aristotle and Epicurus, any and every branch of knowledge or art has its own hypothesis or first principle that cannot be demonstrated, whether by a historical quest or empirical evidence, for this would be but to substitute another first principle in what would lead ultimately to an infinite regress in which no knowledge is possible. First principles are therefore always and in every case accepted on faith.[31] Yet Irenaeus's hypothesis does in fact cohere with the two occasions in which the apostle Paul uses the technical formula of reception and delivery or traditioning: "I received from the LORD what I also handed on to you," that the eucharistic offering received from the Lord himself is to be enacted, "proclaim[ing] the Lord's death until he comes" (1 Cor 11:23, 26), and that "Christ died for our sins in accordance with the scriptures, and that he was buried, and that he was raised on the third day in accordance with the scriptures" (1 Cor 15:3–4). It is not simply the death and resurrection of Christ that is of first importance, but its interpretation "in accordance with the scriptures" in the context of a community that celebrates the eucharist together proclaiming Christ's death. This hypothesis also functions as a criterion or a "canon of truth," by which Irenaeus does not mean, as did Lessing and those following in his wake, a set of doctrines detached from the scriptures and their interpretation, but rather an expression, which can vary depending on context, of the coherence of scripture as a mosaic of Christ. The purpose of the canon was not to demarcate a set of teachings that must be accepted and to curtail reason or further thought, but instead to make further reflection possible. As Eric Osborn puts it: "The rule did not limit reason to make room for faith, but used faith to make room for reason. Without a credible first principle, reason was lost in an infinite regress."[32]

This hypothesis is in fact exemplified in the four Gospels accepted as canonical, in which Christ is always on his way to his passion, and told from that perspective, through the engagement with the scriptures: beginning with Mark, who gives us "the beginning of the Gospel of Jesus Christ" illustrated by a citation from a passage in Isaiah (Mk 1:1–3; Mal 3:1; Is 40:3), continued in Matthew and Luke, where prophecy-fulfillment structures the narrative and the events within it, and culminating in John, where Christ states simply and majestically: "If you believed Moses, you would believe me, for he wrote about me" (Jn 5:46). It is also preserved in the structure of the narrative, where, at least in the Synoptic Gospels, the disciples continually fail to understand who Christ is until after the passion, when the scriptures are opened and the bread broken, and he immediately

---

[31] See John Behr, *The Way to Nicaea*, Formation of Christian Theology, vol. 1 (Crestwood, NY: SVS Press, 2001).

[32] Eric Osborn, "Reason and the Rule of Faith in the Second Century," in Williams, *The Making of Orthodoxy*, 40–61, at 57.

disappears from sight (Lk 24), so that he always remains "the Coming One." The one exception in fact proves the rule: although on the road to Caesarea Philippi Peter confesses that Jesus is "the Christ, the Son of the Living God," he is said to know this by revelation not by flesh and blood, that is, by a merely human perception, and soon gets called "Satan" for trying to prevent Christ going to Jerusalem to suffer. In the Gospel of John, on the other hand, what the disciples learn at the end of the narrative in the Synoptics is known to them from the beginning, when Philip told Nathaniel, "We have found him about whom Moses in the law and also the prophets wrote," and Christ subsequently tells him, "you will see greater things than these" (Jn 1:45, 50).

Read in the light of what God has wrought in Christ, the scriptures provided the terms and images, the context, within which the apostles made sense of what happened, and with which they explained it and preached it. Importantly, in this it is Christ who is being explained through the medium of scripture: the object is not to understand the "original meaning" of an ancient text, as in modern historical-critical scholarship, but to understand the crucified and risen Christ "in accordance with the scriptures," that is, through the terms and images, the events and figures contained in them, so that Christ is the sole subject throughout — the Word of God. As such, the canon of truth does not simply give fixed, and abstract, statements of Christian doctrine — a resolution to "intellectual problems" — but expresses the correct hypothesis of the symphony sung by the Christian community in its exegesis of scripture, so that its members can see in these scriptures the icon of a king, Christ, rather than picture of a dog or fox, to use Irenaeus's image. As canon, the hypothesis also exposes the incongruous character of other hypotheses. By means of the same canon of truth the various passages, the "members of truth" (*Against Heresies* 1.8.1), can be returned to their rightful place within "the body of truth" (*Demonstration* 1). The canon of truth is thus ultimately the presupposition that is the apostolic Christ himself, the crucified and risen Lord proclaimed "in accordance with the scriptures," crystallizing this coherence of scripture, read as speaking of the Christ who is revealed in the Gospels. All this is expressed clearly and profoundly by Clement of Alexandria in his concise definition of the canon: "The ecclesiastical canon is the concord and harmony of the law and the prophets in the covenant delivered at the coming of the Lord" (Clement, *Stromata* 6.15.125.3). The Lord — whose coming is not fixed in the past, for he is known only in his passage out of this world to return in all those who seek him — reveals the symphony of the scriptures by opening the books of the law and the prophets to show how they all speak of him.

Death

"Learning how theology speaks" by returning to "the Word delivered in the beginning," as this was articulated or sung in the symphony of early Christianity, when seen on its own terms, rather than through modern presuppositions, offers us a coherent account of discourse of theology, exegetical and systematic together, as well as all the other aspects that contribute to identity formation in Christ. It also offers a way of seeing the diachronically and synchronically polyphonous character of this symphony, which nevertheless has its own hypothesis and canon. Besides offering a way out of the disintegration of modern theology, by focusing our attention on the crucified and risen Christ as the subject of scripture, returning to "the Word delivered in the beginning" speaks to another perennial, yet peculiarly contemporary issue, and that is the place and role of death.

Reading the scriptures in the light of the passion, and as speaking of Christ, this Christ is, as Paul puts it, "the image of the invisible God" (Col 1:15) such that we can't look elsewhere to "see" God, "for in him all the whole fullness of deity dwells bodily" (Col 2:9), such that there is no surplus of divinity existing elsewhere, as it were, to be discovered by some other means and spoken about in a different discourse. This Christ is the definition of what God is, the *Logos* of God. Probably the most important scriptural passage for the early Christians, as they searched the scriptures to understand how God was at work in Christ, was Isaiah 53, the hymn of the suffering servant. By reference to this passage they concluded that Christ was not simply put to death but went voluntarily to his death, and in this way conquered death, trampling down death by death.

This is perhaps the hardest thing of all for us to hear: Christ shows us *what* it is to be God in the *way* that he dies as a human being. This is stunning! It defies human comprehension. It is not, as it is sometimes thought, that he dies because human, yet because God he is able to conquer death, but rather that by voluntarily going to his death — truly voluntarily, as, since there was no sin in him, death had no claim on him — he shows himself to be stronger than death, such that it cannot hold him.

This is really hard to hear, and so it is not surprising that this is what the great councils of the early centuries worked so hard to affirm. *Nicaea and Constantinople:* that Christ is the Son of God, consubstantial with the Father, that he is what it is to be God, not simply a man who lived in a godly manner, or a way that God chose to express himself at that time (and so could be different another time), but that the one proclaimed by the apostles in accordance with scripture is what it is to be God, yet other than the Father, and this is only known in and through the Spirit, by whom alone we can call Jesus "Lord" (1 Cor 12:3), that is, the one spoken of in scripture. *Ephesus, Chalcedon, and the Second and Third Councils of Constantinople:* that we see what it is to be God and what it is to be human in one, in one *hypostasis*, one concrete being, and in one *prosopon*, with one "face"; that we don't look here to see God and there to see a human being, but that we see them together—without confusion, change, division, or separation. And finally *Second Nicaea:* that he does indeed "image" God in his flesh, such that images can indeed be made of him. And, in turn, this is what all those they struggled with tried to avoid: *Docetism*—that he wasn't really human; *Arianism*—that he wasn't really God; *Nestorianism*—that the Word and the man are two distinct beings, with two different *prosopa*. And perhaps today, the *historicism* that would want to get behind the cross, away from the scriptural presentation of the crucified and risen One, to get to who it is now newly claimed he "really was."

Christ shows us what it is to be God by the way he dies as a human being. This is a vitally important point. Death is that which expresses all the weakness, frailty, and, ultimately, the apparent futility of our existence; we have come into being through no choice of our own ("No one asked me whether I wanted to be born!" complained Kirilov), thrown into an existence in which whatever we do, we will die (again with no choice). So much for human freedom! Death is, in fact, the only thing common to all human beings from the beginning of the world onward. And so it is here, and nowhere else, that Christ shows us how to live divinely, to be gods, by "using death," in the striking phrase of Maximus the Confessor, to turn death inside out, so that rather than being the end, death in fact becomes the beginning—of life and freedom, resulting from a free decision to no longer live according to "this world," to sin, to passions, "in Adam," but rather to live for one's neighbor, living the same life of sacrificial love that Christ has shown to be the very life and being of God.

Moreover, Christ, in this way, not only shows us the life and being of God, but also of the human being, together, in one—without confusion, change, division, or separation. As such, we have yet to become human. Writing to the Romans, urging them not to interfere with his coming martyrdom there, Ignatius of Antioch states this dramatically:

> It is better for me to die in Christ Jesus than to be king over the ends of the earth. I seek him who died for our sake. I desire him who rose for us. Birth-pangs are upon me. Suffer me, my brethren; hinder me not from living, do not wish me to die. . . . Suffer me to receive the pure light; when I shall have arrived there, I shall become a human being *(anthropos)*. Suffer me to follow the example of the passion of my God. (Ignatius, *To the Romans* 6)

In this reversal of life and death, Ignatius is only now about to be born and only now about to become human. The background for these startling words is Christ's words in John, spoken from the cross: "It is finished." The work that is uniquely God's own project, unlike everything else that is simply spoken into existence with a divine *fiat*, is to make a human being in his own image and likeness; this is now concluded by Christ giving his own *fiat*, confirmed unwittingly by Pilate a few verses earlier (and only in John): "Here is the man" (lit: "human being," *anthropos*) (Jn 19:5). The project, the work of God announced at the beginning, is completed at the end by one who is God and man. For every other aspect of creation, all that was needed was a simple divine *fiat* — "Let it be!" But for the human being to come into existence required us to give our own *fiat* by dying to ourselves and living in Christ.

It is perhaps not surprising that one of the biggest questions in our contemporary society is that of human identity, for it is also this society that, for the last half century or more, has been living with the denial of death (to use the title of Ernest Becker's book). We certainly still die, and so do those around us, whom we have known. But in a very real sense, we in the West no longer "see" death: unlike our relatively recent predecessors, we usually don't grow up with some of our siblings dying in childhood, with one or more of our parents dying before we reach adulthood, and certainly not with the dead corpse lying in repose in our own homes, mourned and celebrated by family, friends, and neighbors, for several days, before being taken for the funeral rites; the cadaver is now removed as quickly as possible to the morticians, where it is made up to look, under the rosy lights of the funeral home, as living as possible ("they have never looked so good"). If Christ shows us, as I have suggested, the face of God in the way that he dies as human, then removing the face of death from society all but removes the face of God as well. The challenge that Christian theology faces, as it learns again how it speaks of God, is therefore all the more difficult today than, I would suggest, ever before. Yet, returning to "the Word delivered in the beginning" may well show us the way forward.

A Response to John Behr

Irenaean Symphony in a Post-Establishment World

Rhys Kuzmic

John Behr has argued that the current situation of disciplinary fragmentation is one of the chief issues facing theology today. He does well to highlight the divisions between scriptural studies and systematic or dogmatic theology, which is the focus of his primary concern. Much of the contemporary disintegration stems from the presuppositions of the interpreters, as Behr elucidates. His focal point in particular is those who approach the biblical text with a modern assumption of historicism, under which the kernel of historical truth can be unearthed and dislodged from later accretions through the methods of modern scholarship. Whether the late patristic scholar Richard Hanson or the numerous historical Jesus questers, the presumption is that one can discover behind the historical sources what is real or essential to Christianity, which is typically understood as singular. In contrast, following Walter Bauer, Behr counters that Christianity has been a diverse phenomenon from the very beginning. With this in view Behr asserts that the "history of Christianity can only be written as a history of these different interpretations, and an account of the identity of the Christian church, in theological as well as sociological terms, must reflect its historical reality as a community of interpretation." In this, Behr takes the call of Karen King to be attuned to such communal history making and development of rituals in the process of identity formation as a summons to theological reintegration. Just as identity formation involves various disciplinary endeavors, theology, which is also a means of identity formation, must integrate multiple disciplines into its project.

Behr also ingeniously uses King's insights to question the assumptions present in current scholarship on orthodoxy and heresy. For example, Marcion provides an excellent illustration of someone who sought to get behind the biblical writings to an essential core message, who did away with the diversity of the Gospels by holding to only one account, and who separated himself from the Christian community by starting his own church. It is quite striking how the assumptions of Marcion align with modern accounts that seek an essence behind the texts and subsume diversity under one conceptual apparatus. Behr argues that the early Christian community actually maintained a certain level of diversity; it was the Marcionites who could not tolerate a plurality of gospel accounts or the differing views of the Christian community and thus chose to separate themselves. Perhaps, Behr suggests, the modern critiques of power in regard to orthodoxy and heresy do not apply to the first two or three centuries.

But following Walter Bauer's insights regarding "varieties of Christianity," how can one achieve the theological reintegration Behr envisions if theological interpretations have been diverse from the very inception of Christianity? Should one look to a consensus? Behr moves away from the *consensus patrum* and turns to Irenaeus's depiction of theology as a symphony of different voices throughout time harmonized by God. Irenaeus is largely unconcerned with historical issues, Behr contends, and focuses instead on the coherence of interpretation with scripture. The task of theology is thus to "revert to the scriptural demonstration given by the apostles" (*Against Heresies* 3.5.1), which requires a hypothesis or first principle accepted on faith. For Irenaeus, this principle is the coherence of scripture as a mosaic of Christ. Scripture provides the terms, images, and context in which one must make sense of God's work in Christ, which is the sole subject of scripture: the Word of God. It is precisely this Word that Behr proposes theology return to in order to bridge the divide of disciplinary fragmentation. In addition to addressing theological fragmentation, such a return can, according to Behr, provide a normative criterion, a canon for theology, as well as speak to the place and role of death. The return is not to an idealized past, Behr contends, but to the presuppositions of the early Christian theologians.

In this regard I want to focus more on Behr's proposal as a response to the problem of fragmentation. My goal is to probe further into what such a return to the Word entails and whether it can speak to the balkanization of the theological encyclopedia. There may be some who would want to press Behr on whether disciplinary fragmentation is even a problem, but I will leave that for other questioners. I, at least, do share sympathies with the task of bringing systematic theology together with biblical studies. Behr has highlighted quite insightfully the difference that presuppositions make in our theological endeavors. Let us turn to the specific issue of scriptural or biblical studies and its relation to theology. What does it mean to replace certain modernist assumptions and goals regarding history with the assumption of textual coherence regarding the scriptures and their witness to Christ? Certainly, both Polycarp and his disciple Irenaeus addressed their injunctions to communities of faith (whether to return to the Word or to revert to the scriptural demonstration). Does Behr's proposal also require faith? Should one say "Extra ecclesiam nulla theologia"? Moreover, would it even make sense to take such a return more broadly than Polycarp and Irenaeus surely envisioned and claim one can simply replace intellectual presuppositions without practical issues being involved? It is not surprising in this regard that Polycarp mentions prayer and fasting immediately following his exhortation to return to the Word.[1] If intellectual presuppositions go hand in hand with practical consequences, as Polycarp and Irenaeus seemed to agree, the proposal to return to the Word should be interpreted as a call to *metanoia*, understood as involving both *nous* and *soma* alike or, in the words of liberation theologians, theology and praxis.

It also seems curious whether the fissure between biblical studies and systematic theology is one felt as significant and in need of redress primarily by theologians of faith and, in particular, those who view scripture as authoritative. This concern would be consistent with the presupposition of scriptural coherence, but the question may legitimately be raised whether those who do not share such assumptions also find this fragmentation troubling. It seems important to raise these issues in hopes of clarifying to whom this call of return is addressed and what it entails. My contention is that the exhortation to return be construed as a call to conversion/repentance, which should not be taken pejoratively; in framing the discussion in this way my aim is to highlight and clarify the stakes involved. To accept the terms of the call to return means to leave beside purely histori-

---

[1] Polycarp, *Letter to the Philippians* 7.2. Likewise, Irenaeus urged reverting to the scriptural demonstration precisely to explicate clearly that "our Lord Jesus Christ is the truth" (*Against Heresies* 3.5.1).

cal interests and subsume those beneath a concern for interpreting scripture as a mosaic of accounts that cohere under the leitmotif of Christ. Although Behr does not touch on this specifically, following Polycarp, such acceptance would also result in practical implications in how one lives in relation to the person of this leitmotif.

In turning to a hypothesis or agreed-upon canon that Irenaeus envisioned, these same issues arise. The interpretation of an agreed upon canon is closely linked to faith—it is a *regula fidei* (although not in Lessing's sense). Behr sees the hypothesis or canon not as a set of isolated doctrines demanding assent, but as an expression of the hermeneutical presupposition he is advocating, namely, the "coherence of scripture as a mosaic of Christ." Can one hold to such a canon apart from faith? Behr acknowledges that first principles such as these are always taken on the basis of faith. This brings to the fore the issue of whether faith as intellectual assent can be separated from faith as spiritual relationship. Behr, following Polycarp and Irenaeus, does not seem to be advocating a notional assent of presumption.[2] It is not simply a matter of trading the assumptions of modern historical-critical scholarship for a proposition on the canon of faith. Polycarp and Irenaeus are not enamored with propositions but center their attention on Christ. The Christ is not a notion one must assent to but a person who must be understood through the accounts and reflections in scripture. Farley, whom Behr cites in discussing the problem of theological fragmentation, views theology as sapiential knowledge,[3] and it appears that Behr largely shares this same disposition. Therefore, the return Behr advocates is not one that can be limited to replacing modern historical scholarship's endeavors with the goals of second-century orthodoxy. Returning to the Word is not simply propositional; there is propositional content to be sure, but the Word refers to the person of Christ. Behr's goal is not to resolve intellectual disputes but to express accurately the identity of Christ.

Beyond the question of what such a return entails, there is the question of how the presupposition of scriptural coherence addresses theological fragmentation. I think one can certainly see how a focus on Christ as the central subject of scripture can bridge the

---

[2] See John Henry Newman, *An Essay in Aid of a Grammar of Assent* (Oxford: Oxford University Press, 1985), 4.1. According to Newman, notions "are but aspects of things" and therefore deductions from one of these aspects may contradict deductions from other aspects.

[3] Edward Farley, *Theologia: The Fragmentation and Unity of Theological Education* (Philadelphia: Fortress Press, 1983).

ever-increasing divide between biblical studies and theology. This can be seen, for instance, in a great many evangelical theologians who affirm this presupposition and seek to ground their respective theologies on biblical exegesis. One can argue that the same cleft in other theological movements between scripture and theology is not felt to the same degree among evangelical thinkers. But I wonder if the disciplinary fragmentation endemic to theology runs deeper than the presuppositions that Behr underlines. For Farley, the primary concern is clerical education and the need to restore theological unity to this process. How does a return to the Word affect the various subdisciplines of theology? Does it eliminate them or reorganize them? What is the fate of feminist theology or liberation theology for example? While there are many issues that can be raised here, the concern I want to emphasize is whether returning to Polycarp's and Irenaeus's presuppositions, which are pre-establishment, can address the post-establishment situation of multiple theological disciplines operating with differing presuppositions and methodologies.

My sense is that participation in the various theological subdisciplines is also connected to one's presuppositions. The presuppositions I have in mind go beyond the primary bifurcation of assumptions Behr focuses on between Hanson and Irenaeus. For example, in the case of feminist theology, when one consults the biblical texts there are very divergent interpretations of what they mean. Some take the view that scripture is dominantly hostile to women and such texts should be ignored. Others seek a redemptive interpretation made in light of a more basic hermeneutical principle that trumps the particular message of a given text. Still others are opposed to the very project of feminist theology and employ biblical texts to counter feminist endeavors. This spectrum of responses aligns well with the wide range of evangelical theologians who would accept the terms of the call to return that Behr advocates.[4] If evangelicals who share with Polycarp and Irenaeus the basic presupposition of scriptural coherence can disagree on the ecclesiastical and domestic role of women, then how do such divergent interpretations of scripture

---

[4] Only the first response of discarding biblical texts altogether would not be shared by evangelical thinkers. For differing evangelical opinions on feminism see (among his numerous books on the subject) Wayne Grudem, *Evangelical Feminism and Biblical Truth: An Analysis of More than 100 Disputed Questions* (Colorado Springs: Multnomah, 2004) for a traditional view, and *Discovering Biblical Equality: Complementarity Without Hierarchy,* ed. Ronald W. Pierce and Rebecca Merrill Groothuis (Grand Rapids, MI: Eerdmans, 2004) for egalitarian conceptions.

function in Irenaeus's symphony? Certainly, sharing Polycarp's and Irenaeus's presuppositions regarding the nature and role of theology does not eliminate a plurality of biblical interpretations, some of which are diametrically opposed. Thus, do such subdisciplines as feminist theology and the complex web of biblical interpretations surrounding its purview serve as harmonious voices in the theological symphony? Furthermore, do they participate in the symphony only in so far as they submit to faith in the divine conductor, or does God harmonize their voices regardless?

As this discussion highlights, a whole host of fundamental issues has been raised, including the nature, task, and domain of theology; the relation of theology to its various subdisciplines; the possible reorganization of the theological encyclopedia and its role in education; and the role of faith in such theological endeavors. While Behr draws attention to problematic assumptions in historical-critical scholarship that, in part, have resulted in theological fragmentation, one may well wonder whether adopting the coherence model of the Irenaean symphony does away with other aspects of fragmentation that arise from interpreting scripture even when there is agreement on more basic issues such as the nature and domain of theology. If agreement on the nature and domain of theology does not inexorably lead to hermeneutical harmony in relation to various theological subdisciplines (as evangelical theology has revealed),[5] should the theological encyclopedia be reorganized? Returning to the pre-establishment presuppositions of early Christian theologians can make significant inroads on the problem of fragmentation. I take it that such a move involves two primary and concomitant features: (1) accepting that the task of theology is to understand Christ "in accordance with the scriptures" as a coherent mosaic of narratives and reflections that expresses accurately the identity of the Word; and (2) treating this presupposition not as an abstract notion but as reflecting a living faith in Christ as a person to whom one responds with Christian practices such as prayer and fasting (as in Polycarp). These two aspects are admittedly grand in both their scope and cost; they require much more than intellectual assent, yet they remain quite broad and may be enacted in diverse ways. Consensus on the basic task of theology does not necessitate agreement on theological method. Thus, even if they are accepted in the call to return, it

---

[5] One could also add Peter Abelard's *Sic et Non* to this as an apt example of patristic disagreements and contradictions over various philosophical and theological questions.

is not clear how Behr's proposal can diminish other fissures within various theological subdisciplines such as feminist theology. Perhaps such subdisciplines would simply be eliminated from the theological encyclopedia. Or the divine conductor may nevertheless harmonize the diversity of their contrapuntal textures in one majestic ongoing symphony. However Behr would resolve this dilemma of theological reintegration, the solution gets to the heart of how the Irenaean symphony functions in a post-establishment world.

2

The Deconstruction and Reconstruction of Christian Identity in a World of Différance

ANSELM K. MIN

Let me begin with a brief explanation of my title. We are living in a world of *différance*, to borrow a term from Derrida. I do not agree with his phenomenological analysis of the ubiquity of difference, but I do accept the ubiquity of difference as a phenomenon, and using the language of *différance* is one way of accentuating that phenomenon. Today we live in a world saturated by references to and concerns over diversity, pluralism, multiplicity, difference. Some even talk about the primacy of multiplicity over unity (for example, Alain Badiou, Paul Knitter). While it has freed us from much oppressive essentialism and totalitarianism, this talk of multiplicity and difference has left nothing intact in its traditional identity including Christianity. The "deconstruction" of Christian identity in the title refers to this destruction of Christian identity that has been going on for several decades under the relentless pressure of the culture of difference that now has become a global phenomenon. It refers to the crisis of Christian identity that I believe surpasses that of any preceding crisis in its gravity, in its challenge, and in its task, a crisis I consider comprehensive and fundamental because it touches Christianity in its totality and depth. The "reconstruction" of Christian identity, then, refers to the challenging task of rebuilding that Christian identity under today's very critical conditions.

I will tackle my task in four steps. First, I show why I consider the issue of Christian identity the most compelling of all theological issues facing Christianity today. Second, I discuss four reasons or causes of the radical erosion of Christian identity, problems internal to each of the communions, the popularization of the anti-Christian secularism of the Enlightenment, the relativization of the churches as institutions, and most important, the globalization of cultural nihilism. Third, I review some current discussions and options for the reconstruction of Christian identity. Fourth, I present some ideas of collective identity and argue that Christian identity is ultimately a matter and task of rejuvenating a tradition. For Roman Catholics I end with a call for the convocation of an ecumenical council, Vatican III, as a most potent catalyst for such a task.

Christian Identity as the Most Compelling Theological Issue Today

To begin with a concrete idea of what I mean by the crisis of Christian identity, let me describe it as follows. Today Christian communities all over the world, but especially in Europe and North America, are in great disarray, uncertain about themselves, confused about what they really believe, fragmented among contending ideological groups, demoralized and without much hope and enthusiasm about what they are and what they ought to be, about their sense of mission and identity. They have been on the defensive from the mainstream culture that has been relentlessly attacking the intellectual content of Christian belief, impugning the integrity of Christian morality, and rejecting Christianity as historically reactionary and humanly oppressive. Christians have been made to feel like a pariah, an unwanted minority, forced either to react in a violent, fanatical way to assert its identity under attack, or to withdraw into impotent inwardness with resignation and without "always be[ing] ready to make your defense to anyone who demands from you an accounting for the hope that is in you" (1 Pt 3:15). Christian communities seem to have lost their spine, their guts, their soul, their spirit. To use a word Jimmy Carter once used, for which he was roundly ridiculed, Christianity today seems to be suffering from a serious dose of "malaise" of uncertainty and despair about itself. It is this crisis of Christian identity that I consider the most compelling theological issue today.

I organized a national conference in Claremont, California, April 20–21, 2012, with eight invited presenters, each with a national reputation (from which this volume originates). I put the theme of the conference deliberately in the form of a question: What is or are the most compelling theological issues today? The first obvious rejoinder, of course, is, by what criteria? As organizer of the conference I deliberately left open the criteria by which one can argue that a certain issue or cluster of issues is the most compelling theological issues today. I left it up to the presenters to define both the criteria and the issue they consider the most compelling.

From the papers presented at this conference (and in this volume) we know what the presenters consider to be the most compelling theological issues. The list of compelling issues I received prior to the conference was no surprise to me. I invited the presenters fully knowing what their main interests and concerns were, and I received a list of issues fully corresponding to my expectations. We are most likely to consider our longstanding concerns the most compelling issue of the day. After all, we would not be spending so much of our time and energy pursuing those issues unless we think they do matter and are compelling in some way. Thus, we had a whole range of compelling issues at this conference: returning to the Word delivered in the beginning, constructing a new theology of the world in the light of globalization and postsecularity, a new pneumatology that speaks to the environmental crisis, decolonizing Christianity, liberation of women and nature, a critique of US imperialism, and the political role of faith in a pluralistic society. I think it is entirely possible to make a case for any one of these as the most compelling theological issue today, although they have been around for some time now. I include all of these concerns in the theology of globalization course I have been teaching as an extension of my original interest in liberation theology.

Without in any way detracting from the compelling and urgent character of each of these issues, I still prefer to highlight the crisis of Christian identity as the most compelling theological issue in the contemporary world, for three reasons.

First, unless Christians are themselves clear and hopeful about who they are, about their own identity and mission, all those compelling issues will remain only issues with no community to press them. Here it is critical to distinguish between agendas and agents. It is easy enough to talk about things to be done, the agendas, and we often lose sight of the question of who are supposed to do those things, the agents. As academics we are more concerned about agendas than about agents, more about what the issues are than about who is supposed to solve those issues, more about things to be done than about who is to do those things that so need doing. There are issues galore today in this age of imperialist globalization, from the widening economic gap between rich and poor nations to the oppression of women and the destruction of the environment to political and military imperialism to the conflict of religions and cultures to the digital revolution to migrant workers, but all of these and more require for their solution the involvement and praxis of a large number of people who are conscious of the problems *as* problems in the first place and willing to participate in any collective action, people who are both awakened to the issue as issue and motivated enough to commit themselves. This is the problem of *agency* as distinct from the problem of *agendas.* Today, as always, the real problem is more the problem of agency than the problem of agendas. The problem of Christian identity is the most imperative problem of agency as far as Christian agendas are concerned.

In this regard it is interesting to recall that in recent years Jürgen Habermas has been saying that secular rational morality is too individually oriented and provides only a weak motivation that can be provided by "good reasons"; it does not provide either good reasons or good motivation for solidarity as citizens so essential to the legitimacy of the democratic state or for collective, global praxis of solidarity so demanded by the emerging multicultural global society. For this awakening and motivation for social and global solidarity one must turn to religious resources. Habermas is here recognizing the problem of agency, of agents awakened and motivated enough to engage in the praxis of civic and global solidarity.[1]

In our case the group to be awakened and motivated is primarily the Christian churches. Theology may also speak to the general public and the academy, but I am inclined to think that the primary public of the theologian is the church, and the problem is how to awaken and motivate the churches. It has been noticed with some scandal in recent decades that mainline churches have been declining, while conservative groups, evangelicals, and fundamentalists have been growing. However, if these different groups, liberal or conservative, are themselves confused, fragmented, and indifferent, without much sense of their mission and their identity, we fail in the matter of agency and therefore in the most fundamental way. We produce beautiful agendas, a compelling list of things to do, without anyone willing to do them, without any agency with a sense of mission and identity vigorous enough to accomplish them. The great

---

[1] Jürgen Habermas, *An Awareness of What Is Missing: Faith and Reason in a Post-Secular Age* (Cambridge, UK: Polity, 2010), 73–76; Jürgen Habermas and Joseph Ratzinger, *The Dialectics of Secularization: On Reason and Religion* (San Francisco: Ignatius, 2006), 21–52.

imperative today is to turn our special attention to the problem of agency, especially the problem of Christian agents, both individual and collective, that is to say, the problem of ecclesiology. This is not, of course, in order to neglect the problems of the world but rather to awaken and motivate the Christian communities precisely in their participation in the struggles and hopes of the world so much in need of redemption today.[2]

Second, I consider the crisis of Christian identity the most compelling theological issue because it has not been recognized in all its gravity as the most important issue and cries out for theological attention. There are many theologians who raise the social, political, economic, and ecological issues and bring them to the attention of the Christian communities. There are also many theologians who write on the theology of the church, what the church is and ought to be, and do so even in the context of multiculturalism and globalization. There are also great scholars who write on the history of the church, the history of Christian doctrines, and even plead for a return to the tradition. There are, however, to my knowledge, not many theologians of any stature who write about the state of the Christian communities today, as their identity has been eroded, impugned, even ridiculed; about the deepening crisis of the very sense of identity of Christianity itself brought about by the culture that indiscriminately pluralizes, relativizes, trivializes, nihilates, and reduces all things to what Kierkegaard once called the aesthetic mode of life. I am afraid that very few theologians are fully aware of the depth of this crisis now affecting Christianity and perhaps all religions as well. We theologians may preach what the churches must do, but what if the churches are themselves so intellectually confused and morally enervated by the systematically relativizing and profoundly aestheticizing culture in which they live that they have neither definite convictions nor much enthusiasm to commit themselves to anything?

The Erosion of Christian Identity: Sources and Causes

The third reason I consider Christian identity the most compelling theological issue today should become self-evident in the reasons and causes I am going to discuss for the erosion and enervation of

---

[2] On the important distinction between the problem of agendas and the problem of agency, see Anselm K. Min, "Toward a Theology of Citizenship as the Central Challenge in Asia," *East Asian Pastoral Review* 41/2 (2004), 136–59.

Christian identity. I venture four explanations for this erosion: (1) problems proper to the internal history of a particular communion, (2) the anti-Christian turn of Western intellectual culture and its popularization, (3) the relativization of the churches as institutions, and (4) the globalization of cultural nihilism.

First, regarding problems internal to a particular communion, let me take the example of Roman Catholicism. In *A People Adrift: The Crisis of the Roman Catholic Church in America*, published in 2003,[3] Peter Steinfels, the *New York Times* religion correspondent and columnist, provides one of the best analyses of the problems facing the Catholic Church in the United States in the decades since the Second Vatican Council. His focus is on the church as an institution, based on the premise that "the Catholic Church can succeed as an institution while failing as a church. But it cannot succeed as a church while failing as an institution." Against the rather prevalent dismissal of the "institutional church" or church as an institution, Steinfels insists that "a people is not a population. A people is not an undifferentiated mass but a group with a sense of itself, a collective memory, a solidarity, an anticipated destiny — all of which must be preserved in formulas, rituals, written or recited epics, lines of authority, prescribed and proscribed behaviors."[4]

Among the problems bedeviling the Catholic Church according to Peter Steinfels are, simply to list them here, the polarization between conservatives and liberals with conflicting interpretations of Vatican II; the clergy sexual abuse scandal; the declining public presence of the Catholic voice and the impasse over abortion; the erosion of the distinctively Catholic identity of hospitals and universities the church operates; the significant decline in Sunday mass attendance and the loss of the sense of transcendence in the liturgy so essential to the Catholic identity; problems with the various ways of "passing on the faith," such as the survival of Catholic schools, inadequacy of the catechetical education for Catholic students in both Catholic and public schools (eight of every ten Catholic students are in public schools), the increasing separation between church authorities and theologians; the issues involving sex, gender, sexist language, and women's ordination; and the failure of leadership at all levels, bishops, priests, and lay ministers, in dealing with these issues.

---

[3] Peter Steinfels, *A People Adrift: The Crisis of the Roman Catholic Church in America* (New York: Simon and Schuster, 2003).

[4] Ibid., 14.

Underlying these problems is the central issue of Catholic identity, which has become rather indeterminate, confused, amorphous, and blurred. Steinfels quotes a statement he heard many times from undergraduates at Notre Dame and Georgetown in the 1990s. "I consider myself a Catholic. I like being a Catholic. I'm proud to be a Catholic. But I don't really know what being a Catholic means."[5] The majority of young adult Catholics, according to one report cited by Steinfels, are described as

> distanced from parish life and church institutions, have little sense of church authority, and are not sufficiently versed in the distinctive symbols, narratives, and vocabulary of Catholicism to articulate to themselves a coherent Catholic identity. Moreover, the fragmented Catholic identity they do possess appears to be less and less central in their lives. . . . Through no fault of their own, they breathe in a culture of religious individualism, while at the same they are no longer tied to the Catholic community by their most important friendships or even their spouses.[6]

For them, it does not really matter whether one is Catholic or not. What counts is a "generic Christian lifestyle."[7] Steinfels rightly attributes much of this decline in the sense of Catholic identity to the impact of the many and significant cultural changes in American society such as dramatic changes in family life and the role of women, the rise of other social institutions, the scope of pluralism and the understanding of tolerance, and the nature of information and entertainment.[8] Despite denominational differences I am inclined to think that with appropriate changes, this description also applies to other communions and denominations to varying degrees.[9]

The second reason for the erosion of Christian identity, I submit, is the increasingly anti-Christian turn of Western intellectual culture and its popularization. This is a point Steinfels only indirectly acknowledges and fails to take seriously enough. For some decades no human group has been able to remain insulated from the deluge of information—good or bad, true or false—unleashed by the media, and

---

[5] Ibid., 204.

[6] Ibid., 209–10.

[7] Ibid.

[8] Ibid., 210.

[9] See Robert Wuthnow, *Christianity in the Twenty-first Century: Reflections on the Challenges Ahead* (New York: Oxford University Press, 1993).

its impact on the faculty of judgment. Sunday preaching, religious education at the parish, Christian schools: these are not the only sources of information regarding what is right and what is wrong, what to believe and what not to believe. Increasingly the Christian consciousness, like the consciousness of any other American, has been exposed to and saturated by opinions, arguments, ideologies, propaganda, and perspectives, some legitimate, others merely tendentious, that diverge from the Christian tradition. What they hear at church on Sunday is routinely contradicted by the *New York Times*. What they learn in high school religion classes is radically called into question by *The Da Vinci Code*. What they study in catechism classes is ridiculed by the secular press, television, and increasingly by what they read on the Internet. Catholics find out what the pope says sooner from the secular press, complete with its own interpretation, not always benign, than from their own pulpits or diocesan papers.

The secularization of Western culture with its Enlightenment prejudice against religion and against Christianity in particular is no longer limited to the intellectuals but has become a widespread popular phenomenon from which the churches can no longer insulate themselves. I don't think I am saying anything new when I say that Christianity has been taking a real battering from contemporary intellectual culture. Science, evolution, genetics, and neuroscience, now popularized with all the efficiency of information technologies, have rendered the traditional doctrine of creation and the soul implausible in addition to rendering the God hypothesis superfluous. Books on atheism sometimes become best-selling non-fiction, as do fiction books about Jesus that contradict all the traditional beliefs and pieties. Historical criticism of the Bible and the discovery of new documents like those at Nag Hamadi have called into question the authority and authenticity of the New Testament canon and along with it the validity of Chalcedonian Christology. Historical investigations into the patristic era have unmasked the violence and patriarchy of the orthodox churches and discredited the distinction between orthodoxy and heresy. Feminism has been unmasking sexism and patriarchy as something inherent in the entire history of the Judeo-Christian tradition. Critical sociologists and historians have exposed the role of oppressive power in the churches and radically questioned the innocence and credibility of all ecclesiastical authority. Some of these criticisms come from well-meaning Christian scholars committed to church reform. Some of these attacks come from groups who have a stake in discrediting Christianity. Other criticisms and attacks come from those who want to mix the business of scholarship and the pleasures of making big money by writing best-selling fiction.[10]

We may now go on to ask: After all the recent ideological, deconstructive, genealogical, and postcolonial critiques of human reason and human knowledge, what still remains of faith, revelation, and the traditional understanding of the relation between reason and faith? After all the historical criticisms of scripture and the sociological critiques of the early development of Christian doctrine, how much of scripture and patristic theological developments still remain credible and uncontaminated? After all the scientific reductions of concrete human existence to the brain and the genes, how much of human dignity and human transcendence still remain valid? Is Christianity not moribund in America as it has already been in Europe in the face of the accelerating prevalence of secularism? In recent decades clergy sexual abuse has all but destroyed the moral authority of the Catholic Church. The Christian faith is no longer intellectually and morally credible. Christianity has been compromised and contaminated beyond retrieval. *Or so it seems.* Why take Christianity seriously at all?

For the third reason for the erosion of Christian identity I would like to mention the relativization of the churches as institutions. There are three aspects to this relativization. First, the matter of identity has become so flexible and the sense of identity itself has become relatively weak. Even in the same family members often belong to different religions. The father may be Catholic, the mother Presbyterian, and the children claim no religion at all. The religion of the spouse no longer seems to be a decisive factor in marriage. Second, churches are no longer the only dominant sources of one's identity. People derive a satisfactory sense of identity from the profession that constitutes their career; the many voluntary associations they join; the ethnic, cultural, and political affiliations to which they belong. Third, and most important, the social role of the churches has been significantly reduced and, in many instances, replaced by other social institutions. The churches are no longer the sole institutions that provide counseling, as there are many nonreligious, professionally trained secular counselors. The relief work of the churches has been dwarfed by the much-better-funded functions of the welfare state. Colleges, Wikipedia, and countless places on the Internet provide knowledge, even religious and theological knowledge, in a way

---

[10] The criticisms of Christianity mentioned in this paragraph are so ubiquitous that I do not feel the need for documentation.

much more accessible than the churches. People find interior peace through meditation centers and new religions. Role models are more available from sports heroes, entertainment celebrities, and social leaders than from the exemplars of sanctity in the history of the churches. Various civic organizations have been leading the movement for social justice, democracy, and world peace. There has been a radical decline in the need for the functions of the churches other than the preaching of the gospel and the celebration of the liturgy. In short, it seems that society can get along very well without the churches.[11]

The fourth and most important reason for the erosion of the sense of Christian identity, I believe, has to do with the globalization of cultural nihilism that attacks both the ability of the intellect to make judgments and the ability of the will to commit itself. The intellectual attacks on the content of the Christian faith mentioned above have definitely contributed to the weakening of the sense of Christian identity, but such attacks are relatively determinate and easily identifiable and can be responded to through careful scholarship. They can be humbly accepted as true, refuted as false, analyzed as sheer propaganda in an ongoing culture war, or at least managed with all the complexity and sensitivity they require. There are, however, other sources that are deeper, indeterminate, and hard to pin down because they operate at the level of sensibility, mood, and horizon. I am referring to the culture of nihilism produced by the Internet and other electronic media during the last two decades.

There are, of course, many positive aspects to the electronic globalization of culture. First, by making all ideas and all values in principle available to all people and exposing them to the critique of all, cultural globalization destroys monopolies, hierarchies, and elitisms in the realm of culture and ideas. It is profoundly liberating. No wonder that oppressive regimes are always trying to find ways of controlling what is communicated on the Internet. Second, it makes so much precious knowledge and information so readily available to all. It is profoundly enlightening and informative, and we academics greatly benefit from it. Third, by making the different cultural and religious heritages of humanity easily accessible to all, it contributes to interreligious and intercultural understanding we so need today. Fourth, by providing a hitherto unimaginable variety of alternatives in styles of living, fellowship, belief, knowledge, and

[11] See Robert Wuthnow, "The Quest for Identity," in *Christianity in the Twenty-first Century*, 183–91.

all areas of life it has radically expanded the scope of our options and possibilities, greatly contributing to the promotion of the quality of life. Fifth and last, by making communication possible and promoting it across all the boundaries of time and space, cultural globalization is profoundly unifying and reconciling, at least in the long run. We can say that it is laying the infrastructure for the peaceful coexistence of all humanity in the future.[12]

There are, however, also many negative impacts to the globalization of culture carried on by the media that make us pause in our unthinking celebration of the sheer positivity of cultural globalization. After all, the Internet too is subject to all the dialectic of power among competing and struggling groups, now on the global level, and one should say that the Internet is especially so subject, as it is perhaps the most potent weapon and site of that struggle as "the fundamental symbol-processing system of our time."[13] In a world that is not only different but also divided, globalization means more than the simple coming together of different human groups into the common space of the world for the sake of mutual understanding and mutual search for truth; it also means intensification of the many struggles among divided and alienated groups to secure recognition and domination in the global public opinion now most effectively materialized in the space of the Internet and television. Every group, and indeed increasingly every individual, has its own website and seeks to dominate the public square of the Internet. Every ethnic group, every religious group, every ideological group, every political interest, all with its partisan agenda, seeks to present certain images of itself and its adversaries to win its legitimacy in the court of world opinion. The battle to dominate public opinion in the name of the freedom of speech and expression, of course, is nothing new. It has been foundational to the modern idea of democracy, but it used to be regional or at most national. Now it has become global. Simplification, exaggeration, distortion, and falsehoods are rampant, as are attempts to mobilize all the recent techniques of manipulation and propaganda. Images and appearances replace realities. Ideologies replace truth. Bias replaces objectivity. Such replacements have become an art and a way of life.

---

[12] For a generally positive and optimistic assessment of the possibilities of globalization for faith, see Hans Joas, *Glaube als Option: Zukunftsmöglichkeiten des Christentums* (Freiburg, Germany: Herder, 2012).

[13] Manuel Castells, *Communication Power* (New York: Oxford University Press, 2009), 4.

In addition to ethnic, political, religious, and national groups each with its own interests and ideologies to defend in the global forum of public opinion, there is and has always been the dominant and overriding interest of all, that is, the interest of the capitalist market with its own logic and imperative of profit maximization.[14] For the sake of success in the global competition without limit literally anything goes, short of outright murder and outright lies capable of legal prosecution. In order to stimulate consumption, capitalism must stimulate desire, obliterating all distinction between needs and desires, and creating a global culture of what Jung Mo Sung calls "mimetic" desire, the desire of the middle class to imitate the consumption habits of the economic elite and the desire of the developing countries to imitate those of the developed.[15] Everything is reduced to an object and projection of desire, where images and appearances replace any sense of reality. By the same token every human being is reduced to the subject of desire, and of contingent desire at that, where contingency of desire is deliberately celebrated: a desire is better, the more variable, the more inconsistent, the more insatiable, the more imperative it is. Capitalism celebrates the sovereignty of desire, any desire, in all its contingency, and seeks the liberation of all desire in its infinity, all in the name of freedom. The human being is no longer a subject of self-determining intellect and will who can shape an identity of his or her own with an intellectual power to make independent judgments and a volitional power to determine his or her own actions and life accordingly. Instead, the human subject is reduced to a mere succession of the moments of desire in all its difference, multiplicity, fragmentation, relativity, and rootlessness. The "death of the subject," which postmodernism tries to theorize with such subtlety and erudition that it is beyond the ken of even many a professional philosopher, the capitalist market has been accomplishing with such efficiency and on the global level. No

---

[14] For a discussion of how capitalism colonizes cyberspace for corporate interests and influences politics, education, the media, and culture, see Dan Schiller, *Digital Capitalism: Networking the Global Market System* (Cambrdige, MA: MIT Press, 2000); Robert W. McChesney, *Digital Disconnect: How Capitalism Is Turning the Internet Against Democracy* (New York: The New Press, 2013); Eran Fisher, *Media and New Capitalism in the Digital Age: The Spirit of Networks* (Basingstoke, Hampshire, UK: Palgrave Macmillan, 2010).

[15] Jung Mo Sung, *Desire, Market, and Religion* (London: SCM Press, 2007), 30–50.

wonder that many have been saying that postmodernism is itself a reflection of the late phase of capitalism.[16]

Another reason I am putting forward for the erosion of Christian identity, then, is the inherent cultural nihilism now being globalized by the capitalist market by means of television, the Internet, and other electronic media. Along with the pressure and temptation to exaggerate, distort, falsify, and vilify, the capitalist market celebrates the death of the subject, weakening and mortifying both the power of intellectual judgment and the power of the will to commit oneself to a consistent, coherent plan of life based on some sense of reality, objectivity, and truth. Contemporary globalizing culture presents us with a sheer multiplicity and plurality of goods, services, and, increasingly, ideas and ideologies, reducing each of them to simply one among other such goods, services, and ideologies, and therefore relativizing and trivializing all to the same level of commodities with nothing noteworthy about any. It presents a variety of goods, services, and ideologies as merely objects of entertainment, desire, and power with none being intrinsically and objectively valuable. The competitive practice of winning attention by provoking and shocking has now resulted in such trivialization of things that, as Slavoj Žižek puts it, "perversion is no longer subversive: such shocking excesses are part of the system itself."[17] In the words of Neil Postman: "All public discourse increasingly takes the form of entertainment. Our politics, our religion, news, athletics, education, and commerce have been transformed into congenial adjuncts of show business, largely without protest or even much popular notice," which makes Las Vegas the paradigm of contemporary culture.[18] In such a world, why should I choose any one ideology or belief over another when all ideologies and beliefs are matters of desire, power, feeling, and at most personal historical situations, all results of contingencies without foundations? They are all relative. Furthermore, why should

---

[16] Terry Eagleton, *The Illusions of Postmodernism* (Cambridge, MA: Blackwell, 1996), 132–33; Michael Hardt and Antonio Negri, *Empire* (Cambridge, MA: Harvard University Press, 2000), 150–56. I provide a lengthy analysis and critique of postmodernism in philosophy, culture, and politics in *The Solidarity of Others in a Divided World: A Postmodern Theology After Postmodernism* (New York: T & T Clark International, 2004), 7–90, esp. 47–64.

[17] Slavoj Žižek, *The Fragile Absolute or Why Is the Christian Legacy Worth Fighting For?* (New York: Verso, 2001), 23.

[18] Neil Postman, *Amusing Ourselves to Death: Public Discourse in the Age of Show Business* (New York: Penguin, 1985), 80.

I commit myself to anything when I can always change according to the contingent imperatives of my very contingent desire? There is no self-identical I or me but only a succession of desires and feelings I may entertain, not of my own informed decision but under the uncritical and indiscriminating assault of images and appearances on my unthinking senses.[19]

This kind of culture has received different names over the years, the "aesthetic" stage of life by Kierkegaard, the "triumph of the therapeutic" by Philip Rieff,[20] a "culture of narcissism" by Christopher Lasch,[21] the "triumph of the superficial," the "empire of illusion" and the "triumph of spectacle" by Chris Hedges,[22] now intensified and globalized. This culture creates a certain sensibility, a mood, an ethos that operates as an a priori for any explicit, particular exercise of judgment and will and affects that exercise with an intellectually debilitating and morally enervating disposition, with a certain hesitation, uncertainty, ambiguity, relativity, and a disinclination to commit oneself intellectually and morally. How can I know for sure? Why should I commit myself to anything? It is this cultural nihilism now globalizing itself that leads to the death of the subject. The notorious "death of God" makes sense only to a subject capable of making intellectual and moral judgments about why "God" is dead, with whom, therefore, an argument is possible. It makes no sense in a world where there are no subjects capable of such judgments. The postmodern uncertainty deliberately cultivated by contemporary cultural nihilism is different from the agnosticism and skepticism of Enlightenment rationalism, which are based on a very definite theory concerning the limits of the human capacity to know. Postmodern uncertainty is based, instead, on an a priori reluctance and incapacity to hold any intellectual or moral convictions. It is more a mood, a sensibility, a disposition that debilitates and enervates our capacity to hold a definite intellectual and moral conviction, now increasingly dominating the very horizon of human consciousness today.

---

[19] For the impact of the Internet on human consciousness and human relationships, see John Brockman, ed., *Is the Internet Changing the Way You Think?* (New York: Harper, 2011); and Sherry Turkle, *Alone Together: Why We Expect More from Technology and Less from Each Other* (New York: Basic Books, 2011).

[20] Philip Rieff, *The Triumph of the Therapeutic: Uses of Faith after Freud* (Chicago: University of Chicago Press, 1966, 1987).

[21] Christopher Lasch, *The Culture of Narcissism: American Life in an Age of Diminishing Expectations* (New York: W. W. Norton, 1979).

[22] Chris Hedges, *Empire of Illusion: The End of Literacy and the Triumph of Spectacle* (New York: Nation Books, 2009).

It is this culture of nihilism with the death of the subject as its substance that I find to be the more profound source of the erosion of Christian identity. What makes it really serious is that it erodes not only the identity of the Christian but also that of any other. If cultural nihilism makes it very difficult for Christians to hold definite convictions about what they believe and what they hope for, it likewise makes it very difficult even for the atheist humanist to hold definite convictions of their own. After all, atheist humanism involves commitment to definite values about human authenticity, responsibility, equality, living without illusions, and so on, which presuppose the existence and capacity of a subject with a certain consistency, self-identity, and self-responsibility capable of action. The same is true of any other position on human life. Cultural nihilism erodes all identity precisely by eliminating the very subject who can care about identity, consistency, and commitment—intellectual, moral, or otherwise.[23] It poses a crisis not only to the truth of a particular dogma or to a particular religion like Christianity but to the very possibility of holding determinate convictions regardless of their content. It is a crisis to the very humanity of the human subject. It is short-sighted to just celebrate nihilism as liberation from the Truth, as does Gianni Vattimo,[24] for in that liberation it also liberates us from the very will to any truth whatsoever by reducing will to desire, something postmodern thinkers seem to ignore altogether.

Speaking of the challenge of religious pluralism in the 1980s Langdon Gilkey said that the challenge is not only to "modernize," "demythologize," or "revise" the *expressions* of Christian symbols but to "relativize" the *symbols themselves* affecting not just some but all theological doctrines.[25] The challenge of cultural nihilism is even more serious: it is a challenge to the very capacity to hold any

---

[23] For a psychoanalytic account of the impact of the Internet on human identity, see Sherry Turkle, *Life on the Screen: Identity in the Age of the Internet* (New York: Simon and Schuster, 1995), esp. 257–69. Turkle speaks of the Internet as a culture of simulation that erodes the boundaries between the real and the virtual, animate and inanimate, unitary and multiple self, where people simply invent themselves as they go along with an identity that is fluid, multiple, emergent, decentralized, and always in process (10).

[24] Gianni Vattimo, "Nihilism as Postmodern Christianity," in *Transcendence and Beyond: A Postmodern Inquiry*, ed. John D. Caputo and Michael J. Scanlon (Bloomington: Indiana University Press, 2007), 44–48.

[25] Langdon Gilkey, "Plurality and Its Theological Implications," in *The Myth of Christian Uniqueness: Toward a Pluralistic Theology of Religions*, ed. John Hick and Paul Knitter (Maryknoll, NY: Orbis Books, 1987), 41.

convictions at all and to the very humanity of the subject who can hold any doctrine, Christian or otherwise.

It is precisely the gravity of this challenge and this crisis that I am afraid is not fully addressed by both those who speak of "secularization" of Western societies, like Charles Taylor, and those who speak of "post-secular" societies. In *A Secular Age,* a most comprehensive and thorough historical narrative, Taylor describes the cultural change of the West from what he calls the paleo-Durkheimian paradigm of belief in which church and state were united, through the neo-Durkheimian paradigm where many of the social plausibility structures were still alive, despite the separation of church and state, to keep belief vigorous and socially anchored, to the post-Durkheimian paradigm in which the lone individual seeks religious meaning, trying to "believe without belonging," to be "spiritual without being religious," searching for authenticity without the traditional assistance of institutional plausibility structures. In today's post-Durkheimian world belief has become one among other options and an embattled option at that, with the popularization of exclusive or purely immanentist humanism closed to all signs of transcendence, which used to be the possession of the intellectual elite in the preceding centuries but now has become a widespread cultural phenomenon. In the Western world becoming a believer today is not an easy thing; there are so many obstacles and challenges such as scientism and humanism, which look upon belief as a relic of childish humanity. A fully mature human being learns to live within the means available in this world, without looking for consolations from the transcendent. If it was impossible not to believe in 1500, it has become difficult to believe today.[26] Against this thesis of secularization there are others who point to the resurgence of religion, especially in the post–9/11 era, and the turn to religion among intellectuals such as Habermas, Derrida, Agamben, Badiou, and Žižek as a refutation of the secularization thesis and speak of the "post-secular" world.[27] However, neither the advocates of secularization nor its critics seem to take seriously enough the corrosive and enervating power of contemporary cultural nihilism that

---

[26] Charles Taylor, *A Secular Age* (Cambridge, MA: The Belknap Press of Harvard University Press, 2007), esp. 505–35.

[27] See Craig Calhoun, Mark Juergensmeyer, and Jonathan van Antwerpen, eds., *Rethinking Secularism* (New York: Oxford University Press, 2011); John D. Caputo, *St. Paul Among the Philosophers* (Indianapolis: Indiana University Press, 2009).

seems to destroy the very subjectivity of human beings with which to hold and stick to moral and intellectual convictions, secular or post-secular. Contemporary capitalist culture relativizes, commercializes, and trivializes all convictions and makes it difficult to hold them with any consistency, regardless of their content, Christian, humanist, or even hedonist.

Searching for Christian Identity

What kind of identity, however, are we talking about when we consider the erosion of Christian identity the most compelling theological issue today? Identity, especially collective identity, is a complicated thing with many different aspects. As something historical, collective identity is something formed in a historical process, undergoing erosions, transformations, and renewals in the dialectic of its many historical encounters with things other than itself. Some aspects of a collective identity deserve to be eroded as, for example, the various oppressive abuses of power on the part of the institutional churches. Many outdated beliefs need to be replaced by new discoveries and advances in human knowledge, as in the case of the literal interpretation of scripture and knowledge of the universe. Challenges from the other can play a constructive role in broadening and deepening one's identity, personal or collective. As Hegel insisted many years ago, nothing is pure identity with itself; everything is a dialectic of the identity of identity with itself and relations with otherness. An identity, therefore, is something always in the process of interaction with otherness. When it cannot sublate this otherness into its own identity, it passes away, as in the case of the human body that cannot control and sublate the otherness of cancer into itself. When an identity can sublate an otherness into itself, as in the case of a young person who struggles and survives the many fears and temptations of youth, such experiences can broaden, deepen, and enrich that person's identity with maturity, complexity, and vitality. I am not, therefore, simply mourning the four sources of the deconstruction of Christian identity, internal institutional problems, the popularization of the anti-Christian secularism of the Enlightenment, the relativization of the churches as institutions, and the cultural nihilism now being globalized. These are not all negative, and whether negative or positive, they are all serious challenges demanding clear recognition and timely responses. Depending on how Christians respond, they can become either debilitating crises and a death knell for many Christian denominations or unanticipated opportunities for the purification and enrichment of the Christian identity.

What kind of identity, then, is it whose erosion or deconstruction I am mourning and considering the most compelling theological issue? What kind of identity is appropriate and feasible to the collective historical identity of the Christian movement? Here I would like to dismiss two extreme attitudes toward Christian identity. One is to define Christian identity in terms of a certain empirical particularity, whether biological, such as a particular race, or historical, such as a particular civilization. Many of the so-called Christian Identity movements such as the Ku Klux Klan and the Aryan Nations identify Christianity with the white race. Western ethnocentrism identifies Christianity with Western civilization. These definitions offend against the transcendence and universalism of the central Christian teachings on creation and redemption.[28]

The other attitude toward Christian identity that I would like to dismiss is the exact opposite of the first, the sheer paralyzing postmodern fear of identity, the fear of defining and talking about the identity of anything and of Christian identity in particular for fear of the possibility of excluding, offending, and oppressing others who do not fit into the identity so defined, and for fear of the sociological and political consequences of essentialism and totalitarianism. This fear was fully justifiable at a time when religion and political power were so closely united that to be outside the religious community was to be excluded from political power as well. It remains fully justifiable perhaps even today when the identity is so narrowly defined as to exclude and oppress certain dissenting minorities not by means of the political power of the state, which remains formally separated from all particular religions, but within the struggle for power within the institutions of a particular religion.

Still, these fears do not justify delegitimizing the right and responsibility of the various Christian communities to define and strengthen their own identity. The only question is how narrowly they define themselves and with what consequences, but there is no question about the right and responsibility of each community to define and strengthen its collective identity. After all, the vitality of life, whether the life of an individual or that of a community, depends on its respective sense of identity and commitment to it.

---

[28] See Chester L. Quarles, *Christian Identity: The Aryan American Bloodline Religion* (Jefferson, NC: McFarland, 2004).

There are many kinds and degrees of legitimate and responsible identity between the two extremes mentioned, between the empiricist particularism of the Christian Identity movement that identifies Christianity with the white race against the universalist dynamic of the Christian tradition and the sheer paralysis of the collective will to define itself, opting instead for an identity that is formless, indeterminate, and therefore diffident and unsure about itself, about what it really believes, what it really hopes for, and what it really loves, in short for an identity that is no identity at all. Between the extremes of a triumphalist, fanatical sense of identity oppressive of the other and the despair to be oneself at all in the world of others, there can be many different forms of mature identity fully aware of its own limits in relation to others but also fully committed to its own mission in relation to them, always in the spirit of dialogue and reconciliation.

The talk about Christian identity has a long history. In some real sense the entire history of the Christian movement is a history of the struggle to define and actualize its collective identity against the many internal and external forces of otherness that differ from and often contradict the heart and soul of the movement. As Enlightenment rationalism intensified its challenge to the traditional identity of Christianity, internal discussions of Christian identity have also increased, continuing to the present day. In *The Identity of Christianity: Theologians and the Essence of Christianity from Schleiermacher to Barth*, published in 1984,[29] the Anglican divine, Stephen Sykes, provided an insightful study of the search for the essence or identity of Christianity in the works of six modern theologians—Schleiermacher, Newman, Harnack, Loisy, Troeltsch, and Barth—and concluded that the essence of Christianity is an essentially contested concept; at the level of doctrine there have always been conflicts and diversity about what constitutes Christianity. The unity of Christianity can only exist in the form of "containment of diversity within bounds."[30] Christianity is not a philosophical system but is a whole with many dimensions, and we need a form of unity that is respectful of differences, which Sykes finds in worship. Worship is more than the liturgical text, and it involves the self-surrender and commitment of the whole person in memory of the self-sacrifice of Christ celebrated at each Eucharist. This worship and spirituality is precisely the context of theology as

---

[29] Stephen Sykes, *The Identity of Christianity: Theologians and the Essence of Christianity from Schleiermacher to Barth* (Philadelphia: Fortress Press, 1984).

[30] Ibid., 240.

well, where doctrine and worship prove mutually complementary. Doctrinal diversity can be contained within the unity of worship.[31]

In more recent times, under the corrosive impact of cultural and religious pluralism, many theologians have been turning to the question of Christian identity, each with his or her own proposals. Terrence W. Tilley argues that a collective identity is not a matter of doctrinal identity but a matter of tradition, which is defined as a set of communal practices with its own grammar that both shapes and is shaped by its participants and is always in the process of inventing and reinventing itself.[32] Kathryn Tanner finds the talk about both traditions and rules as markers of identity ahistorical, naturalistic, and inadequate from the postmodern historicist and constructivist perspective. Christian identity can no longer be understood in terms of "group specificity, sharp cultural boundaries, or homogeneity of practices."[33] Christianity has itself become a subculture, no longer self-sufficient or self-contained, thoroughly pervaded by and exposed to Christians' secular roles and commitments. What unites Christians is "concern for true discipleship, proper reflection in human words and deeds of an object of worship that always exceeds by its greatness human efforts to do so."[34] What unites Christian practices, however, "is not agreements about the beliefs and actions that constitute true discipleship, but a shared sense of the importance of figuring it out."[35] In Tanner's minimalist postmodern account, Christianity "has its identity in the form of a task of looking for one."[36]

The problem of Christian identity is further complicated by the mixing of different cultures and religions in the pluralistic world that produces *syncretism* and *hybridity*. In an important sense this is a universal phenomenon true of all religious identities, Christian, Buddhist, or other. A religion is always rooted or indigenized in a culture that cannot be simply identical with that religion for various reasons. This culture may already embody the values and perspectives of one or many religions. A person converting to a new religion does not simply leave behind the intellectual, moral, and

---

[31] Ibid., 262–86.

[32] Terrence W. Tilley, *Inventing Catholic Tradition* (Maryknoll, NY: Orbis Books, 2000).

[33] Kathryn Tanner, *Theories of Culture: A New Agenda for Theology* (Minneapolis: Augsburg Fortress, 1997), 152.

[34] Ibid., 152.

[35] Ibid., 153.

[36] Ibid., 155.

religious habits and views of the culture and its religions in which he or she has grown up. Christians in America are not Christians pure and simple; their Christianity is mixed up with the materialism of American capitalism and the individualism of American political culture. American Christians are hybrids. A Korean Christian is a hybrid of Christianity, the Western culture that comes with that Christianity, and the Confucianism and Buddhism constituting the horizon of the Korean consciousness. Long before the emergence of theories of hybridity the religious life of all humanity has always been hybrid and syncretistic by the very necessity of cultural existence, something theologians are still ignoring, taking instead each religion as a separable system of beliefs in its purity and determinacy uncontaminated by any otherness and advocating greater mutual understanding and mutual dialogue among such reified systems.[37]

"Multiple religious belonging," therefore, has always been a fact of human religious life, at least at the implicit, unreflective level. Today, with the heightening of pluralistic sensibility, it has become something conscious and explicit, and it has been raising a number of theological issues. Catherine Cornille observes that the more comprehensive a religion's claim is to efficacy and truth, the more problematic becomes the possibility of multiple religious belonging: such a religion tends to endorse only those beliefs and practices of other religions that are compatible with its own. For Cornille, there are three ways in which multiple religious belonging may be legitimized. The most common way is to consider all religions as manifestations of the same ultimate reality in the fashion of John Hick's pluralism. The second way is to remain faithful to the symbolic framework of one religion while accepting the hermeneutical framework of another, like Christianity adopting the categories of Greek philosophy or Indian philosophy in the process of inculturation. The third way is to recognize the legitimacy and complementarity of other religions, like Christianity recognizing other religions as anonymous forms of Christianity (Rahner).[38] Cornille's view is still governed by a certain intellectualism that regards religions as

---

[37] On globalization as hybridization, see Jan Nederveen Pieterse, *Globalization and Culture: Global Mélange* (Lanham, MD: Rowan and Littlefield, 2004); on syncretism, see Leonardo Boff, *Church: Charism and Power: Liberation Theology and the Institutional Church* (New York: Crossroad, 1985), 89–107. In this work Boff defines the catholicity of the church as its capacity for "true" syncretism, its capacity to incarnate itself in cultures without losing its Christian identity.

[38] Catherine Cornille, *Many Mansions? Multiple Religious Belonging and Christian Identity* (Eugene, OR: Wipf and Stock, 2002), 1–6.

cognitive systems that need adjustment at the intellectual level if multiple religious belonging is to be possible. It ignores the continuing survival and operation of the implicit cultural habits, values, and dispositions converts necessarily bring with them to their new religion, no matter what this new religion may be.[39]

I do not have the space to go into all the methodological and systematic issues concerning Christian identity, a most complicating issue, to say the least. Instead, I will spend the rest of this essay noting certain relevant features of identity and of Christian identity in particular as a matter of a living tradition, and simply making a proposal, holding an ecumenical council, for catalyzing the beginnings of a solution to the challenge of Christian identity in the globalizing world.

Christian Identity as a Task of Rejuvenating a Tradition

There are four features of identity that I would like to note as particularly relevant to the question at issue. The first is that identity is not simply some external, verifiable fact, a reified, simple, unchanging, purely objective, homogeneous property possessed by all who share the identity, a mere "presence," according to deconstructive postmodernism, but a dynamic trait or movement that touches the core of our being, the core in terms of which we act and think. Merely to know certain empirical facts about ourselves is not yet to know who we are deep down. They fail to identify the core of our being, the sources and springs that generate such manifestations and which in turn such manifestations express and concretize. All such external manifestations become relevant as markers of identity only when they are shown to emerge from and express the core of our being. The search for identity is the search for this core and depth of our being, which in turn can only be defined or identified in terms of the fundamental tendencies and sensibilities out of which we act and think and that allow of many internal variations.

The second feature of identity is that it expresses what we have been. We cannot think of our own identity apart from what we have been, apart from our collective past expressed in our culture, history, language, and religion. To think of our own identity apart from our collective past would be to uproot ourselves, alienate ourselves from

---

[39] For another view of multiple religious belonging, see Peter C. Phan, *Being Religious Interreligiously: Asian Perspectives on Interfaith Dialogue* (Maryknoll, NY: Orbis Books, 2004), 60–84.

the conditions of life that have defined us, and reduce ourselves to unanchored, momentary existence, the reason why oppressors are always so quick and anxious to wipe out the collective memory, the collective past of the peoples they oppress. No peoples are more pitiful than those without a collective memory. In this sense, we are defined by what we have been, by our facticity.

The third feature of our identity is that it also expresses what we ought to be, our future, our ideality. Our past, our facticity, does not tell us what we ought to do under the changing circumstances of the present. We also need a vision of the future, of what we ought to be, in order to guide our actions and thoughts in the many challenges and ambiguities of the present. Our identity is not something given and fixed once and for all but something always in need of growth and adaptation according to the demands of changing situations and contexts. In this sense our identity is not simply what we have been but also what we ought to be, what in fact we would be proud to be in the depth and core of our being, not simply, therefore, our facticity but also our "ownmost" or "authentic" possibilities of being (Heidegger). Our identity is not only facticity but also "ideality" that demands realization in the future, precisely on the basis of that facticity but also from the call of the future. Our integral identity, therefore, always remains in part a future, a task, a challenge, in fact, a dialectic of the past and future, of facticity and possibility, of reality and ideality.

The fourth and last feature of identity relevant to the present issue is that it is an unintended outcome of actions and thoughts over a long period of time and as such the unanticipated result of responses to the contextual challenges of our historical existence. What we can intend is the performance of a specific action or thought, which itself emerges from the kind of people we have been, from the core of our basic orientations and sensibilities already there. We may desire and work hard to acquire certain tendencies and characteristics and acquire an identity as certain kinds of persons, like "generous," "loving" persons, but we cannot aim at and achieve becoming such persons in the same direct way in which we intend to posit certain acts such as driving to New York City, going to the polls on election day, or speaking to a friend. There is no particular act called "becoming a loving person." However, particular acts not only emerge from and express the kind of persons we are, that is, our "being," of which identity is a modality, but they also shape and produce the kind of persons we want to be. It is only through the many concrete acts of generosity and love that we become generous and loving persons. In this sense, our identity, our being, is the indirect outcome of various actions we can directly intend and posit over a long period of time, as the classical doctrine of virtues has long insisted.

All this is to say that Christian identity, the collective identity of the Christian communities, can only be understood in dialectical, historical terms. It consists of a certain core or depth of being, a certain set of fundamental tendencies and sensibilities, a certain spirit out of which Christian communities think and act, which are also externalized, objectified, and institutionalized in verifiable historical achievements, which in turn also manifest and shape, reveal and actualize the core tendencies and sensibilities. As a collective identity the Christian identity involves the dialectic of individual and communal, internal and external, ideal and real, spiritual and material, transcendent and historical, subjective and objective, enduring and transient, unifying and diversifying, past and future. It is this dialectic as a concrete totality. In more specific terms the core of Christian existence, the basic tendencies and sensibilities, refer to the faith, hope, and love of the Christian communities empowered by the triune God through the incarnation of the Word and the relating, reconciling activity of the Holy Spirit. This core is objectified in scripture; the ecumenical teachings of the churches; the liturgy and sacraments; the history of exemplars of faith, the saints; and the institutional history of the churches. This is but another way of saying that the collective identity of Christianity is a matter of a living tradition, and the problem of Christian identity is how to rejuvenate and revitalize the tradition already there.[40]

I said earlier that this tradition seems to have lost its vitality under the fourfold pressure of institutional problems specific to each denomination, the relentless critique of the intellectual content of the Christian faith by Enlightenment rationalism, and the global culture of nihilism that enervates the Christian faith and all other faiths as well by indiscriminately pluralizing, relativizing, commercializing, trivializing, ideologizing, and reducing all things to objects of entertainment, to images and illusions. The Christian communities are unsure about themselves, diffident about what they really believe, what they really hope for, what they really love, fragmented among

---

[40] *The Meaning of Tradition* by Yves Congar (San Francisco: Ignatius, 2004; originally published in English by Hawthorn Books, New York, in 1964) still remains an unsurpassed masterpiece as a theory of tradition. I only try to make it more explicitly dialectical.

themselves, without enthusiasm about their future, temporal or eschatological. As pointed out, we cannot rebuild or revitalize a tradition at will or overnight. There is no mechanical rule for revitalizing a tradition. The task of rebuilding a tradition is a matter of a long process, the unintended result of the communities faithfully attending to what they should do in the context of contemporary challenges on the basis of the best resources they do possess out of their own past.

If it is true that we cannot rejuvenate a living tradition overnight, that we cannot have a five-year plan for revitalizing the tradition, we can still think of certain ecclesial acts that may catalyze a series of actions that may contribute to the revitalization of the tradition, and such acts will vary depending on the peculiar history and genius of each denomination. Here I am speaking of the Roman Catholic Church. In its theological weight, its ecclesial scope, its historical reach, and its universal impact I cannot think of a catalytic action more significant than the convocation of an ecumenical council, Vatican III. An ecumenical council presided over by the pope is the highest teaching authority with the greatest prestige in the Catholic Church. It involves the whole Catholic Church from the pope and the Vatican to the parishes and the various levels of the hierarchy to the many different religious and lay groups all around the world in various stages of its preparation as participants, observers, experts, and active audience. The splendor of the liturgy with which the sessions will begin, and the arguments, authorities, and symbols the participants will invoke to make their case will be saturated in the tradition of the church from scripture to the fathers and doctors to the confessors and exemplars of sanctity. The deliberations of the council, the arguments pro and con, the conflicts that will inevitably surface among different perspectives, and the unity of the entire assembly at prayer: all these will be watched by the entire world, Catholics and non-Catholics alike, to a universal, global impact beyond anyone's prediction. Those who are old enough to have lived through the anticipations, the actual progress, and the immediate aftermath of Vatican II from 1962 through 1965 still vividly remember the sheer excitement, the revolutionary awakening, the global expansion of Catholicity, the exuberant demonstration of ecclesial vitality that only an ecumenical council can be. It was a living embodiment of what it meant to be a Catholic Church, and it was a time when Catholics were truly happy and proud to be what they are, Catholic. The council was Catholic identity at its most authoritative, most communal, most traditional, and most universal. I think that Vatican III will be even more so.[41]

There was much talk by theologians such as David Tracy, Hans Küng, and Johann Metz in the late 1970s about convoking Vatican III,[42] but that talk seems to have petered out for lack of response. Now the time may be ripe for another council. The church today faces an abundance of problems internally and externally, problems far more complicated, far more intractable, far more extensive, and far more radical than those faced by the church at Vatican II. Externally, the world presents plenty of big global issues from injustice, hunger, imperialism, militarism, ecological disasters, religious conflicts, secularization and cultural nihilism, and international migration. Internally, tensions remain between clergy and laity, between conservatives and liberals, between the particularity of different cultures and the universality of the church, and between inherited teachings and postmodern claims. All these internal and external problems, radical and comprehensive, converge to raise the central issue of Christian identity: What does it mean to be a Christian community today? What does it really believe, what does it really hope for, and what does it really love? There are issues galore, and an ecumenical council would be the sole venue for the discussion of these issues appropriate to the gravity of their significance and the scope of their challenge. In executing a council and performing an internal dialogue with itself about itself the church engages the totality of its history, its resources, its personnel. For the duration of the council the whole church will be engaged in meditation, prayer, and dialogue about what it is, its identity, the memory of its founder, its eschatological hope, how it should act in the present moment of its pilgrimage on earth. Going beyond all the tensions it will suffer, beyond all the spectacle and excitement it will generate, a council is above all a collective meditation of the church about itself, its own past, its own future, and what it should do in its present. A council will be the most compelling form of at least one Christian community, the Roman Catholic Church, in search of what it should be, a most dramatic form of Christian identity in action. It goes without

---

[41] On the Second Vatican Council, see Xavier Rynne, *Vatican Council II* (Maryknoll, NY: Orbis Books, 1999), which is a one-volume edition of the four volumes of the famous *Letters from Vatican City*, an insider's report of the workings of the council by the author, a Redemptorist, who also participated in the council as a peritus or theological adviser.

[42] David Tracy, Hans Küng, and Johann Metz, *Toward Vatican III: The Work That Needs to Be Done* (New York: Seabury, 1978).

saying that the council will incorporate essential ecumenical and interreligious concerns in its structure and deliberation in a way most appropriate to the global catholicity of the church in the twenty-first century.

A Response to Anselm Min

São Paulo I or Vatican III?

Joseph Prabhu

*It is not difficult to see that ours is a birth-time and a period of
transition to a new era. Spirit has broken with the world it has
hitherto inhabited and imagined, and is of a mind to submerge
it in the past, and in the labor of its own transformation. . . .
Just as the first breath drawn by a child after its long, quiet
nourishment breaks the gradualness of merely quantitative
growth — there is a qualitative leap and the child is born — so
likewise the Spirit in its formation matures slowly and quietly
into its new shape, dissolving bit by bit the structure of its
previous world, whose tottering state is only hinted at by isolated symptoms. . . . But this new world is no more a complete
actuality than is a new-born child; . . . it comes on the scene for
the first time in its immediacy or its Notion. Just as little as a
building is finished when its foundation has been laid, so little
is the achieved Notion of the whole the whole itself.*

—Georg W. F. Hegel,
Preface to *Phenomenology of Spirit*

There is some historical irony in this response of mine. When I first
responded orally to Anselm Min's fine paper at the time of the
conference in late April 2012, and specifically his concluding suggestion of convening a possible Vatican III, my counter suggestion,
deeply felt but somewhat hazily seen at the time, was that what the
Catholic Church most needs is a radical shift of perspective, both
geographical and intellectual. A year later we found ourselves with
an Argentinean pope who suggests the possible realization of such

a perspective. While it is still very early in his papacy, and while I
argue in this essay that it is more the time of the laity than the hierarchy in the continuing life of the church, there are at least signs
of hope to suggest that what was a wish in 2012 may well become
more of a reality now. Pope Francis seems to be moving in a different direction from his four predecessors and is moving, one hopes,
to dissolve "bit by bit the structure of [the] previous world." It is
significant that among his first announced travel plans was his intention to go to Brazil in July 2013 to attend the World Youth Festival
in São Paolo.

Coming back to Min's essay, there is much that I continue to
agree with, in particular his choice of Christian identity broadly and
dialectically articulated as perhaps the key issue within the context
of a discussion devoted to the most compelling theological issues affecting Catholicism and the Catholic Church in the twenty-first century. Min asserts that Christian identity as he sees it is a dialectical,
historical matter, an identity that "consists of a certain core or depth
of being, a certain set of fundamental tendencies and sensibilities . . .
a certain spirit out of which Christian communities think and act,
which are also external, objectified, and institutionalized" as part of
a living tradition. Min's central thesis is that this identity is being
"deconstructed," or gradually but nonetheless relentlessly destroyed
under the quadruple threat of (1) internal institutional problems,
(2) the secularization that followed in the wake of the eighteenth-
century Enlightenment,[1] (3) the relativization of the churches as
institutions, and (4) "the culture of nihilism" that Min believes is a
prominent feature of late capitalist postmodernity.

It is gratifying also to observe the form and style of Min's overall
argument, one that places theology in what Germans call a *Sitz-im-
Leben*, a contextualization of theology within the broader currents of
culture and society. While theology is by no means reducible to social and economic life, it is undoubtedly affected by it. Min astutely
points to the commodifying power of late capitalistic culture, which,
as he says, "presents a variety of goods, services, and ideologies as
merely objects of entertainment, desire, and power with none being intrinsically and objectively valuable." To adapt Oscar Wilde's

---

[1] It seems important to stress this historically particular Enlightenment
of the eighteenth century because there are other epochs both in the history
of the West and that of the East that are equally deserving of the designation
"enlightenment." Indeed, given the troubled history of the West in the wake of
that so-called Enlightenment, there should be at least a note of irony attached
to that description.

famous words, capitalism is that form of life which knows the price of everything but the value of nothing. This partly explains the contemporary phenomenon of religion and religious commitment being looked upon as a matter of consumer choice, as when we hear such expressions as "shopping in the religious supermarket" and the various styles of "cafeteria religion," where the consumer mixes and matches religious beliefs, symbols, and practices to his or her satisfaction.

In the midst of the changes wrought by secularization, cultural nihilism, and the problems internal to the post–Vatican II history of the Catholic Church, Min believes with Peter Steinfels that Catholics in America, and by extension the Western world, are "a people adrift" without a clear sense of their identity, their distinctive beliefs, and practices, and with a very diffuse sense of what they stand for. This more particular loss of Catholic identity is situated by Min within a more general and more pervasive loss of subjecthood, the "incapacity to hold any intellectual or moral convictions" firmly, and this incapacity in turn is connected with the celebration and manipulation of desire that is a characteristic feature of late capitalism and the postmodernism it spawns.

As indicated before, I agree in broad outline with Min's analysis but not with his prognosis, and I feel impelled to take the underlying logic of his argument in a different direction. Much of what I write here should therefore be seen more as an extension of and complement to his text rather than a direct engagement with it. In the past two years much has changed, new energies have been released, and "Spirit in its formation" is indeed maturing slowly and quietly into its new shape. Given that we thinkers and activists are embodiments of Spirit, it seems to me not very productive to engage with problems and concerns that are not of the greatest urgency. A new era is dawning, and in my judgment our energies are better spent trying to shape it as humbly but also as courageously and forthrightly as we can. And while this era is still very much in its infancy and therefore impossible to speak about authoritatively, the more urgent task is to engage with it in a spirit of hope and new possibility.

In this spirit I take up three interconnected themes in Min's essay and make brief remarks about them: identity, catholicity (more fully developed in Min's original conference paper), and the emerging Christian community. I argue that the logic of my observations about these themes point more toward São Paolo I rather than a possible Vatican III.

The first point I wish to make is demographic. According to the latest reliable estimates of Catholic populations by region for 2010 made by the Pew Research Center, there were 488.4 million Catholics in Latin America and the Caribbean, 257 million in Europe, 177.6 million in Africa, 130 million in Asia, and 88.5 million in North America, out of a total global Catholic population of 1.1 billion. By these estimates only about one-quarter (24 percent) of all Catholics live in Europe in contrast to 39 percent in Latin American and the Caribbean. If we aggregate the Catholic populations of Latin America and the Caribbean, Asia, and sub-Saharan Africa, more than two-thirds of the global Catholic population (67 percent) lives in the so-called Third World. The center of gravity of the Catholic world has clearly shifted to the Southern Hemisphere, and according to demographic trends the growth rates of Catholics in that hemisphere far outstrip those in the Western world. Brazil is also the most populous Catholic country in the world; hence my choice of São Paolo as the site of a possible new council.

Philip Jenkins, basing his analysis on the well-respected World Christian Encyclopedia, which has collected demographic data for the Christian world as a whole, asserts:

> If we extrapolate these [demographic] figures to the year 2025, and assume no great gains or losses through conversion, then there would be around 2.6 billion Christians, of whom 633 million would live in Africa, 640 million in Latin America, and 460 million in Asia. Europe with 555 million would have slipped to third place. Africa and Latin America would be in competition for the title of the most Christian continent . . . [and] these two continents will together account for half the Christians on the planet. By 2050 only about one-fifth of the world's 3 billion Christians will be non-Hispanic and white.[2]

If we ponder the implications of these demographic changes, it is quite clear that there is a serious imbalance in what we might term the geopolitics of power and the production of knowledge that power enables, as manifested in current discourse about trends in Christianity. Postcolonial theory has brought to our attention the epistemological significance of the location from which the world

---

[2] Philip Jenkins, *The Next Christendom: The Coming of Global Christianity* (New York: Oxford University Press, 2011), 2–3.

is viewed and knowledge is produced.[3] All too often universalistic expressions like "what Catholics believe" or "the Catholic Church" in fact represent the view of a particular though of course immensely powerful minority and moreover a minority that is steadily shrinking. The center of power and the Vatican hierarchy continue to be dominated by Europeans who hold on tightly to the power they possess of making major theological, ecclesial, and liturgical judgments and decisions. But these judgments and decisions are seriously out of touch with and non-representative of social realities.

The election of the first Hispanic pope in Catholic history and one of the very few non-European popes represents both a long overdue change and an opportunity. This change of global identity from the North and the West to the South and the East represents a major political and cultural shift that poses significant challenges to what for centuries has been a Eurocentric church.

As this is meant to be a brief response and not a full-fledged essay, let me merely indicate some of the main challenges that this geopolitical shift brings along with it. I should make it clear that I see the election of the first Hispanic pope as a symptom of this larger change and neither believe nor expect that the new pope by himself can bring about the desired changes that I am going to sketch. The Catholic Church remains a highly hierarchical and centralist church with a papacy resembling an absolute monarchy. The center of power still remains in Rome, with the Roman curia, predominantly European in character, determined to hold on to the power it has and to resist the pressures of reform. And yet if the Catholic Church is not to become "an increasingly irrelevant sect," as Hans Küng has described it,[4] it is clear that certain changes are desperately needed. Here I shall mention and outline four such desirable changes.

1. *The matter of faith and culture:* It is clear as Christianity spreads in Asia, Africa, and Latin America that these cultures are going to exert an increasing influence. Will the mass celebrated in predominantly Hindu India be inflected by Hindu-Buddhist practices of meditation and by yogic practices of one-pointedness? Will the sacraments celebrated in Africa respect some of the animist tenden-

---

[3] Among many books on this topic, see Homi Bhabha, *The Location of Culture* (London: Routledge, 1994); and Enrique Dussel, *Beyond Philosophy: Ethics, History, Marxism, and Liberation Theology,* ed. Eduardo Mendieta (New York: Rowan and Littlefield, 2003).

[4] Hans Küng, "A Vatican Spring?" *The New York Times,* February 27, 2013.

cies of the local culture? Will the liturgy in the Caribbean include Santería elements of ancestor worship and sacred drumming and dance? If the matter of faith and culture is seen in broad historical perspective, it is clear that Christianity in its evolution has been a fusion of cultures from its Hebraic roots to Greek philosophy to Roman law and European manners. And just as the early Christian church decreed that one did not have to be circumcised in order to be a Christian, so also one may hope that twenty-first-century Christians in the non-European world will not have to undergo "European circumcision" in order to be admitted into the Christian fold.

2. *Ecumenical relations with other Christian churches and with non-Christian religions:* The Second Vatican Council moved far beyond the exclusivism of *extra ecclesiam nulla salus* in the council document *Nostra aetate.* Speaking of relations with Hinduism and Buddhism it says, "The Catholic Church rejects nothing that is true and holy in these religions. She regards with sincere reverence those ways of conduct and of life, those precepts and teachings which, though differing in many aspects from the ones she holds and sets forth, nonetheless often reflect a ray of that Truth which enlightens all men" (no. 2). The practice of interreligious dialogue in the years since the council ended in 1965 have made still clearer "the ray of Truth" existing not just in Hinduism and Buddhism but in many other non-Christian faiths, to the point where multiple religious belonging is becoming an increasingly common phenomenon. Even when Christians may not regard themselves as "belonging" to other faiths, it is clear that purportedly non-Christian practices like yoga, meditation, drumming, and sacred dancing are being increasingly taken up by Christians as part of their religious practice. In such circumstances, criteria of Christian or Catholic identity will necessarily have to become more elastic. Min quotes Peter Steinfels as saying, "The Catholic Church can succeed as an institution while failing as a church. But it cannot succeed as a church while failing as an institution." If that is so, and I agree that the institutional character of the church needs to be affirmed, the institution itself will have to become more open to and accommodating of the "ray of the Truth" that manifests in non-Christian faiths.

3. *A shift away from the monarchical and highly hierarchical model of church governance to the more democratic habits of the early church:* Much ink has been spilt about the issue of "collegiality" and its

many levels and dimensions from the autonomy of local bishops and priests acting on their own authority rather than of the Roman congregations overseeing them, to the increasing role of the laity. Students of church history from John O'Malley to Garry Wills have pointed out that it was only with the so-called Gregorian Reform put in place by Pope Gregory VII in the eleventh century that the highly centralist and monarchical patterns of current church governance were put in place.[5] Prior to that, the church of the first millennium functioned collegially in the absence of compulsory clericalism. In the wake of the scandals of child abuse, and the financial and other corruptions revealed by the "Vatileaks" affair, one is reminded of Lord Acton's warning that power corrupts and absolute power corrupts absolutely. The eschewing of the pomp and circumstance of the papacy by Pope Francis, who describes himself simply as the bishop of Rome, is a step in the right direction, as is his choice of an advisory council comprised of cardinals from around the world, which one hopes may be able to bypass the Roman curia. The Second Vatican Council document on the constitution of the church, *Lumen Gentium*, emphasized the "priesthood of all believers" and spoke of the church as the entire people of God working in partnership and collaboration. It is to be hoped that the election of a pope from the Southern Hemisphere and the increasing participation of the laity in both the ecclesial and other church-run institutions will usher in a new democratic spirit that will fulfill the hopes of collegiality stirred but alas not fulfilled by the Second Vatican Council and its aftermath.

These three challenges of cultural pluralism, ecumenicity, and democratic freedom will finally, one hopes, introduce a new style, a fresh spirit that the church presents to the modern world.

4. *A new style:* Talking of style, John O'Malley writes:

A style choice is an identity choice, a personality choice, a choice in this instance about the kind of institution the [Second Vatican] council wanted the church to be. . . . The shift in style as proposed in Vatican II thus entailed changing behavioral patterns, but the change in those patterns as in the adoption of

---

[5] John W. O'Malley, *What Happened at Vatican II* (Cambridge, MA: Harvard University Press, 2008), 308; Garry Wills, *Why Priests? A Failed Tradition* (New York: Viking Press, 2013).

dialogue as a preferred mode of discourse was not a technique or a strategy, but an outward expression of the adoption of an inner pattern of values.[6]

It seems clear from all that I have written above that such a decentralized, pluralistic, democratic, and ecumenical church will have to shed its imperial pretensions and its pomp and become "the leaven in the dough," a witness to the redemptive love preached and practiced by Christ. Here too the style of simplicity, humility, and service adopted by Pope Francis is encouraging, and one hopes exemplary. But it is also a style that fits, expresses, and promotes the other three issues I have previously highlighted.

These, then, are some of the concerns that I would put on the agenda of São Paolo I. The shift of location from Rome to São Paolo is symbolic of the move away from the center to the peripheries. It is clear that there will also have to be much more on the agenda in terms of doctrines, beliefs, norms, and practices, but the four issues I have emphasized will, I am confident, create a congenial space and set the proper tone for the discussion of other matters.

---

[6] O'Malley, *What Happened at Vatican II*, 305–6.

3

The Repositioning of a Theology of the World in the Face of Globalization and Post-Secularity

Prophecy and Crisis

ROBERT SCHREITER

Introduction

The most compelling issue for me in theology today is a big-picture one, namely, how the church relates to the world in its current circumstances. What this means today can best be seen by looking at some of the changes going on in different interpretive frameworks of the global scene. These changes all call into question, in various ways, how the church is to relate to this world.

First of all, there are geo-economic, social, and political ones, raised as part of the consequences of globalization. One out of every thirty-five people is in migration, and slightly over half of those migrating are women and are Christian. Neoliberal capitalism and advances in communication technology have knitted the world together whether denizens of any given area like these arrangements or not. While the United Nations announced recently that the Millennium Goal of halving the number of people on the planet who live in extreme poverty had been reached, the gap between a moneyed few and those most poor has continued to grow. What kind of international social order will need to be in place to address some of these compelling issues?

Second, there are demographic realities. Among economically developed countries the United States is the only country that is replacing its population with new births. For those countries that do not, there will be great social challenges to be faced. The longer-term financial support of the elderly (who are also living longer in those countries) will be imperiled as people of working age have to engage in triage—between supporting their children and support-ing their parents (and grandparents). In countries that experience a majority of their population being under the age of twenty-five (as is the case in much of the Global South), the potential for unrest looms largely if there is not suitable employment. The experience of the Arab Spring and of the mass protests of young people in Western Europe in 2011 provides evidence of this. An equally urgent mat-ter is raised by the demographics of women. Slightly over half the world's population is female, but selective abortions have reduced the proportion of women to men in parts of the world, especially in Asia. Thus, in China, there are in the current younger adult popu-lation 118 men for every 100 women. Such imbalances encourage trafficking in women, as is also happening, especially from Asia. Moreover, economic pressures have greater impact on women than men. I have already noted that the majority of people in migration are women. Moreover, it has been frequently noted that the most effective means of relieving poverty is the education of women. Increasingly it is seen that women involved in small business op-erations of their own choosing can dramatically change the face of poverty. And the role of women in peacebuilding around the world is also beginning to be acknowledged.

Third, there are ecological realities. While debate continues on the exact extent of global warming, it becomes harder and harder to avoid the fact that it is happening and will have unavoidable consequences for the very survival of life on this planet. The effect of climate change on world food supplies is already beginning to be felt (the drought that contributed to the uprisings in Egypt in 2011 and in Syria in 2012 portend what may happen in the future with climate change). It will heighten the pace and size of migration as people in low-lying areas face rising seas, and those in the interior seek food. Whether such changes will within a relatively short time make the material conditions for life on the planet is still a very real and unanswered question before us.

Fourth, there are religious realities. While Western sociologists were still predicting Max Weber's hypothesis about the decline and privatization of religion until two decades ago, the general picture, at least on the global scale, now looks different. If anything, religion plays a more visible role worldwide than it did just twenty years ago. A number of factors have contributed to this. One of these has been the increasing implausibility of secular ideologies to provide an adequate framework for human flourishing, epitomized in the fall of the Berlin Wall in 1989. If current changes continue, China could well be the largest (in terms of numbers) Christian country by the middle of this century. If this hypothesis is paired with China's growing economic power and geopolitical significance, one can imagine considerable shift in how the world will be construed. Another factor is religion's being adjoined to other social movements, especially for purposes of war and for nationalism, but also for peace. What this points toward is the different ways religion is being mobilized in the public sector, for both good and malevolent purposes. Yet another feature in the Global North is the emergence of a discussion of post-secularity, triggered in different ways by Canadian philosopher Charles Taylor and German philosopher Jürgen Habermas. Post-secularity is not a univocal concept, but what it implies is that secularity in and of itself can no longer be seen as the regnant ideology of economically developed countries. It must share public space with religion. There is no agreement on how this public space is to be shared by the two, but at the very least religion can no longer be a fortiori excluded from the discussion. In the same manner the place of religion in international affairs is also being acknowledged, even if not yet adequately theorized. And a final thing to mention here is how religions relate to one another. Religious pluralism is a fact with which we must deal, since globalization and migration have brought them all closer together. Moreover, religion by itself is an abstract concept. There is no definition of *religion* that adequately encompasses all the phenomena we bring together under this one word, nor will it in effect give us a single recipe for how the various religions interact with the other perspectives already mentioned or with their relations among one another.

These four perspectives or frameworks — socioeconomic, demographic, ecological, and religious — could be augmented by still others, but that would (for now) make a discussion of the relation of church and world even more impossible than it may already be. The ones presented here take up a host of issues in themselves, more than can be engaged in any single presentation. The intent has been here, rather, to give an indication of the breadth of issues any of these perspectives are grappling with, as well as the range of things that must be taken into consideration in any reframing of a theology of the world and of the church.

I now turn briefly to the other side of this picture, namely, the church. Christians make up approximately one-third of the world's population. Together with the House of Islam, the two faiths constitute more than half of the world's population. Among Christians, Roman Catholics amount to slightly more than half of all the Christians. In speaking of the "church," it is the Roman Catholic Church that I wish to focus upon here.

I do this for several reasons. First of all, besides sheer numbers, Roman Catholics have the widest geographical spread. Thus what this church does has perhaps the greatest possible impact. Second, it is the most integrated — horizontally and vertically — of all religious bodies. While this has led to laments among Catholics in the Global North, it is seen as a source of strength in other parts of the world, especially those where solidarity with other parts of the world is essential for survival. Third, as a religious body the church has formal relations with approximately 190 countries as well as key sites within international bodies such as the United Nations. Again, while this might be decried as remnants of a Constantinian mindset, it provides entry into sites that no other religious institution has to influence policy. Consequently, from my perspective, the Roman Catholic Church is uniquely positioned to have an impact on the world, for better or for ill. The fact that it can have an impact in either direction simply affirms the potential it has for shaping the questions and the delivery of some level of possible solutions to the problems the world faces. It is this mix of our contemporary realities — the changes happening in a globalized world and the potential of the world's single largest religious body to respond to them — that makes for me a rethinking and repositioning of a theology of the world the most compelling theological issue we face today.

What I hope to do in this essay is to try to move the discussion of a theology of the world along a bit within the framework of the world as we now find it, and how a body such as the Roman Catholic Church might engage that world. The compelling issue I see is the Catholic Church's relation to the world, especially as seen through its theology of the world and theology of the church. Such theological positions will shape both analysis and response to the world and the challenges the world presents. To be sure, our pluralist and postmodern setting in the West may press us to think of "worlds" rather than "world." There is a point to this, but "unity" has been a long and cherished feature of the Catholic Church's self-identification (as it has been in some measure for all Christians). That unity can be coercive, but it is also the basis for solidarity, an important way of coming together in a pluralized world. Hence, I think there is some merit in speaking of "the world." Finally, this presentation can only focus upon one part of the compelling question, namely, how the church is viewing this changing world. Compelling questions, to my mind, do not admit of easy solutions and generally find themselves embedded in a host of relationships—both positive and negative, at once ambiguous and ambivalent. A single presentation can but address a fraction of what is at stake. My hope here is the fraction that I will dwell upon will help advance the discussion.

That discussion will be in three parts. The first is to offer where I now find myself in this discussion of repositioning of this theology. This is intended to serve the purpose of providing a context as well as offering some of the principles and motives that are guiding my argument. In the second part I focus on one perspective from which the relation of world and church might be further illuminated. That single point focuses on the church's responsibility to read the "signs of the times" as it shapes its response to the world. Focusing on this topic yields a perspective on how the relation of church and world is being understood from the side of the church. The third section looks at two ways of receiving such a reading: as prophecy or as a summons to confront a crisis. While prophecy and crisis overlap in significant ways, they are sustained over a longer period by differing views on the state of the world. Those differing views are addressed, along with some concluding observations about possible next steps in this discussion.

Repositioning a Theology of the World: The Story Thus Far

In this first part I ask your indulgence to intertwine my own story with the issues I am presenting. It is a commonly held position today that theology is never done from some Archimedean point outside the situation addressed or from some neutral place within. Consequently to understand the argument I am trying to make here, the pre-history of this "compelling question" has to be located in some of my own earlier work. In 1997 I published *The New Catholicity: Theology Between the Global and the Local*, a book that deals with the impact of globalization on the church and its response to a world that was being reshaped by the multivalent forces globalization and the ascendancy of a single economic order.[1] Besides taking up the challenges that globalization put to theology on the macro level, it explores as well themes of globalization's impact upon local settings. Consequently, themes such as intercultural hermeneutics, global forces reshaping religious identities, the fate of liberation theologies, as well as the state of contextual theologies in different parts of the world are explored.[2] The final question raised there was how to construe theologically these changes in the world in a way that would encompass both the global and local dimensions of what was happening, and thereby provide a way for the church to think about these issues and about itself in light of them. That construal was found in the theological category of catholicity, which had roots going back to the early second century and could address how the church saw itself both externally (as extended throughout the entire "known" world of the time), as well as internally (as custodian of the revelation of God given through Jesus Christ and transmitted through the apostles and their successors). I suggested that a continuing articulation of catholicity might help the church (and here was meant the "church catholic") find its place and calling in the world today. In addition, I suggested a third element may be added to these first two, namely, a concern for communication, that is, a conscious effort to ensure that both the local and the wider trans-regional and even worldwide voices of the church might be brought into communication with one another in order that the extension of the church throughout the world and the fullness of faith lived out concretely in each locale might together be respected.

In the meantime, 9/11 and subsequent events, as well as the growing sense of ecological instability, added other elements to this mix. The sense of contingency and the instability that terrorism caused, the increase of a different kind of warfare, the stumblings of global capitalism, the increasing impact of migration, and the reimagining of globalization not as a new phenomenon but a recurrence of one that had presented itself at least twice in the last

---

[1] Robert Schreiter, *The New Catholicity: Theology Between the Global and the Local* (Maryknoll, NY: Orbis Books, 1997). The book began as a series of lectures delivered at the University of Frankfurt in 1995, intended to address future directions in inculturation.

[2] This last point is more evident in the German edition, which reproduces the lectures as a whole. There is a chapter on contextual theologies in the United States, which is omitted in the English edition (see *Die neue Katholizität: Globalisierung und die Theologie* [Frankfurt: IKO Verlag, 1997]).

half-millennium called for further adjustment of the picture of what living in a globalized world might mean.[3]

These additions did not immediately call forth a rethinking of the use of the concept of catholicity as a way of coping with those changes from a theological point of view. But another factor, internal to the Roman Catholic Church, did urge such a rethinking. There had been a large-scale debate going on in Western Europe, North America, and Australia about how to chart the future direction of the church both within the world it was living in and within itself as to its identity and self-constitution. The emblematic center of this debate was how to interpret the teaching and resultant directions the church had been taking since the Second Vatican Council (1962–65). One side saw Pope John XXIII's convoking of a council with a pastoral orientation as aimed at bringing the church to an *aggiornamento* (updating) so as to engage more effectively the modern world. A consequence of all of this was a turning away from the stance the church had taken since the sixteenth-century Reformation and the Enlightenment and a re-engaging with the world by listening seriously to that world. No document from the council epitomized this approach more clearly than the *Pastoral Constitution on the church in the Modern World (Gaudium et spes)*. This entailed sweeping reforms within the church, and new attitudes toward other churches and faiths as well as to the modern world itself. Changed positions on individual religious freedom, ecumenism, and interreligious dialogue were all part of this. Over time, for better or for worse, this approach came to be called a hermeneutics of rupture with the church's immediate past (that is, especially since the reign of Pius IX, from 1846 to 1878).

Another position had consolidated around a different reaction to the impact of the council upon the church. In the 1960s a number of theologians in Europe (including some prominent ones who had been active at the council) felt that some of the changes in the church that were being enacted went beyond the brief that the council had given the church for reform.[4] Their argument was that the reforms that were to be enacted were only "course corrections" rather than a

---

[3] I presented this addition to the picture in a series of four articles published in *New Theology Review* in 2007 under the common title "A New Modernity: Living and Believing in an Unstable World." They had been first given as the 2005 Anthony Jordan Lectures at Newman Theological College in Edmonton, weeks before the death of Pope John Paul II.

[4] A clarion call came from Hans Urs von Balthasar with his *Cordula oder der Ernstfall* (Einsiedeln: Johannes Verlag, 1966).

turn-about of the church. A key factor in moving beyond the brief of the council was, many believed, the self-indulgent or anarchic spirit that had hit Europe and North America in that period, especially in the year 1968. The legitimate changes the council proposed were within a framework of *ressourcement* or return to the sources, not a license to propagate novel changes that were not somehow rooted in tradition. This position came to be known as the hermeneutic of continuity, opposed then to a hermeneutic of rupture.

The position received an official endorsement when the newly elected Pope Benedict XVI clearly allied himself with the hermeneutics of continuity in his speech to the Roman curia on December 22, 2005. A rift within the church that had been growing through the late 1990s and in the first decade of the present century was now clearly acknowledged, with the papacy aligning itself with one side of the debate.

How was this widening gap to be overcome? Besides my work as a theologian interested in questions of the interaction of the local and the global, going back to the mid-1970s, I have been engaged since the mid-1990s in international peacebuilding. This has involved work at the global level in developing what contributions Christian faith can make to peacebuilding, especially for those individuals and communities that are sustained in this difficult work of post-conflict reconstruction and reconciliation, as well as for concrete local communities who are struggling with these issues. This work has taken me to all six continents, to be confronted with a wide array of challenging issues. The work continues to teach me many things and make me think through and articulate at best incomplete answers to the questions posed to me. A consistent theme I am asked to address is how to bring opposing sides together, a challenge that lies at the heart of reconciliation. It began to dawn on me that perhaps what I was learning in the field about reconciliation might be of use in addressing these two seemingly opposed ideas of how the church should position itself in the world today in light of the teaching of the Second Vatican Council.

This, in turn, led me back to the theme of catholicity. It began to strike me that the two opposing positions might be able to be rearticulated as divergent yet also converging construals of the church's catholicity. Catholicity is part of the self-identification of all Roman Catholics. Thus, how best to express catholicity in the present time—either in extension (the phenomenon of being for the first time a genuinely worldwide church) or in inner fullness (a reading of change as continuity with the past) might be a way of getting a different entry into this debate. It is often the case that when opposing positions are presented in terms of ideas, they each represent deeply shared values, some of which (as values) overlap.[5] Trying to articulate what catholicity means in both camps might be a way of reentering this discussion that would help each side see the other's argument better in terms of both its internal coherence and deeply held values.

I tried this idea out first in an academic institution in Manila six years ago.[6] The debate about the council is not carried on with the same intensity there, although it is well known in academic circles. Incidentally, the Philippines (or to be exact, in the armed conflict in Mindanao) is a place where I continue to do peacebuilding work even today. I have since tried it out in a series of lectures in the United States and Europe. Although I would be aligned by most more closely with the first position (catholicity as extension), a considerable number of those in the second position have been able to see themselves in what I have presented and, I hope, see their opponents in a different way.

To sum up briefly where the thinking on catholicity stands with regard to this difference of interpretation and its meaning for interpreting the world, I might say this. For the first position, for the church to be truly catholic means that it engages and goes out into the whole world (Mt 28:19–20) through practices of solidarity, dialogue, inculturation, and the pursuit of justice. It believes that the creator God continues to be active in the world through the workings of the Holy Spirit. The world is to be seen through a sacramental imagination as a place that is grace laden. There one finds what the council called — harkening back to Justin Martyr in the second century — the *semina Verbi* or "seeds of the Logos." Thus, this position sees the world as the place where the triune God is working out and unfolding the *missio Dei* to which the church must be committed. The church itself has tremendous resources to bring to this work out of the revelation it carries in the tradition, to be sure. But those treasures are always in dialogue with what God is doing today. This, from this point of view, was what the council

---

[5] I derived this idea from John Paul Lederach, *The Moral Imagination: The Art and Soul of Building Peace* (New York: Oxford University Press, 2005). It is expressed also in the work of moral psychologist Jonathan Haidt in *The Righteous Mind: Why Good People Are Divided by Politics and Religion* (New York: The Free Press, 2012).

[6] Robert Schreiter, "Two Forms of Catholicity in a Time of Globalization," *Himig Ugnayan* 8 (2007): 1–17.

was trying to do: to bring out both the old and the new. It is not enough simply to present the church's rich faith as unchanging truth in an ever-changing world; there must also be a listening to the world in order to be aligned with God's work in the world. The world is indeed a sinful place. But God's grace is greater, and God has not left the world but continues to love it and sustain it. So how might the world be positioned in relation to the church, seeking to cooperate in the *missio Dei*? The world is at once a place where the effects of sin must be healed and where justice realigns the relationships with God and with the created world. And it is also a site of prophecy, a place where God chooses to speak, even to the church itself. *Gaudium et spes* is the charter document for both this vision and this hermeneutic.

In the second position, for the church to be truly catholic it must offer the revelation about God and the world given in Jesus Christ and commended to the church by Christ. This revelation presents a view of the human being and of the world—a lens, as it were, through which to view and rightly construe the world.

The proposal on theological anthropology in chapters two and three of the first part of *Gaudium et spes* was intended to impart this vision of the church—although many who hold this second position find this section of the document deeply flawed. Rather, this vision of God for the world is better stated in the *Dogmatic Constitution on the Church (Lumen gentium)*, where one sees the concrete form this revelation has taken in the church. By coming in and dwelling within the church and participating in its practices, especially the liturgy, one attains the vision for seeing the world and its problems and possibilities. This second position takes a much darker view of the world and its sinfulness, but also sees its capacity to rescue and redo itself. The utopian constructions of the nineteenth and twentieth centuries, fueled as they were by Enlightenment optimism about the human being, have been shown to be hollow and even harmful. The beauty and the truth that the church proclaims are based on a centuries-old wisdom that touches not just the minds but the hearts of people as well. To find this in unalloyed form in the fallen world is a futile search. It is found in the beauty and truth of the church, especially in the liturgy. By allowing one's soul to be converted and transformed by this truth and allowing the soul to dwell in this beauty, the world might gradually become a better place through the working of God's grace. In the meantime the only productive and true way to look at the world is as a site of crisis. As the etymology of the word *crisis* implies, it requires making a choice: conform to the world or be conformed to the church so as to dwell in truth and beauty in order to transform the world. The church might be seen here as a new ark, to which we must retreat from the impending doom so as to be transformed for the sake of new beginnings. Those new beginnings are the coming and realization of the reign of God. Returning, then, to the hermeneutics of rupture and continuity, there is a rupture, but it is with the world, and a seeking of continuity with what the church has been at its best. But that continuity calls for a return to the world as well, that the world might become part of the New Jerusalem being created by God.

I have proposed these two positions in the broadest and starkest of strokes. Among most participants in this debate, people on both sides can see merits in the position of the other. The intent of the presentation here was to probe some of the most deeply held theological positions and articulation of values that seem to guide and sustain those who align themselves with one side or the other. It is easy for one side to demonize the other, as so often happens in conflict. But I hope this brief sketch outlines some of the fundamental issues that are at stake in this matter. For example, just how fallen is the world? The church has always had an ambivalent view of the world, ranging from confessing that God has so loved the world as to send it God's only son (Jn 3:16) while at the same time admonishing Christians not to conform themselves to this world (Rom 12:2). With that, what will it take to repair the world? Is it principally a matter of structural justice? Or is it first of all a matter of the conversion of human hearts? And depending upon how one answers these two questions, then comes the question of the church in all of this. Just how should the church position itself, both as herald of the reign of God and (rather more ambiguously) to some measure its fulfillment? What does it mean to say that the Eucharist, for example, is a foretaste of the heavenly banquet? Does life in the church prefigure and propose a certain way of ordering the world and of human society within it? If so, what are the practices that sustain that way of life? Both positions grapple with these questions in different ways. Both have insights to contribute, experiences to share and wisdom to impart, but both have limitations to face. I cannot go further into those things here. What this first section has been intended to do is to sketch the domain in order to focus on development of one further point: what is entailed in reading the "signs of the times"?

Reading the Signs of the Times

Gaudium et spes states, "To carry out [its] task, the Church has always had the duty of scrutinizing the signs of the times and interpreting them in the light of the Gospel" (no. 4). This sets reading the signs of the times as an important part of the agenda of the church as it engages the world. The origins of the phrase can be traced to Matthew 16:1–4 (and parallels in Mark and John), where the Pharisees ask Jesus for a sign. Jesus points to natural phenomena (the state of the sky in the evening and in the morning) and berates his interlocutors for not even being able to read meteorological signs. How, then, are they to be able to read signs from God? He then gives them the sign of Jonah to be read in light of himself.[7]

In the first half of the twentieth century the "signs of the times" became a phrase for indicating the need for social analysis for both Protestant (Christian Socialists) and Catholic (the circles around J. Cardijn) activists. Pope John XXIII took it up in his encyclical *Pacem in terris,* as did Paul VI in his inaugural encyclical *Ecclesiam suam.* A special sub-commission on Schema XIII (which was to become *Gaudium et spes*) worked in September and October of 1964 to elucidate the potential theological meaning of the phrase and its eventual inclusion in the pastoral constitution.[8]

The use of "signs of the times" elicits a whole range of questions to investigate. *Times* does not bespeak a mere chronological sense of time, as a mathematically measurable succession of moments that can be quantitatively discerned and presented. It sees time "bunched," as it were, in constellations that evoke clusters of meaning about history and human existence, more in the sense of the "lived time" *(temps vécu)* of Henri Bergson or the time in the conjunctural sense as proposed by Fernand Braudel and the *Annales* school of historians. In this manner one would speak of "economies of time," in the sense of time ordered by some external source and internal principles. Christianity speaks of "salvation history" as an

---

[7] A brief account of this phrase in theological usage may be found in the article "Zeichen der Zeit," in *Lexikon für Theologie und Kirche* (LThK), 10, 1403; for a more extensive account, see Giuseppe Ruggieri, "Zeichen der Zeit: Herkunft und Bedeutung einer christlichen-hermeneutischen Chiffre der Geschichte," in *Das Zweite Vatikanum und die Zeichen der Zeit heute,* ed. Peter Hünermann (Freiburg: Herder, 2006), 61–70.

[8] Thus M.-D. Chenu, "Les signes des temps," *Nouvelle Revue Théologique* 87 (1965): 29–39. Chenu is widely credited with bringing this to the attention of the council fathers.

economy in this regard. So time is more than chronological compu-
tation; as history, it can reveal deeper meanings about human life
and societies.

Likewise, *signs* can carry multiple meanings. Signs were the
source of intense scrutiny in semiotics and in structuralist and poststructuralist literature in the 1960s and 1970s, largely apart from
which the texts of the council were drafted. Putting it in more general, non-specialist categories,[9] one might speak of *natural, conventional,
historical,* and *theological* signs. Natural signs would be, for example,
meteorological ones: looming dark clouds signify approaching rain;
the state of the sky at dusk and dawn bespeak the weather situation
for the next day. Conventional signs are objects that take on specific
meanings as the result of social agreement; thus a red, octagon sign
with white letters announcing STOP instructs automobile drivers to
halt at a given site. Historical signs point to special places or social
configurations as well as to meaning-making events. The image of
the Eiffel Tower calls Paris to mind, or war monuments or memori-
als to the Holocaust take us back to certain crucial moments in time.
Within religious traditions certain objects become carriers of broader
and deeper meaning, such as the lotus for Buddhists, the cross for
Christians, the Star of David for Jews.

Signs of the times speak especially of the latter two kinds of signs,
embedded in concrete histories and in religious and theological traditions. It seems that it is never a matter of simply identifying signs
as signs but of identifying them and locating them within economies
of time. If one goes back to Jesus' invocation of the signs of the times
in response to the Pharisees' request for a sign, the economy seems
to be an apocalyptic one, especially when one sees the sign of Jonah
as prefiguring the death and resurrection of Jesus.

Two major sets of questions can be seen to have emerged in the
subsequent discussion of the signs of the times as articulated in
Gaudium et spes. The first had to do with to what extent the signs of
this age (the *saeculum*) could be seen as bearing messages of God's
purposes. On the one hand (here sometimes found in the first position on catholicity outlined above), there was at some points an
overly enthusiastic identification of signs of this age with the voice
of God. This no doubt grew out of a robust enthusiasm for the world

---

[9] Here I am simply following Chenu, "Les signes des temps." He does not
trace the then-available literature in semiotics and other fields but restricts
himself to some common understandings of *signs.* Presumably it was this more
commonsense understanding that would have influenced the fathers in *Gaudium
et spes.*

after some two centuries of the church's having turned its back on that same world. There was a sense that some more finely honed criteria needed to be in place. Not every occurrence might be called a sign. Chenu himself asked the question whether, for example, atheism (a key concern of the council fathers) could be construed as a sign. His response was negative; atheism was an ideology, not a sign.[10] This response would suggest, however, that a more elaborated theory of signs has to be in place before one begins pointing to this or that sign. How and who determines something as a sign needs some form of theoretical legitimation.

On the other end of the discussion—to be found among some extreme proponents of the second position—was a question as to whether history yields any signs of God's action at all. In its most extreme form this arises from an extrinsicist approach that utterly separates grace from nature. While such an approach was still widespread in mid-twentieth century Catholicism, it was an approach losing ground. But especially for those who would see themselves in the second position on catholicity just mentioned, the question raised was what value does secular history have in revealing God's purposes, or is it only in the light of revelation that any godliness can be discerned in secular history at all? This would be an extreme formulation, but it does raise the question of how much grace can nature reveal, a question lying beneath the anthropologies and theologies of history of those on both positions on catholicity.

The second set of questions was of a hermeneutical nature. While there may be a certain consensus on how to elaborate a hermeneutics for dogmatic interpretation, there is no clear one for a hermeneutics of pastoral interpretation.[11] There is a kind of consensus on both sides about the lack of a hermeneutics of pastoral interpretation, although not on the procedures that would effect an adequate answer to the question. To go back to the quotation from *Gaudium et spes* at the beginning of this section ("scrutinizing the signs of the times and interpeting them in the light of the Gospel") "light of the Gospel" is code, as it were, for a delicate balancing of scripture, tradition, and theological history. But does the gospel pre-discern the signs to be read in the first place? For example, the continuing dispute about

---

[10] Chenu, "Les signes des temps," 38.

[11] There are differences, of course, of dogmatic interpretation, most notably on history and historicity. The dispute between the Doctrinal Commission of the US Conference of Catholic Bishops and Professor Elizabeth Johnson in 2011 gives plenty of examples of differences. Yet the point here is that there is at least some general agreement on the issues.

the possible ordination of women. The contested methodologies are evident in a number of instances in the life of the church. Pope John Paul II in *Inter signores* in effect stated that the possible ordination of women is not a sign of the times, and cannot be seen in the light of the gospel because the Lord had given no permission to the church to consider it. This might be seen as aligned with the second position. From another perspective, the widespread dispute of this contention might indicate that there has been no adequate reception by the people of God, since there are laity, clergy, and bishops who contest, in one way or another, this papal statement. This approach, more likely aligned with the first position on catholicity, might hold that the call for such ordination is indeed a sign of the times. To follow this out in another instance, the methodologies for bringing about a genuine inculturation remain uncertain. The church at the Vatican level has taken up the question somewhat piecemeal in a number of statements on culture, but there is still widespread dispute about proper modes of inculturation.[12]

In this particular question of a pastoral hermeneutics, the central matter is what and who build the connections between the signs of the times and the gospel? If one were to survey the literature, it would be possible to say that those taking the first position on catholicity would be eager to protect and ensure that the voices of the "times" are heard and not predetermined by the church's hermeneutic. The second would be especially concerned about the integrity of the church's self-understanding in all of this, even while acknowledging the relative autonomy of earthly affairs (see *Gaudium et spes*, no. 36). It would be too simple to reduce the differences to a concern only for cultural integrity, on the one hand, and theological integrity, on the other. But there still remains no agreement on how to exercise a pastoral hermeneutic.[13]

In his commentary on *Gaudium et spes* Hans-Joachim Sander has proposed a distinction that might shed light on this immediate matter of a pastoral hermeneutics and larger issues of how to bring together signs of the times with the light of the gospel. He proposes

---

[12] A recent assessment is found in Gerald Arbuckle, *Culture, Inculturation, and Theologians: A Postmodern Critique* (Collegeville, MN: Liturgical Press, 2010). For an anthology of papal statements on culture, see Consiglio Pontificio de la Cultura, *Fede e cultura* (Vatican City: Libreria Editrice Vaticana, 2003).

[13] There have been isolated instances of calling even some texts of the council itself pastoral in the sense of subject to change and not on the level of the dogmatic documents. This is perceived by those in the first position as an attempt to roll back reforms mandated by the council itself.

that what I have called the first position here is preoccupied with seeing the matter topologically, that is, as a "where" question.[14] To the English-speaking world, this "where" question is one of social location. Sander notes that the council fathers were preoccupied with the battle against atheism and the ongoing march of secularism— North Atlantic concerns. A minority voice was raised by Cardinal Lercaro and from Latin America that dehumanizing poverty should be the locus from which to see the signs of the times to be interpreted in the light of the gospel. While the language of social location is often proffered, it often does not admit into its circle what alternate interpretations might be. In the third and concluding section, I hope to highlight a few such differences from the Global South, where the majority of Christians now live.

The other suggestion that Sander proposes along with the "where" question is a "who" question that focuses on issues of identity. This would be more prominent in the second position on catholicity where maintaining the integrity of the church's witness and identity is of paramount importance. If the church is to provide a clear response to the crisis the world faces, then it must have a clear and consistent identity. One sees this exhibited in those clerics who style themselves "John Paul II priests."

What Sander's proposal suggests is that it is difficult if not impossible to put the two positions on the question of reading the signs of the times in a symmetrical relationship. In other words, to try to bring them into conversation, as such, may result in category mistakes, confusing questions of location and perspective with questions of identity. It may at the very least suggest that the methodological approaches that each position may prefer allow only partial dialogue between the two.

Interestingly, "signs of the times" is itself a more preferred hermeneutic for reading the council among those of the first position on catholicity. A 672–page tome appended to the Herder Commentary on the documents of the Second Vatican Council, published in Germany to mark the fortieth anniversary of the close of the council, is evidence of that.[15] By contrast, a more recent volume written from the second position spends little time on the question and draws

---

[14] Hans-Joachim Sander, "Theologischer Commentar zur Pastoralen Konstitution zur Kirche in der Welt von heute *Gaudium et spes*," in *Herders Theologischer Kommentar zum Zweiten Vaticanischen Konzil*, vol. 3, ed. Peter Hünermann and Bernd Joachim Hilberath (Freiburg: Herder Verlag, 2006), 587.

[15] Hünermann, *Herders Theologischer Kommentar zum Zweiten Vaticanischen Konzil.*

principally on critiques written by Joseph Ratzinger in the Vorgrimler Commentary from the 1960s and an article from the mid-1970s.[16]

This section on interpreting "the signs of the times" has tried to
illustrate concerns about how to position the church with regard
to the world. It has generated not only two not entirely compatible
modes of thought, but also raised further fundamental questions
about how a theology of the world and the church's response to it
is to be constructed today. In the concluding section I return to the
themes of prophecy and crisis, and touch again upon the four areas
of a widened perspective about the world and select some issues
from each area to illumine the options—and the questions—that
still remain.

Prophecy and Crisis

I have proposed that the two positions on how to express and enact
the catholicity of the church as it faces the world can be characterized
as looking to the world as a site of prophecy and looking to a world
in crisis. Prophecy and crisis share common ground; both see a situation to be addressed. In this sense, both are engaged in reading the
signs of the times—readings that elicit responses to what is seen. A
significant part of that reading is done through the lens of how each
position constructs its theology of the world, and a theology of the
church to respond to what it sees.

A significant part that shapes what the first position seeks and
perceives is that prophecy—God's word to us at this time—often
comes from beyond the circle of the church. Just as in ancient Israel
the prophets pondered the meaning of exile and of foreign rulers
as mediating God's word in some way to Israel, so too today signs
and voices come to the church from where it would not expect them.
These signs and voices can indeed be from God in that God is the
creator and sustainer of the world. Of course, not everything seen
or heard is necessarily from God; to think so would be hopelessly
naive. But the possibility can never be ruled out that a prophetic
sign or word is coming to us from a place least expected, a place
we might even dub as profane. In a rapidly moving and changing world such as ours, finding ways of discernment—the classic
discretio spirituum—becomes more important than ever. Given the

---

[16] J. Brian Benestad, "Doctrinal Perspectives on the Church in the Modern
World," in *Vatican II: Renewal Within Tradition*, ed. Matthew Levering and Matthew Lamb (New York: Oxford University Press, 2008).

first position's "where" preoccupation, we might ask from where we might best seek the signs of the times. In the geo-economic and political spheres, is it still the poor? Or is it in the middle classes that are rising in some national economies and shrinking in others? Or is the migrant the sign of our times? In demographic spheres, what of the paradox of the declining birthrate in Europe, Asia, and the Americas, while the rates in Africa remain at a very (and likely socially unsustainable) high rate? Is the plight of women the sign of our times? Where might we seek the signs of prophecy in eco-logical spheres? In the religious sphere, what signs speak to us of post-secularity in the North Atlantic? And perhaps most important, what signs help us construe religious pluralism and where it fits into God's *missio* in the world?

To view the world as in crisis—the prevailing view of the second position on catholicity—means that the world needs the message of Jesus Christ and his church more than ever before. In order to be able to deliver that message, the church must purify and focus its self-understanding in a way that will renew those within the church as well as be compelling for those who are seeking truth. It must be reasserted that the faith the church offers is not beyond human reason but is in deep harmony with it. Most important, because the world is in crisis, the church must project a clear and unified mes-sage that touches the most profound depths of the human spirit and its yearning for meaning and for God. There is diversity in the world, but one must seek especially those points of unity that will hold the world together as it faces the crises that lie before it.

What are the signs of those crises? In the geo-economic and political spheres the worldwide recession of recent years may por-tend even greater upheavals to come, just as the rebellions against repressive governments in the Middle East and in places like Burma and Thailand may portend growing social chaos and disorder. The potential collapse of developed countries' economies because of the lack of adequate young people to maintain the social networks nec-essary for caring for the elderly and those unable to work is a crisis coming upon the demographic sphere. How will the impending ecological crises be met? And will an accommodating religious plu-ralism obscure truth, thus producing an unintended effect; instead of helping people live together peacefully, will it drive groups into confusion and violence?

The church must prepare itself for a potentially difficult time. Proposed solutions of changing social structures of all kinds will have but a minimal positive effect in stemming these crises, and may even make them worse. The grace of God, flowing from the church to purify, enlighten, and transform the hearts and minds of the men and women of this world, is what will be needed. Transformed souls may find a way through all of this and ameliorate the worst of what is likely to happen. The church stands as a beacon in these chiaroscuro times with the beauty of its liturgy, the splendor of its truth, and the life of grace it offers.

Conclusion

How will the necessary repositioning of a theology of the world and its implied theology of the church work out in the years ahead? There are two visions—sketched here in the boldest of strokes—that draw differing configurations of the Catholic faithful in overlapping yet different directions. Put from a more secular point of view, is an emphasis on diversity and pluralism or an emphasis on unity the best way through the challenges the world will face in the coming time? In either instance (and these binaries do not do justice to the complexity being addressed), a clear rationale needs to be articulated. For the church, that rationale has to be theological. Can we read the signs of the times? We will perhaps only know in retrospect how effectively we have been able to do so. But I would suggest that either of the positions on reading the signs of the times within the frame of catholicity will be inadequate without learning from the strengths and the shortcomings of the other. Pope Benedict said on occasion that true catholicity leans more to a "both-and" rather than an "either-or." A critical attitude of "both-and," I suggest, is the only way forward.

A Reponse to Robert Schreiter

The Church of the Global South

Not What We Bargained For?

JAMES FREDERICKS

Robert Schreiter makes an important point when he draws our attention to the need to rethink catholicity in the church today. A "new catholicity" will be necessary not only for the Roman Catholic Church, but for the future of the entire Christian community. With this in mind, I want to think about the challenge of catholicity in light of the emergence of what I take to be a development of real importance, what Schreiter calls the church of the Global South. I define Global South as Schreiter does: sub-Saharan Africa, Latin America, and Asia. Of course, Southern Christians are migrating to the North, and they must be counted as well. My intention is not to evaluate the orthodoxy of the Southern Christians or the authenticity of their faith. I have two reasons for extending the conversation about catholicity to the Global South. First, the South is the future of Christianity. This is due not only to the fact that Christianity is in the midst of a monumental shift in population from the North to the South and that the churches of the South are far and away more vibrant than those of the North; but it is also the case that many churches of the South have developed in ways that do not always conform to the expectations of the liberal Christians in the North. This has major repercussions on the need for a new catholicity.

Christianity is moving south. What theologian Agbonkhian-meghe Orobator calls "the church's southward movement" means that the Christian community does not actually look the way most Northern Christians are accustomed to think it looks. The average Christian is no longer a European, or someone who can trace his or her ancestors back to Europe. Actually, this has been the case for some time. In his essay Schreiter takes note of the fact that the fertility rate for many women in the industrialized societies of the North is well below the replacement level of 2.1 (the United States is an exception to the rule because of immigration—from the South). In the last century the increase in the number of Southern Christians has been astounding. In 1900, there were 10 million Christians in sub-Saharan Africa (9 percent of the total population). Today, there are roughly 360 million Christians in Africa out of a total population of 784 million (46 percent of the total population). Mexico had a population of 15 million people in 1900, almost all of them Christians. Today, Mexico's population is roughly one-hundred million. Presuming this dramatic demographic shift continues, and there is no reason why it should not, the AIDS epidemic notwithstanding, 50 percent of the Christians in the world will reside in Africa and Latin America. Another 17 percent will reside in Asia by mid-century. In 1998, more than three-quarters of all the baptisms in the Roman Catholic Church were in Africa, Latin America, and Asia. That year, the total number of baptisms in the Philippines was higher than the totals for Italy, France, Spain, and Poland combined.[1]

Not only is the population center of Christian faith shifting away from the North, but the denominational makeup of Christianity is changing as well. This transformation can be seen most obviously in the rise of Protestant churches in Latin America. Evangelical and especially Pentecostal groups are growing the most rapidly. The successes of Pentecostal Christianity can also be seen in sub-Saharan Africa and Asia. Current estimates place the number of Pentecostal Christians at 400 million. Some observers estimate that their number could approach 1 billion by mid-century. Statistics such as these are admittedly difficult to verify. The astounding success of Pentecostalism, however, is undeniable and of great significance to the future of global Christianity.[2] One reason for this is that Pentecostals and other Christian sects in the South embrace beliefs and practices that are at best bewildering to Northern Christians. This point leads to the second issue I want to address.

Let me start by stating what should go without saying. Southern Christianity is not monolithic. The comments that follow should keep this in mind. My position is that Northern Christians often have

---

[1] Philip Jenkins, *The Next Christendom: The Coming of Global Christianity* (New York: Oxford, 2007), 93–124.

[2] Harvey Cox, *Fire from Heaven: The Rise of Pentecostal Spirituality and the Reshaping of Religion in the Twenty-first Century* (New York: Da Capo Press, 1995).

romanticized views of the Christianity of the South, and this will pose a considerable challenge to achieving a new catholicity. The Roman Catholic Church in the South is more hierarchical, doctrinally rigid, politically conservative, and devotional in its practices than much of the literature of the theology of liberation would indicate. Many Protestant churches, especially some of the independent evangelical and Pentecostal churches, embrace a fideism and fascination with the supernatural that Northern Christians would find baffling. In addition, these Roman Catholic and Protestant congregations of the South tend to be more concerned with personal morality than with social justice.

Churches of the South evince an interest in the supernatural that is unsettling for many Northern Christians. Let me concentrate on faith healing and its two close relatives, demon possession and exorcism.[3] Southern Christianity is peppered with charismatic religious leaders waging spiritual warfare against the spirits of vengeful ancestors, local demons, and the "powers and principalities" of this world. In the Universal Church of the Kingdom of God, a Pentecostal church in Brazil, ministers promote themselves by claiming to have "strong prayer to destroy witchcraft, demon possession, bad luck, bad dreams, all spiritual problems." These ministers can also invoke the Holy Spirit to provide "prosperity and financial breakthrough." The Cherubim and Seraphim Church of West Africa offers "conscious knowledge of the evil spirits which sow the seeds of discomfort, set afloat ill-luck, diseases, induce barrenness, sterility and the like." Ministers of the Zulu Zionist Church in South Africa call for the confession of sins before they expel demons.

Faith healing takes a variety of forms and has a number of social consequences. Northern Christians should think twice before dismissing this form of faith as simple superstition. In Brazil, the overwhelming reason why men convert to Pentecostalism is the perceived ability of Pentecostal ministers to cure alcoholism.[4] The salutary effect this has on women should not be underestimated. Men who have had the dark spirit of "demon rum" cast out of them stay home and take more responsibility within the family. Families become more prosperous because paychecks are no longer squandered in drinking binges on payday. The practice of exorcism also helps women by addressing the dangers of sorcery in a nonviolent

---

[3] Candy Gunther Brown, ed., *Global Pentecostal and Charismatic Healing* (New York: Oxford University Press, 2011).

[4] R. Andrew Chestnut, *Born Again in Brazil* (New Brunswick, NJ: Rutgers University Press, 1997), 58.

manner. A charismatic exorcist can save a woman's life by converting her from witchcraft.[5]

In Africa, the cure of AIDS is a major reason why Christians seek
out charismatic faith healers.[6] The expectation of Northern Christians, worshiping in congregations that have long ago traded the
enchanted cosmos of the medieval world for the disenchantments
of modernity, would be that the failure of faith healers to cure AIDS
would make faith healing a relic of a prescientific past. At the least,
Northern Christians would expect that faith healing and exorcism
would retreat before the advance of the scientific worldview, the
availability of medical treatment, and increased opportunities for
education. This is not the case with many Southern Christians.
Schreiter takes note of Weber's famous thesis about the decline of the
supernatural through rationalization. Weber may not be completely
incorrect in what he has to say about the spirit of Protestantism, but
his thesis is too simple. The continued belief of Southern Christians
in supernatural phenomena proves this point. In fact, the practice
of faith healing and exorcism increases with urbanization in parts of
Africa, Asia, and Latin America. Once again, the Northern impulse
to dismiss the faith of Southern Christians as superstitious seems too
hasty. No matter how Northern Christians evaluate the practices of
faith healing and exorcism theologically, these practices need to be
recognized as genuine expressions of Christian faith. Welcoming
these practices into what Northern Christians consider the fold may
be difficult. But this leads back to my two basic claims: Northern
Christianity is no longer the dominant face of the global Christian
community, and Northern Christians can be naive about the beliefs
and practices of the South. With Schreiter, I agree that the challenge
of a global catholicity to the church is considerably more daunting
than some in the North might believe.

Some have tried to interpret all of this as the resurgence of pre-
colonial religious behaviors. Another interpretation would be to
take these practices at face value as expressions of Christian faith.
After all, faith healing, exorcism, apocalyptic expectation, visions,
and prophecy are all found in the Bible. In fact, without too much
difficulty, a case could be made for saying that these phenomena
are more prominent in the New Testament than the Hebrew Bible.
These biblical realities live on in the faith struggles of contemporary

---

[5] André Corten, *Pentecostalism in Brazil: Emotion of the Poor and Theological
Romanticism* (New York: MacMillan Press, 1999).

[6] Lamin O. Sanneh, *West African Christianity* (Maryknoll, NY: Orbis Books,
1983).

Southern Christians. The African prophet Johane Masowe (1915–73), who recovered from a near-death experience and subsequently identified himself as a messiah, is reported to have said:

> When we were in these synagogues [that is, the European churches], we used to read about the works of Jesus Christ . . . cripples were made to walk and the dead were brought to life . . . evil spirits driven out. . . . That was what was being done in Jerusalem. We Africans, however, who were being instructed by white people, never did anything like that. . . . We were taught to read the Bible, but we ourselves never did what the people of the Bible used to do.[7]

There is a postcolonial resentment in this text that is not hard to discern (to say nothing of an implicit anti-Judaism). I take this as an indication that a new catholicity will be a challenge not only because aspects of Southern Christianity are difficult for Northern Christians to accept, but also because postcolonial criticism of the North is legitimated by what is now being called a post-secular world. Christians of the North have taken Jefferson's scissors (and Bultmann's as well) to the New Testament to purge it of its supernaturalism. This is not the case with many Christians of the South. In some respects I think we must admit that the South takes the New Testament more seriously than the North. Southern Christians are saying that the kingdom of God is not only a future reality but a present reality as well. This is entirely in keeping with New Testament accounts of the teaching of Jesus. When asked to identify himself to the disciples of John the Baptist, Jesus did not talk about Christology. Instead, he drew their attention to the presence of the kingdom here and now: "the blind receive their sight, the lame walk, the lepers are cleansed, the deaf hear, the dead are raised, and the poor have good news brought to them" (Mt 11:5).

The tension between the North and the South has erupted into open conflict within the Anglican Communion. In the North, Anglicans tend to be quite liberal in their theology and pastoral practices. This is especially the case in the United States. The Episcopal Church was among the first Christian congregations to admit women clergy, for example. A threshold, however, was crossed with the ordination of an openly gay bishop. Anglican bishops in the South threatened

---

[7] Cited in Elizabeth Isichei, *A History of Christianity in Africa* (Grand Rapids, MI: Eerdmanns, 1995), 255.

schism. Led by Bishop Moses Tay of Singapore and Bishop Emman-
uel Kolini of Uganda, various Southern bishops offered to bring conservative Episcopalian congregations under their jurisdiction. This
has led to nasty discussions in London and expensive court cases in
the United States. At the Lambeth conference of 1998, Bishop John
Spong said that the African bishops had "moved out of animism into
a very superstitious kind of Christianity"; these Anglicans were now
being led by an "irrational Pentecostal hysteria."[8]

Schreiter also reflects on the church-world relationship in terms of
politics. Here again, the presuppositions of Northern Christians and
the practices of Southern Christianity can be in conflict. In general,
Christian clergy are more overtly entangled in politics in the South
than in the North. This is due in part to the legacy of colonialism,
when church and state were closely aligned. After the council a
number of Catholic bishops took public leadership roles in opposing governments. Episcopal appointments during the papacy of
John Paul II tended to favor bishops who did not pose difficulties
for local governments.

However, I think the most important change has gone on at the
grassroots level. Liberation theology is waning. Some have claimed
that it has been put out of business by Pentecostalism. Whether the
decline of liberation theology is due to Pentecostalism or whether
Pentecostalism has simply filled the spiritual void left by the fading
of liberation theology is difficult to assess. In any event, the passing
of liberation theology and the dramatic rise of Pentecostalism has
had discernible political consequences. Liberation theology was
built on grassroots organizing, social analysis, and a dialogue with
Marxist thought. Pentecostal and evangelical Christianity stress
personal religious experience. Sin has to do with individual moral
lapses, not oppressive social structures. However, to say that these
forms of Christianity are a purely privatized religiosity with no
social consequences is simplistic.[9]

How will tensions between Christians and Muslims shape the
Christianity of the global South? Conflict between Christians and
Muslims has been a reality in parts of Africa and the Near East for
some time. It is increasingly a problem in Asia as well. Instances of
Christians instigating violence against Muslims can be documented,
but the core of the problem lies with the inability of some Muslims

---

[8] Jenkins, *The Next Christendom*, 142.

[9] Philip D. Wingeier-Rayo, *Where Are the Poor? A Comparison of the Ecclesial
Base Communities and Pentecostalism – a Case Study in Cuernavaca, Mexico* (Eugene,
OR: Pickwick Publications, 2011).

to tolerate religious diversity. Violence against Christians (and sometimes Christians retaliating against Muslims) can be seen in Nigeria, Sudan, Ethiopia, Egypt, Indonesia, and the Philippines. This is by no means a complete list of conflict areas. Some of the tension can be attributed to aggressive proselytizing by evangelical Christians. In the North, Muslims are a minority. In the South, Christians are either a minority or on an equal footing with the Muslim population. In areas of conflict, religious affiliation becomes a major identity marker. This is a very foreign phenomenon for Northern Christians. The impact of Islam on Southern churches will be dramatic and, in all likelihood, less than salutary.

Schreiter notes in his essay that the Second Vatican Council was largely concerned with what he calls the "North Atlantic issues" of atheism and secularism. The tension of *aggiornamento* and *ressourcement* arose out of this context. Schreiter's hopes for a global catholicity, however, have to be mindful of the considerable challenge Southern Christianity poses. Schreiter notes that prophecy is "God's word to us at this time." Prophecy, therefore, calls us to be attentive to "the signs of the times." He goes on to note that prophecy sometimes comes to the church from without. He is quite correct, of course, and this is yet another reason to be attentive to the signs of the times. But in responding to Schreiter, I want to emphasize that prophecy can come from within a part of the church that we do not know well and do not understand. Here, I mean the Christian faith of the Southern churches. The faith of Southern Christians cannot always be easily reconciled with the faith of liberal Northern Christians. Schreiter also calls for a "new catholicity" for the global church. This catholicity, if it is to be authentic, will have to find a way to embrace both the Christianity of the North and that of the South. As Schreiter says, "The church must prepare itself for a potentially difficult time."

4

Faith and Political Engagement in a Pluralistic World

Beyond the Idols of Public Space

FRANCIS SCHÜSSLER FIORENZA

A crucial issue in theology currently is the relationship between faith and political engagement within a pluralistic world. Such an issue is fundamental because it is not merely a question of social or political application but rather one that involves the very claims of faith and assertions of theological reflection in the face of contrasting faiths and conflicting viewpoints. It is as much an issue of fundamental or foundational theology as it is of social or political ethics. This thesis can be shown by comparing current debates on the relation between faith and political engagement with earlier Roman Catholic theological approaches within the second half of the twentieth century that strongly advocated a political theological engagement. In this respect both German political theology and Latin American theology provide a backdrop for examining recent Roman Catholic theological statements about the public and political nature of faith. This brief historical sketch aims to show not only the diversity and strengths of these Roman Catholic positions, but also to test their relevance for our very different contemporary situation.

The fundamental question is this: how does one actively affirm the political implications of one's faith within a political and social world that is normatively and religiously pluralistic? *Pluralism* does not refer only to religious pluralism (though it indeed includes that), but also to differences in basic values, in fundamental moral options, in comprehensive metaphysical worldviews, and in diverse moral convictions about the good and even the common good. Hence, I shall examine how some recent Roman Catholic traditions of theology, especially political theologies, understand the public space of society in their support for a political advocacy. Do they criticize or even demonize this public sphere as laden with hostile values and conflicting idols? Or can they envision it in a positive manner, as a pluralist and agonistic space that one enters for the sake of a constructive engagement? How do these theologies fit within the current context of discussions about religious convictions and liberal democracy?[1] How do these theologies relate to the issue of human rights so prominent in public space? What should such an engagement of public space entail in the case of political advocacy?

Political Theology as a Corrective of Existential Theology

In the 1960s, Johann Baptist Metz reintroduced the notion of political theology in Germany at the same time as Jürgen Moltmann was developing the main outlines of a theology of hope.[2] This development can best be understood against the background of the post–World War II situation in Europe, especially Germany. Both Metz and Moltmann had experienced the war as young teenagers. They were conscripted in the last months of the war and became prisoners of war. They belonged to the group of theologians who reflected back critically upon the past decades of Christian theology from a Catholic (Metz), Reformed (Moltmann), or Lutheran (Dorothee Sölle) perspective. Their advocacy of a political theological engagement was clearly their reaction to the German political past.

These political theologians questioned whether the churches had adequately responded to National Socialism and whether the leading postwar theologians had dealt adequately with the Holocaust. In addition to this intent, several elements of their diagnoses need to be highlighted. They interpreted contemporary society as secularized. On the one hand, in a quasi-Weberian sense, they affirmed that the dominance of a scientific-technological rationality has led to a desacralization of nature and reduced the sphere of religion.

---

[1] See the comprehensive collection of essays in J. Caleb Clanton, ed., *The Ethics of Citizenship: Liberal Democracy and Religious Convictions* (Waco, TX: Baylor University, 2009).

[2] Johann Baptist Metz, *Theology of the World* (New York: Herder and Herder, 1969); idem, *Faith in History and Society* (New York: Seabury, 1980); idem, *Memoria Passionis* (Freiburg: Herder, 2006). See also, Jürgen Moltmann, *Theology of Hope* (New York: Harper, 1967).

On the other, they interpreted modern society as dominated by the capitalistic market economics. Within this capitalistic market, religion became privatized and reduced to an individual's consumer preference, becoming but another consumer object.

This interpretation of their contemporary society as dominated by the market economy, in which religion is both privatized and a matter of consumer choice, influenced both their criticism of previous theologians as well as their constructive proposals. They criticized the previous generation of theologians for existentialism, personalism, or transcendentalism.[3] Rudolf Bultmann's existential interpretation of Christian eschatology came in for the strongest criticism.

These theologians argued that the proclamation of the kingdom of God within the Gospels indeed has social and political connotations, while an existential interpretation had reduced its meaning to the urgency or immediacy of an individual decision. Rather than challenging the societal reduction of religion to the personal and private sphere, the existential and personal theologies valorized the very privatization of religion. Political theology was therefore an attempt to retrieve the social and political dimensions of Christian eschatology.

Metz's political theology immediately encountered criticisms and misunderstandings. One objection questioned whether his political theology entailed an advocacy for a return to a more integralist model of church and society. Could it not be seen as renewed advocacy for "Christian political parties" that already existed in Germany?[4] In response, Metz underscored the eschatological proviso and the category of "interruption." In a similar manner Moltmann drew on Karl Barth's participation in the Barmen Declaration to safeguard political theology. However, Metz argued further that a political theology should not take up concrete political advocacy positions. Instead, it should serve almost as a negative theology or as critical theory to underscore the inadequacy of all political solutions and social programs. In this way he sought to counter the charge of integralism. Another criticism, brought to the fore by Hans Meier,

---

[3] The criticisms are not necessarily with complete justification; especially those of Karl Rahner and Karl Barth are perhaps less justified. The more political interpretation by Helmut Gollwitzer and Ferdinand Marquardt has shown the political implications of Karl Barth's thought. Rahner has addressed his political theology in his later writing (see Karl Rahner, *Politische Dimensionen des Christentums*, ed. Herbert Vorgrimler [Munich: Kösel, 1986]).

[4] For the debates concerning political theology, see Helmut Peukert, *Diskussion zur politischen Theologie* (Mainz: Matthias-Grünewald, 1969).

pointed to Carl Schmitt's political theology, which had criticized the liberal democracy of the Weimar Republic and advocated on behalf of Hitler's National Socialism.[5] In response, Metz renamed his theology a "new political theology" and emphasized the memory of the suffering of Jesus, the unjust suffering of victims in the past, and the importance of the Holocaust. In this way Metz clearly separated his political theology from Schmitt's anti-Semitism and his political alliance with the National Socialist party. With this emphasis upon the suffering of victims and the lack of justice for them in history, political theology shows that its political advocacy has a concrete interest in solidarity with the victims of injustice. Political theology and the quest for justice become interrelated.

Three features of Metz's development and defense of political theology should be noted. First, his emphasis upon the categories of eschatological proviso and apocalyptic interruption, while preventing an integralism, nevertheless makes his political theology less political. This has been pointed out by North American and Latin American theologians.[6] Moreover, it prevents him from giving a more foundational role to the appeal to human rights within his political theology.[7] Second, one must raise the question whether the categories of proviso and interruption engage the public space or avoid it as if it were the locus of idols in need of "apocalyptic interruption." In short, political theology avoids engagement with the public in ways that John Rawls's appeal to overlapping consensus or Jürgen Habermas's elaboration of a discourse ethic seeks to rectify.[8]

A third feature concerns the interpretation of religion within the marketplace—an interpretation similar both to Moltmann and to Moltmann's student Miroslav Volf. Consumer choice is treated as

---

[5] Hans Maier, *Kritik der politischen Theologie* (Einsiedeln: Johannes-Verlag, 1970).

[6] Bryan Hehir, "The Idea of a Political Theology," *Worldview* 14 (January 1971): 5–7, and (February 1971): 5–7, 31.

[7] See Francis Schüssler Fiorenza, "Political Theology and Modernity: Facing the Challenges of the Present," in *Distinktion* 10 (2005): 87–105; and idem, "Prospects for Political Theology in the Face of Contemporary Challenges," *Politische Theologie: Neuere Geschichte und Potenziale*, ed. Michael Welker, 41–64 (Neukirchen-Vluyn: Neukirchener, 2011). For a sustained treatment of rights in the context of pluralism, see the excellent book by Grace Kao, *Grounding Human Rights in a Pluralist World* (Washington, DC: Georgetown University Press, 2011).

[8] See the elaboration of this critique in Francis Schüssler Fiorenza, "Politische Theologie und liberale Gerechtigkeits-Konzeption," in *Mystik und Politik: Johann Baptist Metz zu Ehren*, ed. Eduard Schillebeeckx (Mainz: Matthias Grünewald, 1988), 105–7.

an idol of the market place. But is the freedom of consumer choice and preference the correct analysis of the market society? In contrast, Theodor Adorno and Max Horkheimer, in their classic analysis of modern society, underscore the objectification and commodification of the modern market. The objection is that all products are basically the same.[9] The problem is, then, not so much freedom of consumer choice but the absence of free choice. One might have the ability to choose among many models of an automobile, but the choices are among rather minor modifications. If one looks at what was offered on the American market for a couple of decades, the amount of choice is relatively small. This poses the question for our topic whether free choice or commodification of religion is the issue we face. It becomes more complex because the real question revolves around what commodification of religion entails within a pluralistic society. Questions of pluralism, democratic procedures, and diversity of opinions are not uncontroversial issues when one takes into account the criticism of various aspects of modern democracy and pluralism made by Joseph Ratzinger and others.[10]

Latin American Liberation Theology as a Corrective of Catholic Liberal Political Theory

Within Latin American liberation theology several theologians were influenced by Metz's political theology or by the French theological movement the Nouvelle Théologie that sought a more interrelated connection between the natural and supernatural. These theologians too sought to emphasize constructively the church's relation to the political and public sphere.[11] However, their theologies were in significant ways different from political theology and made significant contributions to the relation between faith and political life.

The differences between political theology and Latin American theology are many. They interpret the public space of theology quite differently. It is not secularization understood as the privatizing

---

[9] Max Horkheimer and Theodor Adorno, *Dialectic of Enlightenment* (Stanford, CA: Stanford University Press, rev. trans. 2007). See also Theodore Adorno, *The Culture Industry* (New York: Routledge, 1991).

[10] See Joseph Ratzinger and Hans Maier, *Demokratie in der Kirche: Moglichkeiten, Grenzen Gefahren* (Limburg: Lahn, 1970). See also Arthur Fridolin Utz, *Glaube und demokratischer Pluralismus im wissenschaftlichen Werk von Joseph Kardinal Ratzinger* (Bonn: Scientia Humana Institut, 1989).

[11] Henri de Lubac, *Christian Resistance to Anti-Semitism. Memories from 1940–1944* (San Francisco, CA: Ignatius, 1990).

of faith within the market place. Instead, it is the extreme distance between rich and poor countries and between the rich and the poor within the same country. Not secularization but rather impoverishment and the relations of dependency that breed poverty characterize the context. In many ways Latin American liberation theologies anticipate some of the postcolonial theories current today.

Because they understood the church to have a strong influence upon the public sphere, they did not criticize the existential, transcendental, and personalistic theologies as the political theologians did. Instead, they criticized the liberal theology that developed in France since the French Revolution and that seemed to dominate the Latin American scene. This liberal theology had two aspects that could be seen as contributing to a distinction of planes, arguing that there was a hierarchy that was responsible for the well-being of the church, whereas the laity was responsible for the well-being of society. For example, Yves Congar's work illustrated this specific definition of the role of the laity in the world,[12] and Jacques Maritain's *Man and State* was paradigmatic for its appeal to the natural law rather than the Gospel as the basis for normative judgments and actions in relation to the state.[13]

Latin American liberation theologians have made several enduring contributions to theology, theological method, and to the understanding of relations between Christian faith and political society. *First* is their emphasis upon the importance of solidarity with the poor.[14] The phrase "preferential option for the poor," as expressed by Gustavo Gutiérrez and adapted by Pope John Paul II with his emphasis upon solidarity and the formulation in *Sollicitude rei socialis* of "the option or love of preference for the poor" (no. 42) is significant as a practical and methodological imperative. As a practical imperative it is a guide for the priority of charity as well as justice that is expressed in the solidarity with the poor as outcasts. It is also a hermeneutical key, central to a theological method that underscores importance of the hermeneutical circle in relation to justice. *Second,* its emphasis on the structures of injustice and the importance of structural sin highlight economic, societal, and cultural conditions that get overlooked in an overly individualistic and personal conception of sin. *Third,* its emphasis on the role of community formation,

---

[12] Yves Congar, *Lay People in the Church* (London: Geoffrey, 1959).
[13] Jacques Maritain, *Man and State* (Chicago: University of Chicago, 1951).
[14] See Gerald S. Twomey, *The "Preferential Option for the Poor" in Catholic Social Thought from John XXIII to John Paul II* (Lewiston, NY: Edwin Mellen, 2005).

especially basis communities, acts as a counterbalancing and over-coming of stifling stratification within the structures of the church.

A few issues of debate remain. One concerns the understand-ing of the eschatological proviso. Such a view appears more neo-Platonic than Christian, as José Míguez Bonino's famous open letter to Moltmann underscores.[15] Insofar as political theology emphasizes critique but does not develop a concrete political program—or, in the vocabulary of Latin American liberation theology, fails to develop a "historical project"—it fails to be political. Another issue concerns the role of political ethics. Gutiérrez criticizes a statement by Metz that ethics links faith and politics, insofar as such a response ap-pears to mirror the liberal Catholic view of politics expressed by Maritain and others. Ratzinger, in his critique of liberation theology, makes the argument that the narrow linking of faith and politics can make faith into a political ideology, though in his writings on Christian ethics he tends to favor a more specific Christian ethics. Nevertheless, he argues that a political ethics is needed to mediate the relationship between the Christian faith and politics. The role of ethics is to attend to the complexities of political practice and to provide criteria or judgments for specific actions. In subsequent addresses Ratzinger has increasingly emphasized the importance of natural law as the basis for human rights. The importance of this point relates to some of the debates in the contemporary American situation. The religious critique of political liberalism for placing constraints on religious arguments in the public sphere overlooks a tradition within Roman Catholic theology that has sought to make an appeal to a public standard independent of faith. This is of course contested. Consequently, the Roman Catholic arguments for natural law or a political ethics—and its contestation—have to be discussed in relation to the contemporary American debates about the role of religion in the public space.

In relation to European political theology, some Latin American theologians have taken up the importance of a concrete stance in the face of the dominance of economic neoliberalism, and have faulted political theologians for failing to take such stances. However, the field has shifted when one takes into account the disintegration of

---

[15] José Míguez Bonino, "Reading Jürgen Moltmann from Latin American," *The Asbury Theological Journal* 55 (Spring 2000): 105–14; and Jürgen Moltmann, "An Open Letter to José Míguez Bonino," in *Liberation Theology: A Documentary History*, ed. Alfred Hennelly, 195–204 (Maryknoll, NY: Orbis Books, 1990). See also José Míguez Bonino, *Doing Theology in a Revolutionary Situation* (Philadel-phia: Fortress Press, 1975).

the Soviet Union and its dominance of Eastern Europe as well as the emergence of BRIC (Brazil, Russia, India, and China). The question of the relationship between liberation theology and economic theory has become a renewed point of discussion in view of the economic developments in Latin America.[16] The developments in Brazil have taken a different model than the path of those liberation theologians who opted for a form of socialism as a way to counter neoliberal economic theory and the lack of a political economic option in Metz's political theology.

Religion and Political Engagement in the United States Today

Political theology and liberation theology can provide a backdrop for the specific issues of religion and political engagement within the United States. Three issues are here highlighted.[17] The first is an ambiguity in the empirical data about the relationship between religious commitment and political engagements. While the data shows the majority of religious persons are more engaged in civic political life, it also shows that a minority are more intolerant. The second is the recent political engagement of some American bishops who have criticized John F. Kennedy's statements as a misguided privatization of religion. Third, there is the parallelism between this critique and a more generic critique of liberalism as placing constraints upon religion in the public sphere.

Religious Commitment Between Civic Engagement and Intolerance

In *American Grace* and its analysis of American society, Robert Putnam and David E. Campbell make an interesting argument regarding the relation of religion and civic and political engagement.[18] In line with the communitarianism of Putnam's earlier work,[19] this more recent analysis suggests that religion is what unites rather

---

[16] Ivan Petrella, *The Future of Liberation Theology: An Argument and Manifesto* (Burlington, VT: Ashgate, 2004); and idem, *Latin American Liberation Theology: The Next Generation* (Maryknoll, NY: Orbis Books, 2005).

[17] This is not to claim they are the only issues. Also relevant on the relation between religion and the market place is R. Laurence Moore, *Selling God: American Religion in the Marketplace of Culture* (New York: Oxford University Press, 1994).

[18] Robert D. Putnam and David E. Campbell, *American Grace: How Religion Divides and Unites Us* (New York: Simon and Schuster, 2010).

[19] See Robert D. Putnam, *Bowling Alone: The Collapse and Revival of American Community* (New York: Simon and Schuster, 2000); and Robert D. Putnam,

than divides Americans and is consequently very important for the development of civic life. It also notes a trend toward less active religious involvement and concludes that if this trend continues, the United States might become much less religious and thus more like Europe today. In their examination of the data about religiosity, in the chapter titled "Religion and Good Neighborliness," they list fifteen types of good deeds that are much more common among religious than among secular Americans. They do not find a single instance that goes in the other direction. Underscoring their thesis, they write: "Every significant generalization in this chapter remains accurate when we control simultaneously for gender, education, income, race, region, homeownership, length of residence, marital and parental status, ideology, and age."[20] In short, religious persons are more generous and altruistic. They give more money to charity; they do more volunteer work; they are more willing to help the homeless and the stranger. Religious Americans are more active in local civic and political life by participating in community organizations, engaging in community problem solving. Similar empirical data about the positive link between religious practice and political engagement have been advanced by others.[21]

Putnam and Campbell argue that religious Americans are more engaged in local social and political endeavors and are more trustworthy. Though they acknowledge that statistical correlations do not necessarily demonstrate or imply causality, they propose reasons that might suggest a causal relationship. The religious commitment to the golden rule — do unto others as you would have them do unto you — fosters altruistic values and leads persons to consider the good of others.[22] Describing a minority of religious believers (approximately 11–13 percent) as "true believers," they nevertheless note that in this particular group people are more intensively religious, consider religion to be fundamental to their personal identity and practice, and maintain what Putnam and Campbell label

---

Robert Leonardi, and Raffaella Nanetti, *Making Democracy Work: Civic Traditions in Modern Italy* (Princeton, NJ: Princeton University Press, 1993).

[20] Putnam and Campbell, *American Grace*, 452.

[21] See Paul Weithman, *Religion and the Obligations of Citizenship* (Cambridge, MA: Cambridge University, 2002), esp. chap. 2, "Religion's Role in Promoting Democracy," 36–66; and Sidney Verba et al., *Voice and Equality: Civic Voluntarism in American Politics* (Cambridge, MA: Harvard University Press, 1995).

[22] The golden rule is expressed in various religious traditions; in Christian scriptures Matthew 7:12 and Luke 6:31. Such a rule should not be limited to actions but should also include one's intellectual convictions and attitudes toward others.

"conservative moral issues." These intensively religious believers are "somewhat less comfortable with religious diversity" and "less convinced that religious diversity is a good thing."[23] Consequently, a higher degree of intolerance toward the other exists.

The problem that these particular statistics pose is that, on the one hand, religious belief and practice appear to contribute to civic, communal, and altruistic practice. On the other hand, however, intensely religious believers and practitioners are often intolerant of the other. Putnam and Campbell refer to the "bridging" that takes place through social interaction or intermarriage. That then raises the question whether it is the "bridging" that makes one more tolerant. To what degree does religion not increase tolerance? Or, how could religion that leads to more generosity also lead to a more generous understanding of others?

Roman Catholic Bishops: Political Activism as a Critique of Liberalism

In 1960 John F. Kennedy addressed the Greater Houston Ministerial Association in order to convince the ministers that a Roman Catholic president would be patriotic, loyal, and not subservient to any foreign power. His argument had some convincing power insofar as he was elected.[24] However, in 2012, Richard Santorum, a Roman Catholic and candidate for the Republican Party's nomination for president, took issue with Kennedy's view. In a television interview with Laura Ingraham he said, "If you read President Kennedy's text . . . there were some things that triggered in my opinion the privatization of faith and I think that's a bad thing."[25] The Most Reverend Charles J. Chaput, OFM Cap, the former archbishop of Denver and more recently archbishop of Philadelphia, addressed the Houston Baptist University on March 1, 2010, and also commented on Kennedy's speech:

> It was sincere, compelling, articulate — and wrong. Not wrong about the patriotism of Catholics, but wrong about American history and very wrong about the role of religious faith in our

---

[23] Putnam and Campbell, *American Grace*, 545; for characteristics of this group, see 542–47.

[24] Shaun A. Casey, *The Making of a Catholic President: Kennedy vs. Nixon 1960* (New York: Oxford University Press, 2009).

[25] Rick Santorum, television interview with Laura Ingraham, February 28, 2012. Available online.

nation's life. And he wasn't merely "wrong." His Houston remarks profoundly undermined the place not just of Catholics, but of *all* religious believers, in America's public life and political conversation. Today, half a century later, we're paying for the damage.[26]

In his analysis of what he calls Kennedy's "theological vapidity," Chaput refers to Mark Massa's interpretation of the secularity of the speech and the "almost-privatization of [Kennedy's] Catholic faith."[27]

In addition to his critique of Kennedy's speech, Archbishop Chaput criticizes the idols and orthodoxy of the American Press with reference to George Orwell's definition of orthodoxy as a set of ideas that people accept without question. That this orthodoxy is "rigorously intolerant" is "nowhere more obvious than our news media's treatment of religion." He writes that "journalism from the *New York Times* down to the smallest local newspaper has its own unstated orthodoxies, its own vanities, prejudices, and targets of disdain."[28]

In one respect Chaput's critique of modern society and modern culture is similar to that of the German political theologians insofar as he decries the reduction of religion to the private sphere. However, whereas their critique focuses on dominance of the capitalist market within modern society, Chaput suggests that America's problems as well as its virtues "come from the same seed. Reformation theology and Enlightenment thought elevate the importance of the individual. But they can feed a destructive individualism and a hostility to any religious authority outside the sovereignty of personal conscience."[29]

---

[26] See Charles J. Chaput, *Render unto Caesar: Serving the Nation by Living Our Catholic Beliefs in Political Life* (New York: Doubleday, 2008). The quotation is widely available online.

[27] Chaput, *Render unto Caesar*, 250n14; Mark S. Massa, "A Catholic for President? John F. Kennedy and the 'Secular' Theology of the Houston Speech, 1960," *Journal of Church and State* (Spring 1997): 297–318. See also Mario Cuomo, *More Than Words: The Speeches of Mario Cuomo* (New York: St. Martin's Press, 1993).

[28] Charles J. Chaput, *A Heart of Fire* (New York: Image, 2012), 8–9. For a basis of his critique of the unstated orthodoxies in journalism in general and the *New York Times* in particular, he refers to William McGowan, *Coloring the News: How Political Correctness Has Corrupted American Journalism* (San Francisco: Encounter, 2002); and idem, *Gray Lady Down: What the Decline and Fall of the* New York Times *Means for America* (New York: Encounter, 2010).

[29] Chaput, *Heart of Fire*, 31.

The Critique of Liberalism as Constraining Religious Discourse

This specific Roman Catholic critique of liberalism in many ways echoes an academic critique of modern liberalism for its failure to accord religion its proper place within society or for placing unjustifiable constraints upon religion in the public sphere. For example, Bryan T. McGraw attacks what he labels the consensus viewpoint that advocates a liberal view of society but places undue constraints upon religion.[30] He attributes this view to John Rawls, Jürgen Habermas, and Robert Audi.[31] This consensus viewpoint argues, in his opinion, that religious citizens should properly bracket their religious beliefs and convictions within a democratic society for the sake of democratic pluralism. If this does not occur, the liberal consensus fears that we are soon back on the path to the religious wars.[32] Ron Thiemann suggests that "these [Rawls, Dworkin, Ackermann, Gutmann, and Galston] interpreters of liberalism believe that the fundamental values of freedom, equality, and toleration are best preserved if religion is removed from public affairs."[33] Nicholas Wolterstorff argues with nuance that a feature of liberal democracies is that, in regard to political decisions and activities, they "are to allow their religious convictions to idle. They are to base their political decisions and their political debate in the public space on the principles yielded by some source *independent* of any and all of the religious perspectives to be found in

---

[30] Bryan T. McGraw, *Faith in Politics: Religion and Liberal Democracy* (Cambridge, MA: Cambridge University Press, 2010).

[31] Of the three authors, Robert Audi most clearly articulates such a constraint. See Robert Audi, "Liberal Democracy and Religion in Politics," in *Religion in the Public Square: The Place of Religious Convictions in Political Debate,* ed. Robert Audi and Nicholas Wolterstorff, 1–66 (New York: Rowman and Littlefield, 1997); idem, *Democratic Authority and the Separation of Church and State* (New York: Oxford University Press, 2011); and idem, *Religious Commitment and Secular Reason* (Cambridge, MA: Cambridge University Press, 2000).

[32] McGraw, *Faith in Politics,* 141–43. McGraw notes that Rawls even makes references to religious war to exemplify the dangers. McGraw's own work presents four cases studies in Europe in order to demonstrate that Christian political parties have successfully led governments without any harm to the political life. For a less apologetic treatment that analyzes the distinctiveness of the United States position, see Noah Feldman, *Divided by God: America's Church-State Problem and What We Should Do About It* (New York: Farrar, Straus, and Giroux, 2005).

[33] Ron Thiemann, *Religion in Public Life: A Dilemma for Democracy* (Washington, DC: Georgetown University Press, 1996), 75.

society."[34] Other critics of liberalism, like William T. Cavanaugh, argue that religious liberalism has excessively enhanced the power of the state:

> Liberal Theorists such as Rawls, Shklar, and Stout would have us believe that the State stepped in like a scolding schoolteacher on the playground of doctrinal dispute to put fanatical religionists in their proper place. Self-righteous clucking about the dangers of public faith, however, ignores the fact that transfer of ultimate loyalty to the nation-state has only increased the scope of modern welfare.[35]

Engaging a Democratic and Pluralistic Public Space

The combination of the empirical data showing the positive role of religious belief that goes hand in hand with the increase of intolerance among those who are most religious raises questions about the adequacy of the criticisms of public space as allowing no room for religion as well as the criticisms of liberal theory for its constraints upon religious belief. Both criticisms need to be challenged. Moreover, the issue of religious pluralism and of the religious voice in the public space has not been adequately faced either by German political theologians or by some of the main representatives of Latin American liberation theologies.

A common criticism is that religion has become privatized within the public space of modernity. As noted above, this privatization is sometimes attributed to the dynamics of the marketplace and secularization or to the Protestant Reformation or to Enlightenment Liberalism. In current American debates this privatization is attributed to political liberalism. Among contemporary political theorists,

---

[34] Nicholas Wolterstorff, "The Role of Religion in Decision and Discussion of Political Issues," in *Religion in the Public Square: The Place of Religious Convictions in Political Debate,* ed. Robert Audi and Nicholas Wolterstorff (New York: Rowman and Littlefield, 1997), 73.

[35] William T. Cavanaugh, "'A Fire Strong Enough to Consume the House': The Wars of Religion and the Rise of the State," *Modern Theology* 11/4 (October 1995): 408. See also idem, *Theopolitical Imagination: Discovering the Liturgy as a Political Act in an Age of Global Consumerism* (London: Continuum, 2002), chap. 1. His fear of the welfare state is difficult to square with the historical experience of the lack of work and food after the Great Depression in the United States that the Roosevelt administration dealt with through its work and welfare programs.

John Rawls and, to a lesser degree, Jürgen Habermas are singled out as primary examples of the relegation of religion to the private sphere and even of a hostility to religion.[36] I would like to disagree with this common opinion. Moreover, I shall argue for a political engagement that is open to liberalism and accepts the importance of a mutual critique. One can ask what religion brings to the political space that is critical, just as one can—and must—ask what political liberalism brings to the table that entails a helpful correction of religious attitudes toward the public. To begin, one can indeed give a more generous interpretation of Rawlsian liberalism as well as of Habermas's position. Their views allow much more of a role for religion in the public space than is usually credited to them.

Liberalism and Restraints of Reason

The basic critique holds that Rawls's argument excludes religion from the public sphere, whereas, in fact, religiously diverse democratic states have been shown to have actually enabled democracy to flourish.[37] In attacking Rawls for an animus against religion, critics overlook the point that Rawls is primarily concerned with a "comprehensive view" or a metaphysical view rather than with religion, although a religious belief is included within such a comprehensive view.[38] His central intention is to develop a political rather than a metaphysical view of justice. This entails that the right is given a justificatory primacy in relation to the good. In addition, Rawls has a very limited, if not unusual, understanding of *public*. Moreover, his technical understanding of the term is confusing because it is counterintuitive. By *public* he does not mean civic discourse in general, but primarily and explicitly judicial decisions and legislative enactments. Legislative and judicial decisions need to be formulated in ways that are not formally and explicitly dependent upon a specific religious beliefs or denominational convictions.

---

[36] John Rupert Read, "Religion as Sedition: On Liberalism's Intolerance of Real Religion," *Ars Disputandi* 11 (2011): 83–100.

[37] For a significant and sustained analysis of Rawls's development, see Paul Weithman, *Religion and the Obligations of Citizenship* (Cambridge, MA: Cambridge University Press, 2002); and idem, *Why Political Liberalism? On John Rawls's Political Turn* (New York: Oxford University Press, 2011).

[38] Ronald Thiemann attempts to give religion a thick description and defines it as a comprehensive view; in his critique of Rawls, he concedes that Rawls goes beyond classical liberalism. See Thiemann, *Religion in Public Life*, chaps. 4 and 5.

However, Rawls gives concrete examples of religious discourse in a civic context that he sees as valuable for society, for example, Lincoln's Second Inaugural Address or Martin Luther King's "I Have a Dream" speech. Such religious discourse appeals to religious symbols in order to foster democratic and equalitarian values and to hinder attitudes and language expressing hostility to others. Rhetoric that is racist, sexist, and discriminatory is excluded. Rawls's exclusion of such hostile language applies to all civic discourse, whether religious or nonreligious. The language of neo-Nazi parties that expressed their biological racism and their attempt to obliterate Jews would come under censure just as much as would religious language that gave an allegedly biblical foundation for apartheid (as was indeed done in South Africa and in the United States in defense of slavery). In raising Rawls's reference to the use of religious discourse to foster democratic values of equality and openness to the other, my point is to underscore that it challenges (and indeed encourages) theological and religious leadership to marshal the resources of the religious tradition to encourage democratic values and virtues. Here is where the observation reported in *American Grace* that the overwhelming majority of religious believers increasingly foster common communal civic goals, whereas a minority of intensely religious do not, is pertinent. This tension should challenge religious leadership regarding the adequacy of their communication of the depth of the religious tradition.

The critics of Rawls overlook the degree to which he distances his own conception from classical liberalism and is quite limited in the restriction he places on religion when, for example, he writes that "under reasonable pluralism the religious believers' good of salvation cannot be the good of all citizens." Instead, he posits liberty, equality, and those primary goods that enable citizens to make use of their political freedom.[39] A more serious objection than hostility to religion would be whether or not it is possible to conceive of justice primarily as political rather than metaphysical or resting on metaphysical comprehensive views. The historical and social situation of human persons serves as a life relation that influences human rationality and affections. Obviously, specific presuppositions enter into his conception of justice, despite his

---

[39] John Rawls, *Political Liberalism* (New York: Columbia University Press, 1996), xli. Note that the paperback printing (not listed as revised) contains an important extended introduction as well as a response to Habermas that is not contained in the first edition of the book.

intention to avoid them.[40] Moreover, as interpreters have pointed out, his method is not so much a narrow reflective equilibrium as it implies a broad reflective equilibrium. This distinction means the method involves not simply a correlation between principles and considered judgments, but that hermeneutical considerations of implicit background theories play a much more important role than acknowledged. Appeals to "thin" theories of the good inevitably are rooted in "thicker" conceptions of the good.[41] In this regard Jürgen Habermas's attempt to think of the role of religion in the public space is more important. [42]

Habermas takes serious issue with Rawls on several significant points. He criticizes the formal artificiality of the "original position"; he points out that an overlapping consensus might be important for the stability of a society's understanding of justice, but that such a consensus cannot serve as a justification.[43] There may have been an overlapping consensus in the southern United States about slavery or among whites in South Africa about apartheid, but these do not suffice. Instead, he proposes an actual discourse and the importance of the principle of universalization in relation to real discourses so that all who are affected can bring their voices into consideration. Such a principle has a justificatory role in a way that overlapping consensus does not. Habermas's discourse ethic has counterfactual assumptions that mean that de facto real discourses and consensus are in principle open to future reasons and counter reasons as well as to unrestricted participation of all who are affected.

Habermas's position on the role of religion is evolving and not without inconsistencies.[44] On the one hand, he has a broader under-

---

[40] His own student Susan Moller Okin has pointed out how gender biases have entered into his description of human goods in her various essays. See *Justice, Gender, and Family* (New York: Basic Books, 1989).

[41] Schüssler Fiorenza, "Politische Theologie und liberale Gerechtigkeits-Konzeptionen," 105–17.

[42] See Jürgen Habermas, *Between Naturalism and Religion* (Malden, MA: Polity Press, 2008).

[43] Jürgen Habermas, *The Inclusion of the Other: Studies in Political Theory*, ed. Ciaran P. Cronin and Pablo De Greiff (Cambridge, MA: MIT Press, 1998).

[44] Jürgen Habermas, *An Awareness of What Is Missing: Faith and Reason in a Post-Secular Age* (Malden, MA: Polity Press, 2010); and idem, *Between Naturalism and Religion: Philosophical Essays* (Malden, MA: Polity Press, 2008). See also his dialogue with Pope Benedict XVI in Joseph Ratzinger and Jürgen Habermas, *Dialectics of Secularization: On Reason and Religion* (San Francisco: Ignatius, 2006). Habermas makes the suggestion that secular people should help religious people communicate. Such a suggestion makes sense to the degree that in every dialogue there are mutual attempts to communicate and to help understand

standing of the public than Rawls and recognizes the significance of religious discourse in society. On the other hand, he talks of the necessity of translating religious language into a language that others in society can understand—though he at times appears to admit the limitation of the translation model. If, however, one takes his model of discourse ethics and the principle of speaking so the other person can understand, then the notion of translatability becomes questionable.[45] The basic principle is reciprocity.[46] On that basis one can argue that religious language can be understood without translation. He himself notes that Martin Luther King, Jr.'s religious language was understood, and he was killed for it.[47] In addition, as Habermas has noted in his essay on Gershom Scholem, "Among modern societies only those that are able to introduce into the secular domain the essential contents of their religious traditions which point beyond the merely human realm will also be able to rescue the substance of the human."[48] He notes that "religious language is a bearer of semantic content that is inspiring and even indispensable, for this content eludes (for the time being) the explanatory force of philosophical language and continues to resist translation into reasoning discourse."[49] This awareness and the fact that such language can be understood raises the question of whether one needs a more nuanced and hermeneutical account as to what counts as reasonable

---

each other's position. It should not be understood—though his formulation is ambiguous—as if nonreligious persons had an epistemic advantage in such communications. See his essay "Religion in the Public Sphere: Cognitive Presuppositions for the 'Public Use of Reason' by Religious and Secular Citizens," in Habermas, *Between Naturalism and Religion*, 114–47.

[45] At times Habermas refers to the importance of translating religious language in the public sphere. Yet one could claim that the more basic principle is reciprocity. One's communication needs to be understood by the other. Translation is an inadequate description of the complex task of communication.

[46] What I am suggesting is that Habermas's interpretation of communication as dialogical and reciprocal should be taken as much more basic and that it undercuts his point about translation, which often refers to a one-directional movement from religious to secular.

[47] See Judith Butler et al., *The Power of Religion in the Public Sphere* (New York: Columbia University Press, 2011). See also my comments in Francis Schüssler Fiorenza, "Prospects for Political Theology in the Face of Contemporary Challenges," in *Politische Theologie: Neuere Geschichte und Potenziale*, ed. Michael Welker, 41–64 (Neukirchen-Vluyn: Neukirchener, 2011).

[48] Jürgen Habermas, "Replik auf Einwände, Reaktion auf Anregungen," in *Glauben und Wissen. Ein Symposium mit Jürgen Habermas*, ed. Rudolf Langthaler and Herta Nagl-Docekal, 366–414 (Oldenbourg: Akademie, 2007).

[49] Jürgen Habermas, "Themes in Postmetaphysical Thinking," in *Postmetaphysical Thinking: Philosophical Essays* (Cambridge, MA: MIT Press, 1993), 28–53.

or as a public reason when one has a non-foundational account of discourse and is aware of the historical and rhetorical conditioning of language and reason. In these respects issues entail foundational questions about language, communication, and rationality. As I shall point out later, the division between religious and nonreligious language is much more complex than any account of public reason and moral norms that does not merely distinguish them but sharply separates them.

Public Reasons, Accountability, and Rationality

What constitutes a reasonable argument in public? From the point of discourse the answer would be that there is not an a priori or an independent foundation for such an answer, but the answer takes place in and through the very act of being reasonable. Let me give an example, not from a "secular perspective" or from a position that might put constraints on religious reason, but rather from the "religious perspective" of my own church, Roman Catholicism.

It has always been a standard argument within modern Roman Catholicism that one can advance Catholic ethical positions in public because they are not based on revelation but rather on a natural-law argument or some form of public reason that is accessible to all. (Such an argument is actually not very different from the secular liberal who argues against specifically religious reasons in public.) The problem with that position is that an argument from natural law is hermeneutically or interpretively insufficiently determined. For example, if one argues that contraceptive birth control is intrinsically evil, as the American bishops have done, the public does not hear such a rhetorical argument as a public reason open to all but rather hears it as a particularistic Roman Catholic claim. This is so because that view is based upon a very specific deterministic and biologically teleological view of sexuality that might *not* be obvious or shared by others. (In fact, Joseph Ratzinger, arguing as a theologian before he became a bishop and then pope, criticized the biological determinism of the argument.)[50] So what might appear as an appeal to nature or natural law is not perceived as such because the very meanings of

---

[50] For references to earlier and later writings, see Francis Schüssler Fiorenza, "Marriage," in Francis Schüssler Fiorenza and John Galvin, *Systematic Theology: Roman Catholic Perspectives* (Minneapolis: Fortress Press, 2011). See Joseph Ratzinger, "Zur Theologie der Ehe," *Theologische Quartalschrift* (1969): 53–74.

human nature, sexuality, and so forth are up for debate or in need of interpretation.

The point of this critique is not to eschew reasoning that appeals to human nature or natural law — it is indeed a longstanding tradition of Roman Catholicism in distinction to Lutheranism, though one that the Calvinist Reformed traditions with the exception of Karl Barth have more affinities with. Instead, the point is that there are diverse conceptions of natural law, and there is the problem of its hermeneutically indeterminate character. The meanings of human dignity and of human sexuality are open to diverse interpretations. Consequently, any appeal to a natural-law argument has to be aware of this diversity and justify its particular interpretation. It is not by accident that there is such a diversity of interpretation of contraception by married Roman Catholics and by a celibate hierarchy. The hermeneutical circle becomes decisive in how sexuality is understood and interpreted.

From this perspective one can argue that appeals to philosophical reasoning as ethical arguments do not necessarily have a greater degree of certitude or a greater openness to public space than religious arguments. The question is whether religious arguments can be advanced with an openness to other religious arguments and philosophical arguments in public reasoning. Here is where a more tolerant and pluralistic conception of religious argument is needed. Yet today it is precisely this quality that is denied by those who exclude religious argument in public solely on the basis of epistemic status. Such considerations rule out any a priori conditions or thresholds of public discourse that are prior to the entering into the public space of discourse with the intent and attempt to engage the other members of the public in discourse about norms and values as well as about policy and practices. Obvious points of conflict and disagreement should be allowed to emerge and to be engaged within public discourse. The very engagement in public discourse gives rise at least to the demands that attempt to listen, understand, and acknowledge the integrity of those with whom one disagrees and to grapple with their arguments.

The Rejection of Religious Pluralism

In *A Public Faith*, Miroslav Volf of Yale University makes a diagnosis similar to Metz and Moltmann insofar as he sees modern society dominated by two tendencies: a marketplace that enthrones personal choice or preference as paramount, and a scientific-technocratic rationality that favors the hard sciences. The result is the privatization of religion and the absence of religion from the public sphere.[51] At the same time he argues for a pluralistic arrangement that can be combined with a monotheistic belief. God relates to all people equally; the command is to love our neighbors as we would want to be treated, and we cannot claim rights for ourselves that we are not willing to grant others. Religion cannot be coerced as a personal belief or outward practice.

Volf combines this advocacy with a critique of liberal democracy. In his view liberal democracy maintains that the "protagonists' religious perspective should no longer be part of their public encounters."[52] As I have argued, I do not believe this corresponds to the views of either Habermas or Rawls. However, Volf's position raises important questions about the advocacy of religion in the public sphere as an issue of pluralism rather than as a separation of spheres and in relation to the basis of one's views of religion and normativity.

In Volf's view a "pluralist account of relations among religions is incoherent" because it basically "tries to reduce religious diversity — that is, diversity that is acceptable on its own terms — to an underlying sameness."[53] In his view this is because the pluralist places religions within the pluralist framework as an encompassing frame. He correctly notes that religions do not have a common core, and he wants Christians to argue from their distinctive configuration. The constructive part of the proposal, in my view, has merit. But it seems that the challenge to religious engagement within a pluralistic society is not answered when one argues that one can give one's religious arguments in public. One needs to take into account how one receives with respect, even mutual respect, and how one takes into account diverse voices, some diversely religious, and others secular — though the label secular is perhaps misleading. The term *secularization* originally referred to the transfer of religious property to the state or the transition of a person from a religious or clerical state to the non-clerical state.[54] However, when applied to a

---

[51] Miroslav Volf, *A Public Faith: How Followers of Christ Should Serve the Common Good* (Grand Rapids, MI: Brazos, 2011), 124–45.

[52] Ibid., 127.

[53] Ibid, 128.

[54] Hermann Lübbe, *Säkularisierung: Geschichte eines ideenpolitischen Begriffs* (Freiburg: K. Alber, 1965). See also Charles Taylor, *Dilemmas and Connections* (Cambridge, MA: Harvard University Press, 2010); and idem, *A Secular Age* (Cambridge, MA: Harvard University Press, 2007).

cultural transformation of ideas and attitudes, the transition cannot be so clearly demarcated. Religious traditions become in part transformed and in part embedded within secular traditions. A clear-cut separation or division between church and state as in the transfer of property rights or between clerical to lay as in laicization is not possible in the realm of cultural values and ideals.

Pluralism Includes Both Religious and Political Pluralism

Obviously a theory of religious pluralism that reduces religions to one core or makes them all centered on an unknown transcendent is an inadequate understanding of religious pluralism. But there are several ways to understand religious pluralism, and many do not necessarily entail the reduction of religion to a common core or sameness, as has been charged. Taking religious pluralism seriously is important for political engagement because many normative values and moral judgments that enter the political arena are embedded in religious traditions. One can, however, approach religious pluralism as an institutional and practical pluralism with the goal of public order and peace, or one can understand religious pluralism as a theoretical issue that entails the intersecting with other religious claims as well as other normative claims within public discourse.

Practical and Institutional Pluralism

One approach to religious pluralism is the practical. It views freedom of conscience in terms of institutional pluralism or the independence of religious groups or institutions. The state should respect institutional pluralism except where public order clearly and unambiguously requires otherwise. An example is Roger Williams's attitude toward Quakers and Roman Catholics in the Rhode Island colony. Religious groups may divide and conflict with one another as long as they do not impair or injure public order or peace. Such an approach does not invoke an overarching theory of religious pluralism but instead makes public order or peace the criterion of institutional pluralism. This is quite different from defining freedom of conscience in individual or personal terms rather than in institutional terms. Even here the state is viewed as protecting the individual from harmful institutions or from an institutional arrangement between religious and governmental institutions that would harm or contravene the individual's freedom of religion.

Another example of a practical approach is the interpretation of Vatican II's *Declaration on Religious Liberty (Dignitatis humanae)*, which Joseph Ratzinger has repeatedly used to defend its affirmations. Faced with the tradition of negative papal statements with regard to religious freedom and consequently religion pluralism (for example, by Leo XIII, Pius XI, and Pius XII),[55] Ratzinger squares the declaration's affirmations with the tradition by arguing that religious freedom and pluralism are understood as a practical and societal solution. In this view the declaration leaves unchanged the Catholic Church's traditional claims in regard to its truth and the uncompromising nature of that truth. Instead, as he affirms, "religious liberty is a matter of social and political co-existence which does not affect man's relation to truth but only affects truth's historical concretization."[56] Such an interpretation fits with the emphasis that the document gives to human dignity and the common good, which, as *Gaudium et spes (Pastoral Constitution on the Church in the Modern World)* points out, is historically understood in terms of the specific conditions of today. Such an approach allows a pluralism of voices in the public arena as a practical resolution to a contemporary historical concretization. Religion is not reduced to the private sphere, and religious pluralism is seen in relation to the public good and the peace of societies today.

Theoretical Pluralism and Dialogue

If one justifies religious diversity and pluralism merely as a practical necessity within the historical contingencies of a pluralist society, then one does not grapple with what religions have positively to contribute to religious pluralism in our changed historical context. As the empirical data presented by Putnam and Campbell show, religious practice does contribute to civic and political life. Nevertheless, a minority — those most religious — tend to be intolerant of the other. This poses a challenge, one that has been well formulated by Anselm Min when he underscored that "considering the often destructive role religions have been playing against bridging differences and building solidarity, it is absolutely crucial that each religion also explore the best of its own tradition that will contribute to the global solidarity of the different."[57]

---

[55] For a recent historical survey on Catholicism and democracy, see Émile Perreau-Saissome, *Catholicisme et démocratie* (Paris: Éditions du Cerf, 2011).

[56] See Joseph Ratzinger, *Theological Highlights of Vatican II* (New York: Paulist Press, 1966), 211.

[57] Anselm Kyongsuk Min, *The Solidarity of Others in a Divided World* (New York: T & T Clark, 2004), 230.

Such a challenge means that religious communities should engage pluralism by drawing on their traditions to strengthen the solidarity with others and to encourage an openness for their life and views. This means that a religious tradition must acknowledge that one can learn religiously from other religious voices as well as other normative voices that if labeled secular might have their indebtedness to previous traditions, including religious traditions, overlooked. That does not presuppose that one has to reject one's own traditions or that one needs an overarching framework or that one needs to reduce all religions to sameness.[58] It does require that one enter into dialogue with others of diverse convictions and be willing to raise normative claims.[59] Such a dialogue entails that one bring one's faith and normative convictions into the public, not with a monolithic or monopolistic conception of faith and truth, but with a genuine reciprocal openness to the other.

The status of arguments in the political sphere is much more complex than a simple division between religious argument and "secular" arguments suggests, as if the former lacked the epistemic certainty assumed by the latter. Political arguments often entail assessments that are more than empirical statements but are often normative statements. The evaluation of normative claims often makes claims that are complex and not easily resolvable. For example, if one argues for a progressive form of taxation as being more just, how does one adjudicate such a claim? One cannot simply do so in terms of economic or empirical factors. Obviously, normative issues are at stake, and these normative issues have long traditions within religious, communal, and civic life. They are central issues also within religious reflection.

Let me take another example. An affirmation of human rights excludes slavery. Many Christians today believe slavery is not compatible with Christianity. A theologian might claim that there is a religious background to the affirmation that all are equal before God and therefore see the religious background of creation as the unique basis for universality. Nevertheless, Christianity existed for centuries without finding slavery to be incompatible with Christianity. Obviously, human equality before God did not translate into equality

---

[58] On sameness and difference, see Jeannine Hill Fletcher, *Monopoly on Salvation? A Feminist Approach to Religious Pluralism* (New York: Continuum, 2005).

[59] Francis Schüssler Fiorenza, "Christian Redemption Between Colonialism and Pluralism," in *Reconstructing Christian Theology*, ed. Rebecca Chopp and Mark Taylor, 269–302 (Minneapolis: Fortress Press, 1994).

among humans themselves. Consequently, for almost two millennia one defined human equality without excluding slavery. However, if one appeals to the Enlightenment, especially its emphasis on human autonomy and freedom, one has to note that Thomas Jefferson, the drafter of the US Declaration of Independence, which begins with an affirmation of human rights, saw no conflict between the affirmation of human equality and his own possession of slaves.

The right of women to vote is another example of a long struggle before it became possible in the United States.

One could point to the contemporary debates about the death penalty or about gay marriage. One cannot simply designate one side of the issue as a religious position and the other side as a secular. The divide runs through religious and secular approaches. What is taking place is a realignment of views within both religious and secular perspectives. The sharp distinction between the religious and the secular does not help in such normative issues. In actuality, there is an overlapping among the distinct backgrounds and sources animating the reasons for positions. The importance of public debate is to enable the disentangling of these diverse backgrounds and sources in order to clarify what is at stake.

Public space has another significant role besides being the place where diverse traditions come together to form normative positions. Public space could be said to be a place where moral ideas are debated. These discussions and debates are important for the formation of normativity. One often hears references to horrendous evils of the twentieth century: the Holocaust, the deliberate use of rape as an instrument of war, or the initiation of young children into warfare in which they are often forced to kill a relative or parent. What is common among these is that they were never discussed in public as actions that could be justified for some other purpose. It is almost as if their evil was such that one kept these actions away from public discussion and hidden. If we look at some of the moral issues that divide us, especially those that could be said to make up the center of the culture wars, then those that are publicly debated (with all diverse voices participating) are issues where we are aware that there is (an often strong) divergence of conviction. The point then becomes the emergence of difference in public space; this requires an awareness that there is disagreement over these issues, and they should not be looked upon as being in the same category as those that one dare not raise in public. This, in my view, is a reason for allowing all voices in public and at the same time having respect for them. I make this suggestion with some hesitation because I am also aware how public space is open to manipulation and is not free standing, especially in our own time, when powerful interests, financial and institutional, have enormous influence upon the public.

Symbolic Praxis as a Form of Public Communication

I have pointed to the analysis of Adorno and Horkheimer, which understands the market as leading not so much to private choice and consumer preference but to commodification. The claim for a diversity of arguments within public space seeks to underscore the view that public reason should not be commodified to one simple type of argument and that all arguments are complex and intertwined. In the Roman Catholic tradition there is a significant emphasis on the importance of the sacramental dimension of life and on the role of symbols and liturgical practice within church life as formative influences. Symbolic action can be a form of communicative action. One has to view such symbolic action as ways of advancing a community's conviction in the public space.

One example is the hospice movement. Its establishment had religious motives as well as ethical reasons.[60] What does the hospice movement communicate? With our technological and scientific successes, there is the temptation to use these means to extend life as long as possible. Insofar as the hospice movement acknowledges the reality of death and focuses on palliative care to prepare the patient for death, it counters the unquestioned reliance on technology to continue life at all costs. Insofar as the high costs of medicine and the suffering of patients can lead us in society to terminate life in order to save the costs of care, the hospice movement goes against this temptation as well. One could view the hospice movement as a form of a communicative action in public space that counters both tendencies.

Another example is the Eucharist. One theologian has argued that the family meal should be a means of retrieving the meaning of the Eucharist. While that may be true, I wish to point out that in the early church, as is evident from Acts and from the Didache, the sharing of the goods with the poor of the community was central to the community's eucharistic practice. One might say today that helping out with meals for the homeless is perhaps a better form of retrieval.

---

[60] Dame Cecile Saunders is known for the establishment of the hospice movement in the 1950s, but the movement had many precedents, among which is the establishment of a hospice in Dublin in 1879 by the Sisters of Charity.

Students in high schools and even colleges often do community service as a part of their education. I am impressed with what Harvard students who have worked in Africa or South America have learned, and how that has transformed their awareness of their responsibility for the other, the stranger, and the poor. I wish our church would require such service of its youth, as some religions do. I mention this because one needs to avoid the impression that churches contribute to the public sphere by advancing rational arguments that are based on religious or natural law traditions, as if some form of rational argument is the only way to contribute to the public sphere.

In conclusion, however, what I want to draw from all the reflection in this essay is that significant moral and normative issues have been debated in the public space. There are religious as well as nonreligious background theories that enter into these debates. Both the religious and nonreligious perspectives change in the course of historical and societal developments. James Madison once wrote: "It may not be easy, in every possible case, to trace the line of separation between the rights of religion and civil authority with such distinctness as to avoid collisions and doubt on unessential points."[61] My point is that religious arguments and nonreligious normative arguments can also not be clearly distinguished. Both belong in the public space. But in this public space both can and should be open to challenge and to criticism. It is important that the public space not be treated as the locus of "idols" under the labels of the economic market, consumerism, privatization, individualization, and secularization. Instead, the public space is a space that needs to be invigorated.[62] The issues raised in this essay concern the nature of theological communication within a pluralistic world. Such issues get at the heart of the challenges that we as theologians face as we look forward to our current century.

---

[61] James Madison, "Letter to the Rev. Jasper Adams," in *Church and State in American History,* ed. John F. Wilson, 77–78 (Boston: C. C. Heath, 1965). See Martin Marty, "The Kingdom of Heaven and the IRS" (March 25, 2012), available online.

[62] See Francis Schüssler Fiorenza, "The Church as a Community of Interpretation: Political Theology Between Discourse Ethics and Hermeneutical Reconstruction," in *Habermas, Modernity, and Public Theology,* ed. Don S. Browning and Francis Schüssler Fiorenza, 66–91 (New York: Crossorad, 1992).

A Response to Francis Schüssler Fiorenza

Pluralism, Persuasion, and Prophets

Paul Miller

Dr. Schüssler Fiorenza presents an illuminating historical sketch that captures and contextualizes some of the most important contemporary issues associated with the role of religious convictions in the public sphere. He begins with an instructive analysis of German political theology, highlighting Metz's reaction against existential theology and its impact on the privatizing of religion in post–World War II Europe. Fiorenza points out that while Metz's political theology attempted "to retrieve the social and political dimensions of Christian eschatology" by showing "solidarity with the victims of injustice," it carefully avoided concrete political positions that could lead to charges of integralism. Latin American liberation theologians, on the other hand, have refused to limit themselves to apocalyptic interruption and the approach of negative theology. Their theological methods focus on advocating concrete political proposals that address economic injustice and other results of "structural sin." These concrete proposals are justified and supported not only by theological arguments but also by sociological analysis of urgent moral problems. By contrasting these two types of faith-based political advocacy, Fiorenza puts us in a better position to understand the theological and moral issues associated with political engagement today.

As he turns his attention to religion and politics within the United States, Fiorenza considers, on one hand, the degree to which religious commitment might lead to intolerance, and on the other, whether modern liberalism places unwarranted constraints upon religion. He uses these two questions to explore the impact of religious pluralism on political engagement within contemporary society. He asks how one can "actively affirm the political implications of one's faith within a political and social world that is normatively and religiously pluralistic." Fiorenza highlights the challenge of advancing religious arguments while at the same time being open to learning from other religious and philosophical arguments that are made in the public sphere.

In my response I address three points that clarify how religious citizens can learn from other religious and nonreligious citizens in the process of political engagement: (1) the need for citizens to acknowledge that they have moral blind spots that can be diagnosed and overcome through dialogue; (2) the theological tension between divine immanence and transcendence; and (3) the relationship between faith-based political advocacy and the persuasive techniques of rhetorical theology. I use each of these points to explore Fiorenza's conclusions about faith and political engagement in a pluralistic world.

My first take-away point from Fiorenza's historical analysis is that *a robust awareness of our own moral blindness is vital* as we seek a foundation of openness and mutual respect in the public sphere. Fiorenza gives a few examples that identify what would be considered moral blind spots in our thinking about the need for global solidarity, a stronger commitment to human rights, and various evils associated with war and violence. According to his analysis, the best way to correct these moral blind spots seems to be public dialogue that begins "with a genuine reciprocal openness" to those who have different perspectives, those who would be inclined to challenge our normative claims.

In the context of partisan politics within the United States, outside observers recognize that both liberals and conservatives have blind spots—some of these blind spots are shared by nearly all politicians and others apply more directly to a particular political party. Such an observation aligns itself well with the Christian doctrine of universal sin and the pervasive reality of corruption of the will. But I would emphasize that we are not necessarily talking here about false doctrine, theological humility, or accusations of spiritual blindness. We are talking about acknowledging a universally flawed *moral perception* that is shaped by one's limited moral horizon, the effects of structural sin, imperialism, and other factors associated with one's sociocultural class, gender, political affiliation, and general historical situation. It seems to me that a humble recognition of possible *moral blind spots* serves as a realistic and acceptable motive for people of faith to engage in genuine dialogue within a liberal democracy —

more acceptable as a prerequisite, I believe, than insisting that religious citizens be open to rethinking their theological positions in light of religious pluralism. Keen moral perception is perhaps better understood as a result of practical wisdom and experience than doctrinal insights—although theology certainly plays a role as well. One of the most instructive historical examples Fiorenza presents to illustrate moral, though not necessarily doctrinal, blind spots is being unable to see the evils of slavery while at the same time upholding the Christian doctrine of human equality before God.

So is the moral perception of religious people generally more flawed than that of nonbelievers? Putnam and Campbell's survey of the data on religious practice and political engagement seems to point in the opposite direction. While a small percentage of extremely religious Americans might be less tolerant of others, religiosity seems overall to have a positive effect on civic life. However, the conflicting influences of religiosity should not necessarily be surprising when we consider the difficulty of universalizing the virtues; we love and embrace those with whom we share things in common, but it is much more difficult to embrace the stranger or to be tolerant of one's political enemies.

My second point can be captured by several related questions: Where is God in the public sphere? Is it possible to maintain a healthy sense of God's transcendence while at the same time affirming God's immanence and active interest in public deliberation? Or are we better off confining talk of God to our private deliberations and then simply translating religious doctrines to enable them to compete on a level playing field with more secular views in the public sphere? If one assumes God's active interest in concrete political issues, policies and movements can quickly become the idols of public space. Indeed, continuing to push for the privatizing of religion might prevent citizens from using God instrumentally in their public deliberation over foreign policy and social issues—especially as these relate to coercive laws within a liberal democracy.

Yet perhaps a more dialogic and dynamic theory of revelation could be compatible with democratic discourse. In this case religious citizens could expect the reality and urgency of divine revelation—unanticipated insights—during the very process of dialogue in the public square. Karl Barth's theology of the concrete particularity of the Word of God might offer a starting point. Barth was himself reluctant to engage directly in ethical controversies or speculations about God's involvement in human history. Nonetheless, he emphatically affirmed the concrete particularity of the Word of

God as the speech of God. According to Barth, God does not speak abstractly or in a general sense. On the contrary, "God always has something specific to say to each man, something that applies to him and to him alone."[1] Perhaps such revelatory insights can occur in the process of human dialogue, correcting the flaws in one's moral perception and leading to solidarity and social justice. If God is aware of each individual's blind spots—as well as the reality of collective or institutional moral blindness—we are probably safe making the assumption that God wants us to talk to those with divergent views.

Now as Christian theologians we are understandably cautious about assuming God's immanence—especially in the messy world of democratic discourse. The temptation to use God instrumentally may be too great. We may end up losing a Barthian sense of the mystery, authority, and judgment of divine revelation. In addition, we must be careful, in Barth's words, that we do not adopt a theory of revelation that allows a moralist "to set himself on God's throne."[2] Theological humility is always in order. As we seek to discern the workings of God's Spirit in the public sphere, we must be careful in applying assumptions about humanity to God. Christian theologians make these assumptions in light of the person of Jesus Christ. Yet we realize that as a transcendent Being, God is not necessarily bound to our sense of proper civic engagement. In fact, what we consider passivity or indifference, on the one hand, or manipulation and coercion, on the other, could align at times with God's purposes. Here again, divine revelation may occur, not only as unanticipated insights into God's will, but also as unanticipated rhetorical techniques that may clash with our sense of vigorous and respectful dialogue in the public square. In other words, theological humility and a sense of God's transcendence will always dictate caution in making assumptions about God's immanence or direct involvement with humanity.

My mention here of unanticipated rhetorical techniques employed by God brings me to my third and final point. It is drawn from a brief reference Fiorenza makes to the problematic reality that the "public space is open to manipulation." My response to this concern is that religious citizens ought to consider more seriously the positive value of *rhetorical theology* as they engage social and political issues in the public sphere. Contrary to the stereotypical

---

[1] Karl Barth, *Church Dogmatics I.1: The Doctrine of the Word of God* (New York: T & T Clark, 2004 <1936>), 140.

[2] Barth, *Church Dogmatics III.4: The Doctrine of Creation* (New York: T & T Clark, 1978 <1961>), 10.

understanding of rhetoric as manipulation or irresponsible soph-
istry, ancient theories of rhetoric describe it as the ability to see
and employ available and appropriate means of persuasion. From
Aristotle's perspective, rhetoric is a neutral art, one that can be used
either for good or for evil. One reason rhetorical theology has positive value is that focusing on the art of persuasion can be conducive
to mutual respect and civil dialogue. It encourages citizens to avoid
engaging in contentious arguments in the public square — because
those types of arguments are usually unproductive and unconvinc-
ing. The art of persuasion includes much more than logic, such as
establishing trust and credibility and rousing positive emotions in
one's audience.

David Cunningham's work on rhetorical theology relies primarily
on Aristotle to illustrate the important role of persuasion in Christian
theology. For Aristotle, rhetoric is closely associated with dialectic
because it begins with common opinions and "calls for attention to
concrete, historical reality."[3] Both rhetoric and dialectic are methods
for examining political and ethical issues. However, dialectic is better
suited for theoretical matters, rhetoric for practical matters: "Dialectic may move a person's intellect, but it does not necessarily bring
about fundamental changes in a person's attitudes and actions."[4] In
other words, while dialectic convinces the intellect, rhetoric moves
the will.

The question about whether concrete political proposals ought
to be supported by religious arguments is really a question about
what tools of persuasion are allowed by religious groups. My suggestion is that religious arguments can and should be *persuasive*.
When used to stir the emotions of the public in support of concrete
political positions, rhetorical theology can appropriately influence
both religious and nonreligious citizens. But faith-based rhetoric
used for political advocacy clearly ought to be employed with the
type of theological humility that is informed by religious pluralism.
Such discourse must not be coercive or manipulative; as Fiorenza
suggests, it should help citizens on a practical level to maintain
public order and to increase global solidarity.

So how can a religious citizen engage in meaningful conversation with a secular liberal about a contentious issue on which they
strongly disagree? Rhetorical theology would be aligned with what

---

[3] David S. Cunningham, *Faithful Persuasion: In Aid of a Rhetoric of Christian
Theology* (Notre Dame, IN: University of Notre Dame Press, 1991), 17.
[4] Ibid.

Jeffrey Stout calls "immanent criticism" in the democratic process. Through sincere, non-manipulative criticism based on the particular premises of an opponent, we actually show respect for a fellow citizen.[5] We give and ask for reasons, participating in a dialectical process of understanding and holding each other accountable. Significantly, the process of immanent criticism depends on the willingness of citizens to be transparent about their real reasons for justifying particular social and political views. This includes being candid about the religious foundations of one's views. Immanent criticism also requires that citizens cultivate civic virtues in their discursive exchanges. Stout points out the important difference between having rights and exercising them in prudent and respectful ways.[6] He suggests that civility, the desire for justice, temperance, practical wisdom and discernment, courage, tact, poise, and humility are all important virtues to be cultivated.[7] In some cases it would be imprudent even to bring religious premises into a political argument.[8]

The promotion of civic virtues in democratic discourse, while it rules out coercion and disrespect, does not necessarily exclude the use of bold prophetic discourse in the public sphere. Amelia Uelmen evaluates the extent to which recent statements from the United States Conference of Catholic Bishops promote "fruitful and constructive dialogue about religious values in a pluralistic democracy."[9] She concludes in particular that "the concept of intrinsic evil holds a compelling power which may be, at least in part, the kind of energetic injection that Catholics need as they reflect on their role in political participation and public life."[10] Uelmen suggests that the prophetic style of discourse within the 2007 document *Forming Consciences for Faithful Citizenship* helps Catholic voters rise above self-deception and embrace the protection of moral absolutes. She argues that "our culture needs powerful language" that calls out against sin and strengthens us against temptation.[11] As Fiorenza clearly points out, even Rawls recognizes certain contexts (for example, abolition in the nineteenth century and the civil rights

[5] Jeffrey Stout, *Democracy and Tradition* (Princeton, NJ: Princeton University Press, 2005), 73.

[6] Ibid, 64.

[7] Ibid, 85.

[8] Ibid, 86.

[9] Amelia Uelmen, "'It's Hard Work': Reflections on Conscience and Citizenship in the Catholic Tradition," *Journal of Catholic Legal Studies* 47 (2008): 333.

[10] Ibid., 334–35.

[11] Ibid, 336.

movement in the twentieth) in which the work of prophets may be indispensable in guiding the practical reasoning of citizens.

From the perspective of religious pluralism, prophetic certainty ought to be avoided out of respect for others. Yet Fiorenza's suggestion that it is difficult to distinguish religious from nonreligious arguments is relevant here. A utopian sense of urgency and intolerance for evil may characterize the language of a secular liberal as well as a "true believer." Neither of these "prophets" can expect to have the final word in a democratic exchange of reasons. Yet if rhetorical theology as an art of persuasion is welcome in the public sphere, prophetic certainty may be expressed at times to reinforce bold, incisive arguments. By encouraging an open exchange of both religious and nonreligious perspectives, we will be in a better position to address the idolatry and moral blindness that characterize public space today.

5

"The Prisons Fill Up"

The Specter of Mass Incarceration as Compelling Theological Issue

Mark Lewis Taylor

Colonial racism is no different from other racisms. Anti-Semitism cuts me to the quick; I get upset; a frightful rage makes me anemic; they are denying me the right to be a man.

-Frantz Fanon, Black Skin, White Masks

And then one fine day the bourgeoisie is awakened by a terrific boomerang effect: the gestapos are busy, the prisons fill up, the torturers around the racks invent, refine, discuss.

-Aimé Césaire, Discourse on Colonialism

Frantz Fanon bears witness to a persistent compulsion at work in the tangled political and moral landscapes of colonial violence and racism. There is in him a compulsion, born of a co-feeling with sufferers of racism everywhere. Another's suffering of anti-Semitism "makes me anemic," writes Fanon, even as he bears his own acute suffering of anti-black discrimination and repression in his native Martinique, in France, Algeria—nearly anywhere. Police often mistook him for an Arab, and upon receiving from police their hasty apologies, Fanon "protested violently" against their claims that being Martinican was better than being Arab. Fanon was compelled by this co-feeling to criticize, to unmask the ways racism gets inside both colonized and colonizer. "I cannot dissociate myself," Fanon testifies as if subject to a compelling force, "from the fate reserved for my brother."[1]

Nevertheless, Fanon is equally clear that some can make, and have made, the dissociation. He names them, analyzes them, in all his works, especially in *Black Skin, White Masks* and *The Wretched of the Earth*.[2] These dissociating groups are the creators and bearers of, and participants in, European colonial racism. But even their dissociation, sustained particularly by the dehumanizing *habitus* of white racism vis-à-vis colonizable Africans, Caribbeans, Asians, Arabs, all as bearers of a supposedly "tolerable" suffering — even this dissociation testifies to powers of human co-belonging. Europeans pay a cost for their dissociation. To dramatize the point, Fanon cites his native Martinican compatriot Aimé Césaire, a former teacher, poet, political activist, and national leader. In a searing indictment of Europe and its descendants titled *Discourse on Colonialism*, Césaire details a "terrific boomerang effect": the violence that colonizers dish out upon the colonized often circles back into the colonizers' worlds. In Césaire's epigraph above this effect is registered in Europe, according to Césaire, in the explosion of Nazism: "the gestapos are busy, *the prisons fill up*, the torturers standing around the racks invent, refine, discuss" (emphasis added).[3]

More recently, Rey Chow, in her study of xenophobia in the United States, argues that the stranger — the cultural, national, religious "other" — becomes today "the-other-as-target." Growing numbers of these are reduced to "bombable others." But "xenophobia can backfire," Chow warns, as its anxiety goes inward; thus white supremacist militiamen turn the xenophobic bombing reflex loose on innocent US men, women, and children, "a violence that erupted from within the heart of the country," as in the Oklahoma City bombing of 1995. She cites, then, a "vicious circle of the-world-as-target . . . returned to its point of origin."[4]

---

[1] Frantz Fanon, *Black Skin, White Masks*, trans. Richard Philcox (New York: Grove Press, 2008 <1952>), 71.

[2] He interlaces the colonizing racism in his descriptions of the architecture and geography of colonial situations. See Frantz Fanon, *The Wretched of the Earth*, trans. Richard Philcox (New York, NY: Grove Press, 2004 <1964>), 4–5.

[3] Aimé Césaire, *Discourse on Colonialism*, trans. Joan Pinkham, new intro. Robin D. G. Kelley (New York: Monthly Review Press, 2000), 36. Originally published as *Discours sur le colonialisme* (Editions Presence Africaine, 1955).

[4] Rey Chow, *The Age of the World Target: Self-Referentiality in War, Theory, and Comparative Work* (Durham, NC: Duke University Press, 2006), 42–43. W. E. B. Du Bois made a similar observation about "tiny Belgium's" experience of

If "the prisons fill up" in the United States today, of what "vicious circle" might it be a part? How does it mark a "boomerang effect" for the United States ? The United States suffers burgeoning prisons in overfull and onerous measure. "Mass incarceration" names US society's commitment, investment of expenditures, and citizen support for the extensive imprisonment of large numbers of its citizens. I detailed the extent and multi-leveled impact of mass incarceration in 2001,[5] and scholars from nearly every discipline confirm the worsening problem today. Since the 1970s, as Harvard sociologist Bruce Western observes, the prison population, now at about 2.3 million, has grown sevenfold, one of the largest, most frenetic prison buildups in the history of world cultures.[6] No other nation incarcerates as many people as does the United States (more populous China incarcerates only 1.5 million, and Russia is third, far behind, at 890,000). No other nation has a higher percentage of its population behind bars. Most egregiously, in a country that vaunts equality and democracy as its creed, no other nation, by far, has a prison population so swelled by its racially stigmatized groups, primarily blacks and Latinos/as (the largest per capita group being American Indian, and Southeast Asians are entering at increased rates).[7] More African Americans are behind bars today than there were slaves in 1830.[8] As early as 1996, the National Criminal Justice Commission declared the racialized prison buildup a "social catastrophe."[9] Legal scholar Michelle Alexander shows how minoritized groups today experience the prisons as a labyrinthine power driving them into a

---

slaughter in the European theater of World War I, seeing in Belgium's suffering, "dimly through the rifts of battle smoke," the twelve million dead in its own African colony, the Congo. So-called "modern humanity," notes Du Bois, comes to this. Having vaunted its "civilization" above Asian, African, and American indigenous ones, wreaking suffering among the colonized, the colonizers themselves now bear in their own lands and peoples the slaughter they had tolerated for others while their "cities were gay, art and science flourished" (W. E. B. Du Bois, *Darkwater: Voices from Within the Veil* (New York: Dover Publications, 1999 <1920>), 22–23.

[5] Mark Lewis Taylor, *The Executed God: The Way of the Cross in Lockdown America* (Minneapolis, MN: University of Minnesota Press, 2001), 18–47.

[6] Bruce Western, *Punishment and Inequality in America* (New York: Russell Sage, 2006), 3.

[7] On these statistics see *One in 100: Behind Bars in America 2008*, The Pew Center on the States (Washington, DC: The Pew Charitable Trusts, 2009), 5–7.

[8] Michelle Alexander, *The New Jim Crow: Mass Incarceration in the Age of Colorblindness* (New York: The New Press, 2010), 271n7.

[9] Steven R. Donziger, ed., *The Real War on Crime*, The National Report of the National Criminal Justice Commission (New York: HarperPerennial, 1996), 31.

stronger racialized "caste" experience in America.[10] University of California sociologist Loïc Wacquant analyzes how the prisons have become the major way the United States deals with its socially and economically insecure groups, replacing the ghetto and state provisions of healthcare, education, and care of the mentally ill.[11] And again, all populations are touched by this. True, among men age 18 and over, 1 in 54 is in prison—of Hispanic men in that age group, 1 in 36; and of African American men in that age group, 1 in 15—but of the entire adult population of the United States in 2008, "one in 100" was locked up.[12]

The problem of mass incarceration deepens even more when we recall the studies of comparative law professor James Whitman, who has shown that US prisons, compared to those of other developed countries, circulate the most onerous levels of harshness and low-status degradation. US prisons feature routinized dehumanization, racial separation, hierarchical conflict, guard brutality, and sexual assault (216,000 cases a year of sexual assault alone, according to the Department of Justice's statistics)[13]—all running at epidemic proportions.[14]

How is it that "prisons fill up" in the United States as they do while Christian theologians largely fail to address the matter, and how might the problem of mass incarceration become a "compelling issue" for those theologians? The argument of this essay responds as follows: mass incarceration will become a compelling issue for US theologians and others in the United States who now tolerate and support it, through a kind of Fanonian/Cesairean "boomerang effect" that creates travail for their society. This will not be the outcome of some divine or metaphysical recompense ("what goes 'round comes 'round"). It is better understood as the outcome of the way memories in present-day communities become specters, and the way perpetrators, acting brutally abroad, become such that they cannot help but enact their brutalities at home. By "specters"

---

[10] Alexander, *The New Jim Crow*, 185–208.

[11] Loïc Wacquant, *Punishing the Poor: The Neoliberal Government of Social Insecurity* (Durham, NC: Duke University Press, 2009), 76–150.

[12] Pew Center, *One in 100*, 6. The Pew report credits the US Department of Justice, Bureau of Justice Statistics, "Prison and Jail Inmates at Midyear 2006" (June 2007) for these numbers.

[13] David Kaiser and Lovisa Stannow, "Prison Rape and the Government," *The New York Review of Books*, March 24, 2011.

[14] James Q. Whitman, *Harsh Justice: Criminal Punishment and the Widening Divide Between America and Europe* (New York: Oxford University Press, 2003), 41–68.

I do not speak of phantasms easily dismissed as superstition. Specters are cultural and historical currents that take on such force, in particular situations, that they can pose as threat, demand, and/or promise of transformation. If mass incarceration is to become more than an occasional agenda item, or a topic of theology, but instead a compelling issue, then it will be because mass incarceration becomes a spectral force.

After clarifying, in a first section, the sense in which I invoke the notion of "compelling issue," the second major section begins a spectral ontology of mass incarceration, a prison "hauntology" (to recall Jacques Derrida's neologism),[15] by treating two specters that long have haunted US history and society. Mass incarceration is a major "sedimentation" of these specters, accumulated remains of routinized US history that, over time, have formed the powerful and expansive prison apparatus accepted by so many today.[16] In a third major section, though, I turn to mass incarceration as itself a specter. Here it becomes a positive spectral force, taking the form of critical movements of resistance, rich with liberating practice. These emerge amid situations of the "boomerang effect" (Césaire/Fanon) or the "vicious circle" (Chow). It is here that mass incarceration becomes, indeed constitutes itself as, a force, and hence as "compelling theological issue." Mass incarceration becomes, then, not just a topic, subject matter, *an issue*, but as specter it *issues in*, compellingly, not only social measures of redress, but also theological discourses, ones that may distill liberating meanings from various Jesus traditions.

What Is a Compelling Theological Issue?

I suggest thinking of compelling theological issues in relation to history's specters. Such issues, then, emerge from crises that come mixed with both challenge and opportunity, both threat and promise. A compelling issue tends to be pervasive of theological discourse. The compelling issue should not be confused with either of the two main interpretive tasks that theologian David Tracy identified in structures of dynamic theologizing: one, the risking of some interpretation of the situation of human and planetary being;

---

[15] Jacques Derrida, *Specters of Marx: The State of the Debt, the Work of Mourning, and the New International,* trans. Peggy Kamuf (New York: Routledge, 1994), 10.

[16] I adapt this notion of "sedimentation" from social phenomenologist Alfred Schutz. See Alfred Schutz, *On Phenomenology and Social Relations* (Chicago: University of Chicago Press, 1999), 322.

the other, the daring of some interpretation of the traditional events, symbols, and discourses of Christian religious traditions. In both interpretations, distinguishable but occurring always in "mutually critical correlation," there is risk and imagination, a constitutive act that gives a particular theologian's discourse, in its social location, a distinctive character.[17] Tracy links the notion of risk and distinctiveness of theologians' constitutive act to his theme of the "journey of intensification," which he stresses throughout his works, particularly in *The Analogical Imagination*. The compelling issue emerges, congeals, becomes ever more demanding as theologians, in their own sites of discourse and along their journeys, intensify and sharpen their senses of crisis and concern. Whether the interpretation is a reading of the situation or of the Christian tradition, it is often animated, focused, and charged with its compelling issue.

Nor should discerning a compelling issue be confused with identifying an agenda item in theology. Agenda items are many and various. Moreover, one person's agenda item may become another's compelling issue. What matters is how either is positioned in its theological discourse. Agenda items are not minor; they may name significant problems like guilt, shame, death, colonial domination, injury and disablement, ecological destruction, gender and sexual justice or injustice, class exploitation, mass incarceration. As subject matter, agenda items are often then treated under larger rubrics used by theologians, that is, liberation, reconciliation, love, justice, and so on. A compelling issue, though, is a matter that charges a theologian's entire theological project and usually throws him or her into relationships of support and struggle with other thinkers and actors.

To exemplify the differences between an agenda item and a compelling issue, consider feminist theology. Here, gender injustice and patriarchy (and often heteronormativity) constitute "sexism" and function as far more than an agenda item. Complexly analyzed sexism becomes a galvanizing concern, a "compelling issue," in my sense. Feminist theologians' agenda items then might become a task of redefining Christology in light of sexism. Perhaps its agenda is a new theological anthropology, a reimagined view of race and gender, of spirituality. Because sexism touches and distorts almost

---

[17] David Tracy, *The Analogical Imagination: Christian Theology and the Culture of Pluralism* (New York: Crossroad, 1998<1982>), 15–26. Tracy is, of course, reconfiguring the theological method of mid-twentieth-century theologian and religion scholar Paul Tillich and his notion of "the method of correlation." Cf. Paul Tillich, *Systematic Theology*, 3 vols. in 1 (Chicago: University of Chicago Press, 1951), 1:59–66.

all levels of social being, it is a likely candidate for becoming a theological discourse's compelling issue. Agenda items do not usually pervade as thoroughly the fabric of theologians' social locations and discourse. Sexism is often spectral for women, and it can also be for men as well.

In theology, of whatever stripe, usually US mass incarceration is barely an agenda item. It may be occasionally referenced by theologians, but usually it is left to a domain of pastoral reference. Christians most often taking up prison issues and working on those issues are those engaged in prisoner visitation as "prison ministry," working as prison chaplains.[18] But few Christian thinkers have addressed the phenomenon of mass incarceration in the United States as a *structural* issue and then have made it a compelling issue for their theological and ethical reflections. The exceptions that I know are T. Richard Snyder's *The Protestant Ethic and the Spirit of Punishment,* my *The Executed God,* and James Samuel Logan's *Good Punishment?*[19] While these books might be viewed as taking up only agenda items—punishment, imprisonment, the death penalty—each did more than that. For Snyder, the way Protestant America views and practices punishment, his compelling issue, sets other topics as his agenda, for example, reconceiving the whole notion of grace in Protestant theology.[20] In *The Executed God* I took the entire complex of "lockdown America"—with its growing mass incarceration, police violence, *and* use of the death penalty (often 90 or more convicts were being executed annually during the book's writing)—as my compelling issue. Christology, then, became an agenda item, wherein I reimagined Jesus as a sufferer of imperial execution, thus redefining understandings of what constitutes participation in the way of Jesus.[21] For Logan, a Christian theologian and ethicist, US imprisonment, a concern that touched his own community life deeply, galvanized a theological ethics broadly in the United States, which addressed fundamental questions of Christians' ontological intimacy with many other groups in US society.[22]

---

[18] Lennie Spitale, *Prison Ministry: Understanding Prison Culture Inside and Out* (Nashville, TN: Broadman and Holman, 2002).

[19] T. Richard Snyder, *The Protestant Ethic and the Spirit of Punishment* (Grand Rapids, MI: Eerdmans, 2001); Taylor, *The Executed God*; James Samuel Logan, *Good Punishment? Christian Moral Practice and US Imprisonment* (Grand Rapids, MI: Eerdmans, 2008).

[20] Snyder, *The Protestant Ethic and the Spirit of Punishment*, 101–25.

[21] Taylor, *The Executed God*, 37–47.

[22] Logan, *Good Punishment?* 201–54.

These books do not just take up the issue of prisons, imprisonment, and mass incarceration as agenda items. On the contrary, they
issue from a sense of compulsion regarding the urgency and crisis
of mass incarceration. That compulsion reshapes their theological
discourse, their very understandings of what Christian practice is or
might become. I mean *compelling issue* in this sense. Etymologically,
it is helpful to recall that to compel (Latin, *com* + *peller*, "to push
together") means not just to force or drive, to submit or subdue, to
overpower, but to do so in a way that constrains toward a new way
of thinking things together, comprehensively, or acting together with
others who are driven together for action, collectively.

Compelling issues so understood ride the force of the specter.
Thus it is that I turn to the prisons as housing a haunted past, and
as force haunting the present and futures of theologians and their
US publics.

A Prison Ontology As Hauntology

When Jacques Derrida coined the now much cited neologism
hauntology, he was referencing the way being has a kind of presence,
wherein, nevertheless, there is something absent, present mainly as
a kind of "seething presence," as sociologist Avery Gordon glosses.[23]
The dynamic structures of mass incarceration, in the prison house,
indeed, with the US as "Prison House of the Nations," make up
such a seething presence. Being "ghosted," US prisons are haunted
by specters past and, as I shall argue, constitute specters future. The
prison house in America thus is both haunted and haunting.[24]

The US prison, then, should be viewed not just as an institutional
phenomenon, then, but also, with apologies to Martin Heidegger,
as a "house of being." It houses in a profound sense the very being
of US political, social, and economic history. Heidegger, of course,
was affirming that "language is the house of being." An element
of confinement and struggle is signaled even here in the "Letter on
Humanism," in which Heidegger offers his phrase:

---

[23] Avery F. Gordon, *Ghostly Matters: Haunting and the Sociological Imagination*
(Minneapolis, MN: University of Minnesota Press, 1997).

[24] In this section I am clarifying usages I have made of the notion of specter
across especially my last two books. See Mark Lewis Taylor, *Religion, Politics,
and the Christian Right: Post-9/11 Powers and American Empire* (Minneapolis, MN:
Fortress Press, 2005), 13–14, 96–109; and idem, *The Theological and the Political: On
the Weight of the World* (Minneapolis, MN: Fortress Press, 2011), 31–35, 181–82,
203–8.

Language is the house of being. In its home man dwells. Those who think and those who create with words are the guardians of this home. Their guardianship accomplishes the manifestation of being insofar as they bring the manifestation to language and maintain it in language through their speech.[25]

Guardianship may take the milder form of oversight (guardians as protectors of something entrusted to them) or, more negatively, the harsher form of confinement and concentration of bodies under cellular confinement ("guardians" as prison guards, supervising and controlling the imprisoned). Between these two notions, but leaning a bit to the latter, is Pierre Bourdieu's notion of "the guardians of symbolic capital,"[26] such as family, religion, educational systems, the state—all effective powers of control and constraint, often involving and enforcing fundamental antagonisms etched into the structured practices of daily living.[27]

The Prisons as Haunted by Specters of US History

The housing function, with respect to human beings, then, is a construction of language and practice that is marked generally by an experience of guardianship. In the case of the prison house, our focus here, this house of guarded being(s) is a distillation of larger forces that have coursed through the history of the nation and constitute veritable social traditions of antagonism impinging on the present. In this section I first make brief reference to three historical lineages in relation to which the prisons must be understood. I then identify two major spectral forces that drive the sedimentation of the prison in the contemporary period.

Historical lineages. First, among historical connections we must recall that US mass incarceration is intimately dependent upon the legacy of slavery and Jim Crow. Whatever else it was, slavery

---

[25] Martin Heidegger, "Letter on Humanism," in *Martin Heidegger: Basic Writings*, rev. and exp. ed., ed. David Farrell Krell (San Francisco: HarperCollins, 1993 <1947>), 217.

[26] Pierre Bourdieu, *Masculine Domination,* trans. Richard Nice (Stanford, CA: Stanford University Press, 2001), 96–108.

[27] Obviously, the "ontology," here, though citing Heidegger's famous phrase on language, is not an onto-theology or an ontology of historical structures. In the terms of Foucault, it is a *"historical* ontology of ourselves," a more fleeting, sociological, and historical approach, rather than one aiming at fundamental structures.

was a routinization of the disposing of black bodies such that the white social imaginary possesses a still near-permanent expectation that black bodies have their "rightful place," or at least "tolerable place," in a position of control and disposability. When slavery was abolished in the mid-nineteenth century, and Reconstruction efforts backslid into new racist structures (sometimes "worse than slavery"),[28] as they did by end of the nineteenth and early twentieth century, the prisons were "blackened," almost overnight.[29] By the end of the twentieth century the prisons had become the major way for dominant groups, particularly the US "white overclass,"[30] to respond to blacks', to other non-whites', and to women's gains in the civil rights movements and social upheaval that culminated in 1968. By 2009, mass incarceration in the United States supplanted the ghetto as the major way of controlling dispossessed African Americans, along with Latinos/as and other poor and stigmatized groups.[31]

Second, historically, the prisons today must be seen against the backdrop of a history of *colonial confinement operations* used by Western powers and the United States. Even the lineage of slavery and caste-making in the US, discussed above, must be seen in the light of what has been termed "the colonial carceral."[32] Slavery, its apparatus, and institutions of confinement were crucial to the emergence of Western colonialism and capitalism. In US history the colonial carceral is strikingly apparent in the confinement and restriction of American Indian peoples after decimation of their nations. Today, American Indians have the highest per capita incarceration rate (individuals per group), and in many of the Plains States Indians' percent of state prison populations is often more than double that of their percent of population in those same states.[33] The prison

---

[28] David M. Oshinsky, *"Worse than Slavery": Parchman Farm and the Ordeal of Jim Crow Justice* (New York: The Free Press, 1997).

[29] Wacquant, *Punishing the Poor*, 207; and Oshinsky, *"Worse Than Slavery,"* 32.

[30] Michael Lind, "The White Overclass," in Michael Lind, *The Next American Nation: The New Nationalism and the Fourth American Revolution* (New York: Free Press, 1995), 152.

[31] Eduardo Bonilla-Silva, *Racism Without Racists: Color-Blind Racism and Racial Inequality in Contemporary America*, 3rd ed. (Lanham, MD: Rowman and Littlefield, 2010).

[32] Graeme Harper, *Colonial and Postcolonial Incarceration* (New York: Continuum, 2001), 1–8.

[33] Marianne O. Nielsen and Robert Silverman, eds., *American Indians in Prison* (Boulder, CO: Westview Press, 1996), see data at www.ncjrs.gov/App/Publications/abstract.aspx?ID=168158 .

function recurs also in the management and confinement of various immigrant populations; it was applied to the Chinese in America before their expulsion in 1882 and to control them during expulsion. The carceral function was also deployed in the internment of Japanese Americans,[34] and also of Italian Americans, far fewer of these interned during World War II, though some 600,000 were put under special surveillance, regulation, and curtailment in that period.[35] Abroad, the United States had also honed the confinement procedures of the colonial carceral—in Korea, during its occupation, taking over from and collaborating with lingering Japanese colonizers, the US military helped imprison thousands after post–World War II uprisings for national liberation;[36] in Vietnam, too, where over forty CIA Provincial Interrogation Centers anchored one of the most onerous, murderous of covert operations, imprisoning and killing tens of thousands.[37]

Third, there is the history of the very *architecture and marketing* of confinement and surveillance technology, crucial to maintaining carceral confinement and current US mass incarceration. One indicator of this is present investment and interests of weapons industries like Lockheed Martin. This corporation makes surveillance and communications technology for the Department of Justice and many US prisons. Lockheed Martin is just one of the key industries with long involvements in the manufacture, marketing, and purveying of military weaponry for US war. For more than one hundred years, just shortly after the invention of air navigation, Lockheed Martin (through the Martin connection) has been developing aerospace and other technologies; today it is the largest defense contractor in the United States, with 71 percent of its contracts being for US defense.

Historical Specters of American Romanticism and Contractual Liberalism

These historical lineages signal major forces that characterize US history and drive it in distinctive ways. Those forces constitute specters

---

[34] Linda Gordon and Gary Y. Okihiro, eds., *Impounded: Dorothea Lange and the Censored Images of Japanese American Internment* (New York: W. W. Gordon, 2008).

[35] Lawrence Di Stasi, *Una Storia Segreta: The Secret History of Italian American Evacuation and Internment During World War II* (Berkeley, CA: Heyday Books, 2004).

[36] Bruce Cummings, *The Origins of the Korean War: Liberation and the Emergence of Separate Regimes, 1945–1947* (Princeton, NJ: Princeton University Press, 1981), 289–92, 351–81.

[37] Alfred W. McCoy, *A Question of Torture: CIA Interrogation, from the Cold War to the War on Terror* (New York: Metropolitan Books, 2006), 64–71.

that have congealed, sedimenting in US mass incarceration as the powerful social form it is today.

The first specter, American Romanticism,[38] reduces the notion of America and American to the borders and history of the project of the United States of America, politically instituted in 1776–89 through war, propertied groups organizing in the North American Atlantic colonies against other constituencies (Indians, slaves from Africa, indentured servants, women, often Irish, the Asian and Arab descendents mixing with these, and others) and then instituting their constitutional Republic. From the US nation's founding to the present, a Romanticism has interlaced this national project with the exceptionalist myth (American exceptionalism),[39] in which the United States is held to be the vanguard nation of Western "civilization's" expansionist project, usually today through projects of "development," promising increased liberty and material well-being to other nations and peoples but often bringing under-development and entrenchment of US interests.[40] An innocence—feigned or genuinely believed—interlaces the notion of the nation being a kind of "light to the nations." This has been driven by Christian religious notions of mission, spurred in early forms by colonial aspirations to be a kind of biblical commonwealth. It can be spurred just as powerfully today by liberals *and* conservatives who lack biblical or any religious conviction, who defend more secularist notions of "American greatness," such that, in much circulated parlance, citizens and leaders speak of a whole epoch as "the American century," which, especially when coined after World War II by Henry Luce, was a euphemism for "American empire."[41]

In short, this destructive specter of American Romanticism presents the nation as a people who, in Reinhold Niebuhr's memorable phrase, are "children of light," a good force arrayed against the more threatening "children of darkness."[42] From the nation's

---

[38] I will capitalize the names of each of these specters to signal the reification and fetishization of the key concepts, by the US popular traditions that embrace them, which sustain their spectral status.

[39] For one presentation and a criticism of American exceptionalism, see Michael Ignatieff, *American Exceptionalism and Human Rights* (Princeton, NJ: Princeton University Press, 2005), 1–26.

[40] Arturo Escobar, *Encountering Development: The Making and Unmaking of the Third World* (Princeton, NJ: Princeton University Press, 1995), 52–54.

[41] David Harvey, *The New Imperialism* (New York: Oxford University Press, 2003), 50.

[42] Niebuhr himself, while critical of the naiveté of "the children of light," had his own version of this binary. See Rienhold Niebuhr, *Children of Light and*

earliest devastating wars to its occupations and war making in Iraq and Afghanistan in the twenty-first century, the "US imperial" has grown ever stronger in this appropriation of this virtuous light and its assumed "liberty defending" role.

How is the prison a distillation of this specter? Especially as a racialized institutional matrix, US mass incarceration creates and sustains the idea of a nation emergent from the "darker nations" and historically colonized groups. The prisons are a result of that history, but more significantly, symbolically reinforce it today by its dramatically massive concentration of racialized groups in a white dominated nation, one with still a strongly entrenched "white over-class" and in which whiteness and citizens' passing as white remain ways to secure privilege.[43] The racially skewed prison population steeps the US populace in a symbolic world that sustains a pervasive ideological ethos that the "children of darkness" are the people of fetters, of labor, of exploitation. The "children of light" thereby claim not only their role as bringers of light to the nations, but also sustain that global imperial ideology with a domestic domination that takes the prisons (earlier, the ghetto)[44] as worlds of the failed human, the exploitable, disposable peoples. As a consequence, mass incarceration constitutes blackness and racialized groups generally as threatening negativity, as fearsome specter. In sum, mass incarceration is constituted and marked as an alternative nation *internal* to the United States, replicating and reinforcing the US constitution of its imperial position among racially marked nations abroad. Hold this first specter to the fore before we turn to consider another. Here, the prisons have first been presented at the heart of a romanticizing US nation-state, arising from and continually reinforcing the legacy of racism, understanding this latter in the powerful sense of Gilmore's definition as "the state sanctioned or extralegal production and exploitation of group-differentiated vulnerability to premature death."[45]

There is, though, a second destructive specter. It is that of Contractual Liberalism. It is the form of progress promised and

---

Children of Darkness: A Vindication of Democracy and a Critique of Its Traditional Defense (Chicago: University of Chicago Press, 2011 <1944>), esp. Gary Dorrien's "Introduction," ix–xxvi.

[43] George Lipsitz, *The Possessive Investment in Whiteness: How White People Profit from Identity Politics* (Philadelphia: Temple University Press, 1998), 24–46.

[44] Wacquant, *Punishing the Poor*, 204–8.

[45] Ruth Wilson Gilmore, *Golden Gulag: Prisons, Surplus, Crisis, and Opposition in Globalizing California* (Berkeley and Los Angeles: University of California Press, 2007), 28.

emphasized, suggesting a unified citizenry that has made a "social contract" to assure the liberality of opportunity and equality for all ("life, liberty, and the pursuit of happiness"). As I have detailed elsewhere, the social contract in the United States, as in Europe, is "contractual" in another sense.[46] As political and economic life is actually structured, the social contract delivers a most twisted form of liberal vision. It "contracts out" opportunity and enablement to a few (from the beginning, in the United States, to a white male propertied elite). At the same time, practice of the social contract functionally "contracts" in another sense, that is, it constricts and reduces the fields of opportunity and empowerment, "contracting" the scope of those who may enter environments of opportunity and empowerment. With respect to women's and racialized groups' experience of the social contract, this invidious side of contracting has been carefully analyzed by Carolyn Pateman and Charles Mills.[47] Practice of the social contract constitutes not only a disempowerment of women and racialized groups, but also a protection and masking of the function of US class structure and the workings of its corporate white overclass.

US prisons and mass incarceration are also sedimentations of this specter. The extensive and intensive use of prisons, what sociologist Wacquant terms "hyperincarceration," is the result of economic policies by the US overclass, working in tandem with participants in a transnational political project to "remake the nexus of market, state, and citizenship from above." This political project is often termed "neoliberalism" and is an intensive economic program, driven by the US and Global North powers to maximize their profit and economic power.[48] Operative here are not just singular, iconic villains who are the bread and butter of conspiracy theorists. To be sure, sociologist Wacquant can identify key agents and organizations of the transnational neoliberalism,[49] but what is operative is a structural functioning of the corporate class interests. As Wacquant and Gilmore stress, since the 1960s this overclass has felt itself under threat in

[46] Taylor, *Religion, Politics, and the Christian Right*, 71–95.

[47] Carole Pateman, *The Sexual Contract* (Stanford, CA: Stanford University Press, 1988); Charles Mills, *The Racial Contract* (Ithaca, NY: Cornell University Press, 1997); and Carole Pateman and Charles Mills, *Contract and Domination* (Malden, MA: Polity Press, 2007).

[48] Wacquant, "Theoretical Coda: A Sketch of the Neoliberal State," in Wacquant, *Punishing the Poor*, 287–317.

[49] Wacquant, "Theoretical Coda," 306–7. Loïc Wacquant, *Prisons of Poverty*. Expanded edition (Minneapolis, MN: University of Minnesota Press, 2009), especially on think-tank projects like the Manhattan Institute, 7–18.

the United States from workers and activists of numerous stripes, emanating from the gains and tumult of the civil rights movement and "black/brown/red/yellow power" movements associated with it.[50] This was a threat to its own social and economic security, yet, political leaders representing that overclas managed to recast their own economic insecurity as a "criminal insecurity" that allegedly threatened the wider public.

The basic neoliberal moves of the transnational overclass, particularly in the United States, have been two: first, to desocialize wage labor, to splinter work and labor so that more Americans have to work at more jobs to sustain a livelihood and at lower wages. At the same time, rights and protections of labor unions are curtailed, and the already economically vulnerable are moved "from welfare to workfare," swelling the ranks of those living in poverty. This has thrown many US citizens and residents into the "world precariate," fraught often with the social despair and desperation that leads to transgression.[51] The second move of the overclass is ready at this point. Having withdrawn the "safety net" of economic protections for socially vulnerable groups, "the dragnet" moves in, the carceral state. It sweeps transgressors into its domain, and the prisons themselves become subject to the profit motive. New draconian sentencing policies and a manufactured "drug war," targeting all groups but communities of color most comprehensively and onerously (much more than white youth, the group with the highest percentage of drug use),[52] then swell the prisons, as has occurred especially between the 1970s and the present. The criminalization of poverty and the rise of carceral "Big Government" generates the carceral state. American economic "liberalism," thus, becomes "contractual" in very insidious forms, that is, it contracts/constricts the fields of opportunity for the poor, and when despair reigns, and the desperation leads to social transgression, or simply labels one as transgressor/criminal *because* one is poor, then the space of living contracts further, to the walled-in and controlled spaces of cellular confinement and "corrections" institutions.

These two specters carry destructive negativity, not only where the prison and mass incarceration proliferate, but wherever the

---

[50] Laura Polio, *Black, Brown, Yellow, and Left: Radical Activism in Los Angeles* (Berkeley and Los Angeles: University of California Press, 2006); and Gilmore, *Golden Gulag*, 24–26.

[51] Wacquant, "Welfare 'Reform' as the New Statecraft," in Wacquant, *Punishing the Poor*, 76–109.

[52] Alexander, *The New Jim Crow*, 96–97.

US state's constant fusion of these two specters move into intense relation with one another. Especially in conditions when the state feels most under threat, the two often unite most virulently so that romantic nationalism and corporate overclass policies often drive states to fascist forms of rule. The most notable examples of this are in the US prisons, where the two specters have sedimented a brutal "institutional corridor fascism"; in 1930s Germany, when corporate powers joined Romanticist German populism into an ethos that led to Nazism; and also in the post–9/11 United States, where key corporate players, many of them die-hard secularists and/or of other religions, made common cause with Christian theocrats among American Romanticists and thus carried the nation into a unilateral war of aggression in Iraq, with lethal consequences, especially for Iraqi citizens, and also in central Asia.[53]

How do these threatening specters become anything but negativity? In the case of mass incarceration, how does the haunted house of the prison become a haunting place, generative of a portentous specter of emancipatory transformation?

The short answer is that mass incarceration generates Critical Movements of Resistance[54] that bear emancipatory effect. This short answer, though, should not be taken as meaning there is anything simple or clean about this specter's emergence. The more emancipatory specter emerges amid the tumult that occurs when the "boomerang effect" takes place, to recall the trope from Césaire and Fanon. To recall a point made above, US mass incarceration is a feature of the colonial carceral, and as US leaders create or compromise with ever-expanding and more dehumanizing enforcements abroad of a lockdown of peoples (political, economic, military, as well as carceral—the latter rampant in US centers of interrogation maintained worldwide), those leaders at home create similarly brutal and dehumanizing carceral institutions. The colonizer abroad, to recall Césaire again, is dehumanized to the point of transforming "*himself* into an animal," and thus cannot help but act accordingly at home. Mass incarceration is, in effect, a reflex, a boomerang effect (Césaire), a vicious circle (Chow) by which the colonial carceral comes home. As the destruction "comes home," though, so does the resistance amid the tumult, just as the Arab Spring (2011) has broken loose against

---

[53] Ahmed Rashid, *Descent into Chaos: The United States and the Failure of Nation Building in Pakistan, Afghanistan, and Central Asia* (New York: Viking, 2008).

[54] I capitalize Critical Movement(s) of Resistance, as I did American Romanticism and Contractual Liberalism, to highlight the spectral power of these formations.

US-backed regimes abroad. As US hyperincarceration increases, the tumult will be society wide, even as efforts and expenditures by guardians of the neoliberal carceral state will increase, with likely increases in brutality and neglect, to hold prison populations at bay, within the walls.

These efforts, though, will be in vain. The simple fact of the revolving door between society and prison assures this. The population of 2.3 million in US prisons and jails is not static. Some 644,000 enter prison every year, while about 625,000 are set back outside.[55] Never mind that many of these are recidivists, often the same people going in as have come out; still, the pathologies of disease and social distortion (racism, sexism, homophobia and class division, and exploitation) all grow stronger throughout the larger society as those coming and going circulate and recirculate their brutalized and brutalizing actions in larger circles of society. The carceral and its pathologies, increasingly, cannot be kept within prison walls.

This upheaval for wider society is foreshadowed in the two decades of research undertaken by scholars detailing the "collateral consequences" of mass incarceration.[56] These include (a) increased social immiseration of children, as offspring of the incarcerated swell the ranks of the impoverished, (b) the stigmatization of communities of color to the point that even after many of their members' release, persisting unemployment, disfranchisement, and lack of healthcare lock them and their families into caste exclusion, and (c) the erosion of law and its force, as groups most susceptible to incarceration become so routinized by it that imprisonment is "depenalized," to use ethicist James Logan's term. As Logan writes, overall mass incarceration has the collateral consequence of destroying "social capital," the "thick networks of social relations and its needed norms of reciprocity, trust and honesty."[57] The transnational architects of the neoliberalism that destroys economic safety nets and constructs the carceral state as dragnet are creating *within* the United States a society siphoning off ever large numbers of its own into the "world precariate," those "underdeveloped" countries of the Global South that are a legacy of European colonizing structural dynamics.

In sum, the prison's ontology as hauntology is such that it "houses being" in US society, in the sense of constituting a social structure in

---

[55] Logan, *Good Punishment?* 62.

[56] Marc Mauer, *Invisible Punishment: The Collateral Consequences of Mass Imprisonment* (New York: The New Press, 2003). See also The Sentencing Project at the sentencingproject.org website.

[57] Logan, *Good Punishment?* 91.

the present that is a culmination of US history's always spectral traditions of antagonism—particularly those of American Romanticism and Contractual Liberalism. How, though, amid the tumult effected by the prison's housing of these specters, does a transformative specter arise, and what is its nature? I turn, now, to these questions.

The Prison and Liberating Spectrality

The prison, and mass incarceration generally in the United States, takes on its own positive, spectral form as it births Critical Movements of Resistance. These movements also have a historical lineage that comes to fruition in its spectral power. Throughout the history of the United States, and during European colonization, and across the tricontinental fields of the Global South (Latin America, Asia, Africa), resistance to Western hegemony has been ongoing. There is operative here a distinctive—often unheralded, denied, and repressed—world revolutionary tradition, with a unique history of movement struggle, subjectivity, and mythic language, which I have detailed elsewhere.[58] It was often labeled and feared as "the Hydra," and heroic Western powers and personalities styled themselves as so many apparitions of Hercules aiming to slay this Hydra. At the time of the founding of the United States, white property owners, while establishing their new government, feared this "mob," this "mobility dangerous to the gentry," as "founding father" Governeur Morris observed.[59] Yet the same elite founders drew much of their own reforming zeal from the "driving revolutionary force" of the multitude of groups pressing for liberation, from slavery, imperial impressments in the navies, and so on. This "mobility," a "motley crew" historically analyzed by historians Peter Linebaugh and Marcus Rediker, represented displaced and dispossessed peoples of all continents. The founders may have tapped the driving force of these revolutionary groups, but they then capped their liberatory aspirations—most notably in the new US government's decision to preserve slavery.[60] But the history of resistance never died.[61]

---

[58] Taylor, *Religion, Politics, and the Christian Right*, 110–23.

[59] Ibid., 110.

[60] Peter Linebaugh and Marcus Rediker, *The Many-Headed Hydra: Sailors, Slaves, Commoners, and the Hidden History of the Revolutionary Atlantic* (Boston: Beacon Press, 2000), 3–6, 331. On the notion of "the motley crew," see 27–28, and as "driving revolutionary force," 212–14.

[61] For a history of these movements across the tricontinental South and their relations to emancipator theory, see Richard J. C. Young, *Postcolonialism: An*

The Specter of Critical Movements of Resistance

The specter of a Critical Movement of Resistance (CMR) amid the tumult of mass incarceration today is made possible by this historical lineage of resistance. Movements of resistance are many, and they are at work from all sides of the political continuum. The movements of resistance we most need, and which in fact are arising amid mass incarceration, are "Critical" movements. As *critical,* I stress that the movement of resistance is marked by an ethos of deliberation and analysis that extends throughout movement work (here, *critical* in the general sense as reflective, thoughtfully attentive to complexity, including an openness to self-criticism). Beyond this general meaning, the notion of *critical* also specifies that movement work will foster and integrate three important impulses of movement life. Without these, a CMR will be neither critical nor effective toward liberation. There are three such critical impulses.

First, there is an *owning of agonistic being,* wherein the communities understand themselves as under pressure, existing in an agonism. There is also, here, a consciousness of antagonism that marks movement members' daily living and sets the terms of their larger projects. Incarcerated persons and groups, for example, their friends and families, and persons of conscience throughout the society of the carceral state, take the antagonism—particularly its generation of rage and lament or mourning—and chisel it into an oppositional stance. That stance can be oppositional and still "critical" in the general sense of dealing with what Avery Gordon terms "complex personhood" and "ensembles of social relations."[62]

Second, there is a *cultivating of artful reflex.* Here a CMR—this, not just as a second step but an impulse simultaneous to the previous owning of agonistic being—expresses and performs its penchant for artful and imaginative vision. The artful reflex may be an almost immediately reflexive move, a subtle gesture, even some "gimmick" (as James Baldwin found so necessary even for the child of color who knows something is wrong in a racist world but has not yet been able to say and think what it is).[63] This might take the form of a pose, a kind of carriage of the body struck by women at times in patriarchal systems, by youth of color on the street, by imprisoned

Historical Introduction (New York: Blackwell, 2001).

   [62] Gordon, *Ghostly Matters,* 4–7.

   [63] James Baldwin, *The Fire Next Time* (New York: Modern Library, 1995 <1962>), 23.

men striking the pose of toughness, by a child alone in a room full of adults. These poses and reflex gestures are a creative arrangement of the body and part of what Bourdieu termed the *hexis*, the symbolizing motor functions of the body under pressures of domination.[64]

In the CMRs that become spectral, though, these artful reflexes are only the starting point. They are further honed for a more creative, dramatic, even theatrical resistance to the incarcerating transnational powers in the United States generating mass incarceration. Indeed, the dramatic, the theatrical, becomes especially important in a media-saturated age wherein information technology wields media images to create spectacles that assure domination, enlisting citizen fear and fascination for fealty to state powers. Most of all, the artistic reflex, thus cultivated, offers to CMRs, amid their agonistic sensibility, a celebratory function, a foretasting of the futures they dream and for which they struggle. Prisoners taking up the paint brush, the pen to create poetry and prose while confined, or the song while they are on the chain gang, are cases in point. So also are the activists readying the singers, the artists, the rhetoricians for social movement gatherings, which are designed to engage the agonistic community in pressing toward its goals. The artful reflex, a first gesture of survival under repression, is cultivated, here, as a strategy for highlighting and sharpening a resisting movement's protests, criticisms, and organizational structure. These reflexes also are essential for knowing a celebratory flourishing. All are crucial for the making of hope and becoming truly spectral amid a mass incarceration system that will not easily or quickly be dislodged.[65]

Third, there is the *fomenting of resistant and emancipatory practices*. This fomenting follows the first mark of critical resistant communities, the *owning of agonistic being*, which, as an owning, is an acceptance, an acknowledgment, one made perhaps reluctantly but with a sense of resolve, a resolution to see one's being as what it is, in struggle, labile, tense, in readiness for tasks, but first known simply as a "being-so-poised." Fomenting practices, now, also follow the *cultivating of artful reflex*. The fomenting, I stress, is dependent upon the owning of antagonism and the cultivating or artful reflex. While

[64] Pierre Bourdieu, *The Logic of Practice* (Stanford, CA: Stanford University Press, 1990), 74.

[65] A point underscored in the conclusion of Alexander's *The New Jim Crow*, 209–48.

fomenting is, as dictionary definitions remind us, a stirring up, an instigating of revolutionary tumult, maybe of strife, it is helpful to recall its etymological roots as "poultice, lotion" (Latin, *fomentum*). So here, the fomenting emancipatory practices are not just liberations from mass incarceration, but also restorative, an effort for new, redressive structures. Fomenting, then, is ultimately the living into practices that bring a salve, a mass that soothes the inflammation of tense, labile pain of agonistic being.

I can sum up all these traits adhering in CMRs by referring to a remarkable passage in Judith Butler's recent work. There, she refers to the power of those encaged at the US base in Guantánamo, who with their poetic skills, published only after strenuous efforts by lawyers and publishers, found a way to connect and foment change. Butler writes:

> The Guantánamo poems are full of longing; they sound the incarcerated body as it makes its appeal. Its breathing is impeded, and yet it continues to breathe. The poems communicate another sense of solidarity, of interconnected lives that carry on each others' words, suffer each others' tears, and form networks that pose an incendiary risk not only to national security, but to the form of global sovereignty championed by the U.S.[66]

The passage powerfully reminds us that communities of critical resistance are not all agony and art. They are that, but as networks whose practices have transformative effect, they put at risk, even pose an "incendiary risk," to structures of global US sovereignty. This is to strike right at the heart of the specters of negativity, American Romanticism, and Contractual Liberalism, which drive mass incarceration today. Here, antagonistic sensibility and artistic expression constitute, through these practices of the CMR, a force of resistance and subversion to exploitative power. Practice gives a certain forceful "hardness" to lament and artistic expression. This is intimated by a lyric from the corpus of US balladeer Bruce Springsteen in an album that targets the post–2008 economic unemployment crisis. While Springsteen's overall project is not free enough from American Romanticism to erode its negative spectrality, he does get the point of art's transformative power under conditions of economic and political antagonism. In one song he advises,

[66] Judith Butler, *Frames of War: When Is Life Grievable?* (New York: Verso, 2009), 61–62.

Now get yourself a song to sing . . .
Yeah, sing it hard and sing it well
Send the robber barons straight to hell.[67]

Still more tellingly, another artist, in another time, suffering the colonial carceral in Vietnam of 1973, signals the spectral challenge. In US detention there, Chim Trang wrote:

The song now rises as high as the flames of hatred
now whispers softly, kind and tender
Now glows like the sun and glitters like the lodestar
Now thunders down the prisons.[68]

The three critical impulses together create a force of networking people, that "power of the people" much referenced in CMRs ("the people" as *el pueblo,* in Spanish, *Atlepetl* in Aztec, *Amaq'* in Maya, *sha'b* in Arabic, *mian* in Chinese, *minjung* in Korean). In Enrique Dussel's language, the people is "a bloc from below," made up of many needs (of say, the imprisoned, immigrant populations; urban communities of color; indigenous people; women of color; men and women of all backgrounds in labor and industry)—all to rival the forces positioned in antagonism against them.[69]

This provides a rough outline of the dynamics that make CMRs a specter of threat and promise. What chance is there for Christians, those constituting themselves in the way of Jesus, to approximate or contribute, along with their theologians, to such CMRs? Is there a Christian theo-poetic that might "sing it hard and sing it well" and so help constitute the specter that "thunders down the prisons"?

Tracing Marks of a Christian Theo-Poetic

A Christian theo-poetic, its artful discourse with emancipatory effect, can be found in the way gospel stories, as informed also by

---

[67] Bruce Springsteen, from "Death to My Hometown," *Wrecking Ball* (New York: Sony Records, 2012). For an invaluable critique of the politics of Springsteen, see Bryan K. Garman, *A Race of Singers: Whitman's Working Class Hero from Guthrie to Springsteen* (Greensboro: University of North Carolina Press, 2000).

[68] Chim Trang, from "The Rising Song," in *Hauling Up the Morning/Izando la Mañana: Writings and Art by Political Prisoners of War in the United States,* ed. Tim Blunk and Raymond Luc Levasseur (Trenton, NJ: Red Sea Press, 1990), 367.

[69] On his theorization of the people, see Dussel, *Twenty Theses on Politics,* 73–77.

pre-gospel biblical tradition(s),[70] support and participate in CMRs, as sketched above. The discourses occurring around the figure of Jesus and its early movement can be interpreted as both a contribution to and participation in the specter of CMRs, so needed in this moment of US governance become carceral state. It is crucial not to idealize Christian discourse and references to Jesus. They have played key roles in the very establishment of the carceral state and its sovereignty today, and helped fuel the specters of negativity we have examined, both American Romanticism and Contractual Liberalism. The way of Jesus and its movement discourse, though, can be viewed as offering — to Christians with broad emancipatory interests, at least — a veritable spirituality of critical movement resistance. This is a spirituality that locates the dynamism of transformation not in a divine outside of history, in a transcendent beyond, which has mesmerized many Christians and offered grounding for the divine rights of kings and exploitative forces. It is more a spirituality that, following philosopher Jean-Luc Nancy's notion of "trans-immanence," works as an unlocking of the world's continual unfolding of itself to itself, and against those structures that would lock it down, lock the world in place.[71] The contemporary transnational project, its neoliberal hyperincarceration, seeks precisely that kind of lockdown, that lockdown of world and history. This Christian spirituality of critical resistance is a *theo*-poetic then, not because of a reference to a transcendent God *(theos)*, but because of its participation in the catalyzing specter eroding that lockdown. This spirituality entails a reimagining of early movements that sought to survive and challenge Roman imperial lockdown, not just as an anti-empire move, but one that sees the anti-imperial social living as also, simultaneously, a resistance to hegemonic constrictions set in this period by race, gender, and sexuality.[72]

Indeed, three dimensions of this spirituality, increasingly explored by recent scholarship, particularly in feminist and counter-imperial studies of Jesus discourse in the Roman period, are roughly analogous to the key dimensions of CMRs. We can discern them in relation to the crucifixion, the mode of Jesus' death.

---

[70] Elisabeth Schüssler Fiorenza, *Jesus: Miriam's Child, Sophia's Prophet* (New York: Continuum, 1994), 109–19.

[71] Taylor, *The Theological and the Political*, 125–38.

[72] For the kind of work on early movements sparked by Jesus and communities of his followers, see Davina C. Lopez, *Apostle to the Conquered: Reimagining Paul's Mission* (Minneapolis, MN: Fortress Press, 2010), 122–24, 227n27.

First, the Christian way of the cross and its sociality is marked by a *politically adversarial* practice. Here, there is opposition. It is difficult to overlook that Christian gospel themes and historical accounts indicating that Jesus' life and way of dying entailed an adversarial stance toward religio-political systems of domination. This was evident, especially, in Jesus' opposition to the practices of the Temple State, which were not only antithetical to his religious views, but also constituted a system inconsistent with the political and economic dimensions of the great Hebrew prophets' vision.[73] To be sure, the very notions of opposition and adversarial practice, at the level of strategies, would be uniquely recalibrated, as I will note in discussing the second dimension, below. There is adversality even in Jesus' oft-noted ethic of love of the enemy, in its very pre-supposition that there *is* an enemy, indeed, a matrix of antagonism and adversarial forces at play.

I doubt there will be any effective Christian practice to take on the spectral forces that sediment in mass incarceration unless Christians understand their faith to be about a state of adversarial resistance to dominative structures. The Jesus who was put to death on the Roman cross, with the support of religious officials and crowds, is a Jesus who suffered an imperial execution. Let me be blunt. It was not a cross he chose to go to intending to make payment or transaction to secure forgiveness for all the world, as many American evangelicals claim. This is a strong universalist claim for Christianity that often resonates with expansionist ideologies of American Romanticism. Such an ideological rendering of Jesus' life and work is largely a later construction of the meaning of Jesus' death. Moreover, it abstracts almost completely from the set of meanings that attach to his con-crete mode of dying, that is, imperially executed. As thus abstracted, the meaning of Jesus' death is taken as a salvific transaction that can occur anywhere, and usually outside the adversarial space of exis-tence limned by Jesus and his early followers. They approximated something like "a discipleship of equals," and constituted, according to Elisabeth Schüssler Fiorenza, "*ekklesia* of wo/man."[74] This is no liberal community touting difference and tolerance, but a commu-nity (a called group, *ekklesia*) accenting egalitarianism against the background of life in antagonism with kyriarchal powers (another

---

[73] For one summary of the literature on the "Temple State," see Ched Myers, *Binding the Strong Man: A Political Reading of Mark's Story of Jesus* (Maryknoll, NY: Orbis Books, 1997), 78–87.

[74] Elisabeth Schüssler Fiorenza, *The Power of the Word: Scripture and the Rheto-ric of Empire* (Minneapolis, MN: Fortress Press, 2007).

name for imperial power, but indicating the sovereign power of diverse lords — *kyrioi* — of state, household, city, and so on).[75] Any love and care associated with Jesus' teaching and being lose their meanings if we lose sight of the politically adversarial contestation at work amid situations of imperial and colonial antagonism.

Second, the social space of the way of the cross is *mimetic*.[76] I choose this word to signal that Christian practices employ a full range of artistic representations, ranging from creative storytelling, to creative actions and dramatic events. The parables and street theater of Jesus are exemplary here, as explored by Ched Myers, Marcus Borg, and John Dominic Crossan.[77] It is with its deployment of the arts, seeking out creativity and drama, that Christian practice marshals most directly a poetics to challenge the powers at work in the theaters of state power. It is in this mimetic dimension that the "theatrical" nature of the Christian way of the cross is developed most fully.

A Christian theatric, especially as focused on Jesus' death on the cross, challenges violent mechanisms of power and unleashes a countervailing power from nonviolent action undertaken with dramatic creativity. In this, it respects the artful reflex of CMRs and cultivates it in a particularly dramatic way. In so doing, the Christian theatric offers up far more than simply a violence-renouncing pacifism. Instead, it taps the power of aesthetic creativity to challenge violent mechanisms of power. In fact, pacifism is not a good word at all for this Christian theatric. It does not allow adequately for reading Jesus' nonviolence *as* a mode of contestation and adversarial practice. It certainly does not do justice to the modes of creative, adversarial practice that Mahatma Gandhi, Martin Luther King, Jr., Larry Itliong, Cesar Chavez, and others have advocated and forged for "nonviolent creative *direct action*," and which we must forge today.[78] Reading King on nonviolence, for example, is

---

[75] See Aníbal Quijano, "Coloniality of Power, Eurocentrism, and Latin America," *Napantla: Views from the South* 1/3 (2000): 533–78.

[76] On the notion of mimesis more broadly, see Eric Auerbach, *Mimesis: The Representation of Reality in Western Literature* (Princeton, NJ: Princeton University Press, 1953).

[77] Marcus Borg and John Dominic Crossan, *The Last Week: What the Gospels Really Teach About Jesus' Final Days in Jerusalem* (New York: HarperOne, 2007); and Myers, *Binding the Strong Man*, 294.

[78] Readers seeking a "uniqueness" for Christian contributions to CMRs may find it in this particular way of theatrically nurturing the artful reflex. But I hasten to say that while Christians, at their best, lift up this feature of Jesus' way, they are not the only ones among religious communities who can do so.

always to be reminded again that the hallmark of nonviolent love is not passivity, not even first of all nonviolence, but instead creativity and imagination become dramatic actions that rally a public to its sense of conscience.[79]

This creative drama, this mimetic second dimension is key, so let me elaborate further. Jesus' death on the cross, itself, was theatrical both in its nature, an imperial execution, but also as to its effects, the ways later Jesus movement followers, and pre-gospel and gospel writers, experienced from it a strange dramaturgy. As to its nature and function, recall that Jesus' execution by crucifixion was one of many in his period. Their function was not unlike lynchings in the United States, as noted most recently in James Cone's *The Cross and the Lynching Tree*.[80] Crucifixions were, as early Christianity scholar Paula Fredricksen points out, like a "public service announcement" saying, in effect, "do not engage in sedition, as this person has, or your fate will be similar."[81] But the effects of Jesus' imperial crucifixion were not limited to those intended by the penal state. Followers and later interpreters would exploit a theatrical reading that intensified the contrast between so ignominious a political end (executed, low-status criminal), on the one hand, with a life lived beforehand marked by creative actions and teachings about radically inclusive love that transgressed the ways of the religio-political state. So, Jesus' death was a lifting up, a theatrical uprising of sorts, in ways that galvanized audiences and set them in motion. As I explained at length in *The Executed God*, this way of conjuring the site of torture, the cross, for ends that were unplanned by imperial powers, constitutes a "stealing of the show" in the realms of spectacle. Paul, and later the gospel writers, would conjure the cross for audiences that knew it to be a tool of the torture state.[82] Part of the stealing of the show was to galvanize audiences in their living against, alternative to, the *Pax*

Almost *all* religious traditions have thrown in their lot with violence, but many, too, deploy highly creative modes of nonviolent resistance, for example, Islam. See Eknath Easwaran, *Nonviolent Soldier of Islam: Badshah Khan, A Man to Match His Mountains* (Tomales, CA: Nilgiri Press, 1999).

[79] Martin Luther King, Jr., "Nonviolence: The Only Road to Freedom," in *Testament of Hope: The Essential Writings and Speeches of Martin Luther King, Jr.,* ed. James M. Washington (New York: HarperSanFrancisco, 1986), 54–61.

[80] James Cone, *The Cross and the Lynching Tree* (Maryknoll, NY: Orbis Books, 2011).

[81] Paula Fredricksen, *Jesus of Nazareth, King of the Jews: A Jewish Life and the Emergence of Christianity* (New York: Knopf, 1999), 233.

[82] Taylor, *The Executed God*, 99–126.

Romana. This, now, points us to the third dimension of the way of the cross.

In a third dimension I stress that the sociality intrinsic to the way of the cross is *kinetic;* that is, it is moving and dynamic. It embeds its adversarial and mimetic strategies in concrete movements for change in history. Movements are about forming new relations and coalitions for some transformative purpose. A multitude of Jesus' teachings and concerns lend themselves to movement building in their continual references to social relations, indeed, to a *basileia tou theou* (a kingdom of God) as alternative to dominative rule. This entailed raising profound themes of love and justice, again from especially Hebrew traditions. In this way, like good CMRs, the social theatricality of the way of the cross forges relations into practices, fomenting practices through its adversarial arts. A Christian theatric that would really counter the powers of a penal state today is not content with mere personal stances or with occasional actions of creative nonviolent drama. No, it presses further and seeks to embody these in the organizing of movements, seeking to sustain life-renewing activity and communal work. It is this movement-oriented character of the theatric that prevents the way of the cross from becoming a mere aestheticism. Walter Benjamin warned that "all efforts to render politics aesthetic culminate in one thing: war."[83] He feared especially the aesthetic becoming a tool in the hands of the state, and indeed the Nazi rally throngs exemplify Benjamin's worry. What saves a Christian aesthetic from that end is not only its qualitatively different mode of contestation, in contrast to fascist state violence, but also the fact that its mimesis, its aesthetics, is situated in CMRs to such hegemonic (kyriarchal) state powers. Its sociality is informed by ideals of justice and love, not those of national or transnational projects that impose conditions of the carceral or war-making state. Again, we know too many cases of Christians taking the Constantinian way, underwriting and invigorating the most destructive punitive and military acts of state.[84] But the way of the cross can be construed differently, highlighting another political track that has historical precedent. If political theorist Michael Doyle is correct, then we do

---

[83] Walter Benjamin, "The Work of Art in the Age of Mechanical Reproduction," in Walter Benjamin, *Illuminations: Essays and Reflections*, ed. Hannah Arendt, 217–52 (New York: Schocken Books, 1969; original essay published in German in 1936), 241.

[84] On the long history of Christians supporting torture, punitive systems, and war, see James J. Megivern, *The Death Penalty: An Historical and Theological Survey* (New York: Paulist Press, 1997).

well to recall that early Christian movements helped sap the military and civic power of Rome's imperial and conquering aspirations.[85] Similarly, sociologist Rodney Stark describes the rise of early Christianity as "one of the most successful revitalization movements in history."[86] We wait amid these latter times of *Pax Americana* – its powers waning amid its own generated imperial hypertrophy – for those Christians who will lend their presence to such CMRs today.

Conclusion: Mothers on the Move in the Carceral State

I close with an example from a group working in California against the neoliberal state, not only involving people of faith, but also those of many backgrounds in CMRs. Christians were involved here, but this largely extra-Christian movement exemplifies for Christians and others what the emancipatory specter sparked by mass incarceration can look like. This movement bears witness to the compelling force of the specter of CMRs. Moreover, we might say, *this*, below, is what mass incarceration becoming a "compelling theological issue" looks like. Again, the compelling issue rides the force of the specter.

Mothers Reclaiming Our Children, or Mothers ROC (even more briefly, MROC), is the name of this group, and its story is narrated in a sixty-page chapter by Ruth Wilson Gilmore in *Golden Gulag,* about neoliberalism's penal state in California.[87] MROC "evolved from a self-help group that formed in response to a crisis of place – a police murder in South Central Los Angeles."[88] In 1992, when first formed by Barbara Meredith and Francie Arbol, a crisis was looming, and it would only become worse with time: "the state locking their children, of all ages, into the criminal justice system."[89] MROC was certainly an adversarial group, mothers opposing what was done to their children and "organizing opposition to the state's form and purpose,"[90] living in the agonism and antagonism with which this situation is fraught. MROC generated a host of practices that are ongoing. Founded first by African American mothers, it attracted hundreds of mothers and family members of the incarcerated into its work.

[85] Michael Doyle, *Empires* (Ithaca, NY: Cornell University Press, 1986), 98.
[86] Rodney Stark, *The Rise of Christianity: A Sociologist Reconsiders History* (Princeton, NJ: Princeton University Press, 1996), 9.
[87] Gilmore, *Golden Gulag,* chap. 5, 181–240.
[88] Ibid., 239.
[89] Ibid., 181.
[90] Ibid., 247.

Soon, its campaigns "brought Chicanas, other Latinas, and white women to Mothers ROC for help. A few years into its existence, the group had Black, Brown, Asian American and white women and some men."[91] As the very different groups represented shows, MROC is reflective of a spirit of coalescing action reaching back to the third-world spirit of Bandung, where Asians, Africans, and Latin Americans met in 1956 to find a way beyond US imperialism and the Soviet system. As Vijay Prashad advises, this project of Bandung failed eventually, and should not nostalgically be embraced by activists today.[92] But neither should we foreclose the power of that legacy to haunt and transform the devastated landscape of America that recycles repression of the poor "Third World." Gilmore writes, "Mothers ROC consciously identified with Third World activist mothers, the name deliberately invoking South African, Palestinian, and Central and South American women's struggles."[93] If it is true that today's carceral state is, in part, a response to the mix of third-world nonalignment struggle and civil rights movements in the United States—"the era of 1968"[94]—then the lesson here is that such a mix is still a strong potion for change.[95]

As Gilmore treats MROC, though, what is crucial in terms of its participation in the specter of CMRs is the way MROC's acceptance of antagonism and agonism, generative of practices counter to the neoliberal carceral state, features that middle, enlivening dimension of drama, creativity, and imagination—the artful reflex, the mimetic power. In the very beginning MROC "convened its activism on the dispersed stages of the criminal justice system." The very tools of the repressive state, these places, like the sites of the cross, were reinhabited by the sufferer as a stage sending out an "unconditional invitation to all mothers and others struggling on behalf of their children."[96] They "stole the show" from the carceral state. They also leafleted the streets and took to the media, these venues themselves already theatrical. MROC made these sites *its* stage. Funerals of slain youth of color were fully that, full of mourning and lamentation and group solidarity, but also sites for rallies to be announced against

---

[91] Ibid., 184.

[92] Vijay Prashad, "Bandung Is Done: Passages in AfroAsian Epistemology," in *AfroAsian Encounters: Culture, History, Politics,* ed. Heike Raphael-Hernandez and Shannon Steen (New York: New York University Press, 2006), xi–xxiii.

[93] Gilmore, *Golden Gulag,* 184.

[94] Wacquant, *Punishing the Poor,* 287; see also Gilmore, *Golden Gulag,* 24–25.

[95] Prashad, "Bandung Is Done," xxi.

[96] Gilmore, *Golden Gulag,* 182.

police violence.⁹⁷ What emerged was what Gilmore terms "oppositional political arts centered on creating an order different from the one built by the state out of more and bigger prisons."⁹⁸

Many of the members of MROC were Christians, alongside many of interfaith communities, as well as peoples of conscience from humanist and other persuasions. The way prayer functioned at some MROC meetings is illustrative of the spectral power of the Critical Movement of Resistance. Gilmore notes that prayer had a way of "framing," setting MROC actions in a context full of deep significance. It involved bodies clasping hands, standing and sitting in circles, a listening among women gathered, especially to those with powers of the rhetorical art that churches would call preaching. Crucial in this, according to Gilmore, was a fostering of the sense of difficulty and urgency, a meditative pondering on power and powerlessness, also a play of mutual encouragement flowing between speakers and the gathered collective. Prayer "helped span the visible and invisible social distances among people for whom, in most cases, organized religion was a vital aspect of life."⁹⁹ In this space of meditation and resultant action, not only race, but also gender, sexuality, and especially class, all under the powers of neoliberal political economy, were brought to consciousness in varied and changing modalities.

Here among these mothers on the move is an exemplar of the CMRs needed today: agonism and antagonism, emancipatory practice, artfully woven to galvanize a countervailing specter. No wonder Gilmore places at the start of her chapter on MROC a women's political chant that was part of the anti-pass law movement in South Africa in 1956: "Now that you have touched the women, you have struck a rock, you have dislodged a boulder, and you will be crushed."¹⁰⁰ This is not only an art or song that sings "it hard and sings it well" (Springsteen), but it also begins to form the specter that "thunders down prisons" (Trang).

---

⁹⁷ Ibid., 202.
⁹⁸ Ibid., 236.
⁹⁹ Ibid., 222.
¹⁰⁰ Ibid., 181.

A Response to Mark Lewis Taylor

The Adequacy of Trans-Immanence for Decolonial Struggle

WILLIAM A. WALKER III

For many it might seem that the issue of mass incarceration in the United States, while it may be disquieting in some respects, is hardly "most compelling" as a subject for theological reflection. Mark Lewis Taylor makes a forceful and cogent case, however, that the expansive prison apparatus indeed marks a "boomerang effect" (Césaire) generated by the vicious legacy of US racism, unilateral military aggression and the "historical specters" of what he aptly dubs "American Romanticism" and "Contractual Liberalism." Mass incarceration is the product of "sedimenting" and "accumulated remains" from these lineages. As "prisons fill up," these histories as specters persist in the memories of present-day communities. In this way they "haunt" and remind us that the repression and discrimination of the past has not so much been abolished as it has assumed a new form.

Of all the alarming figures, perhaps most stunning is the fact that more African Americans are behind bars today than there were slaves in 1830. Taylor references Michelle Alexander's contention that the experience of the "carceral state" by minority groups today has created a racialized "caste" system. He notes, from sociologist Loïc Wacquant, how the prisons have become the primary means of managing socially and economically insecure populations. Moreover, once in prison, sexual assault and guard brutality are rampant for inmates. The question for Taylor, then, is how this crisis can become a positive force that issues in critical movements of resistance and liberating practice. First, though, his preliminary methodological clarifications are worth underlining toward this end.

Neither a mere agenda item nor an interpretation of a traditional theological or contemporary existential subject matter, mass incarceration becomes a compelling theological issue when it "charges a theologian's entire theological project and usually throws him or her into relationships of support and struggle with other thinkers and actors." Following David Tracy, Taylor asserts that the compelling issue gives intensity, animation, and distinctive character to the theologian's discourse in light of a particular social location. The compelling issue of sexism is one such example. The concern is galvanizing, pervasive, and "spectral," constituting a reimagination of the theological enterprise in terms of the compelling issue. Its urgency produces a sense of compulsion that reshapes one's very understandings of faithful Christian practice. As Taylor demonstrates in the remainder of his essay, mass incarceration is a candidate because, like sexism, it touches and distorts almost all levels of social being in the US context.

Moving from methodology to ontology, the use of Derrida's neologism *hauntology* evokes for Taylor the sense in which the prison is symbolic of society's guardianship—how it "houses," controls, and disposes of bodies, "enforcing fundamental antagonisms etched into the structured practices of daily living." It is a "house of being." Moreover, the prison house must be seen against the backdrop of Jim Crow, colonialism, slavery, and conquest. How telling that Native Americans have the highest per capita incarceration rate. Furthermore, mass incarceration indicates the present investment and interests of weapons industries in the architecture and marketing of confinement and surveillance technology.

The specters already mentioned of American Romanticism and Contractual Liberalism name and signal the major forces that drive and characterize US history, referring specifically to the American exceptionalist myth and Christian religious notions of mission, on the one hand, and the ideological promise of life, liberty, and the pursuit of happiness for an enabled minority, on the other. About the latter, this US "overclass," in keeping with Wacquant and Gilmore, has felt itself under social and economic threat by the still limited progress of workers and civil rights movements, incentivizing the recasting of these groups as evidence of an imminent "criminal insecurity" endangering the greater public. The result has been the development of a transnational neoliberalism that withdraws social support services and augments deregulatory economics.

Accordingly, Taylor calls for a response in theo-poetic fashion, which is not reducible to the level of political economy but is also concerned with affecting culture and stirring artistic expression of creative storytelling, dramatic and performative acts of resistance to both express and catalyze a social movement against the oppressive force of mass incarceration. So, an appropriate Critical Movement of Resistance (CMR) will take broader and deeper forms than mere advocacy for change in policy at the political-economic level. It will be more total than that, consisting of at least three visible marks of critical resistance. The specter of a Christian decolonizing effort, according to Taylor, is constituted by dynamic social existence moving from (1) owning of agonistic being, (2) cultivating of artful reflex, and (3) fomenting of counter-colonial practices. The fomenting, Taylor stresses, is dependent upon the owning and the cultivating.

Finally, tracing the distinctives of a Christian theo-poetic challenge to mass incarceration, for inspiration Taylor deliberately makes no reference to a transcendent Other or to knowledge that is dependent on some kind of revelation from beyond or outside. Instead, Taylor wishes to invoke a neither fully immanent nor a transcendent mode of trans-existence or trans-immanence (Nancy) that is infinite, opposing any attempt to lockdown the world as is or close it off, as it were, and envisaging the world as unfolding.

A theo-poetic challenge, however, is nevertheless firmly grounded in the way of the cross for Taylor, and there are three main features to this way. It is (1) *politically adversarial*, analogous to Jesus' own life and ministry; (2) *mimetic* and theatrical, off-setting the unpredictable, theatrical performance of the state, and creatively dramatic—crucial, Taylor says, for unleashing a countervailing power much like Jesus's crucifixion did by challenging violent mechanisms of power, and finally, (3) *kinetic*—moving and dynamic—which sets in motion an organized embodiment that seeks to "sustain life-renewing activity and communal work" by extending Jesus's own "radically inclusive love that transgressed the ways of the religio-political state." Thus, Taylor firmly believes that the power of a vulnerable, networking people who bear the weight of produced social suffering is sufficient and more suited than traditional transcendent references to ignite and organize a counter-carceral movement, and he finishes by highlighting poignant contemporary examples of this in the Mother's Reclaiming Our Children (MROC) movement, noting the significance of its extra-Christian character.

In my view, Taylor successfully demonstrates that mass incarceration meets the criteria for a compelling theological issue. More than this, Taylor gives his own succinct and coherent justification for what should constitute a compelling theological issue as such. Consistent with the rest of his corpus, Taylor shows a remarkable aptitude for inventive and original political and theological thought on matters of ultimate and urgent social concern. In both Taylor's style and substance, one is presented with conviction and erudition. Perhaps most pertinent is Taylor's deliberate attention to concrete and imitable CMRs. His is a method of exemplary theological praxis. For the sake of this volume's interest in theology proper, then, and although it is not the focus of his essay, I have chosen to limit my response to what Taylor alleges ontologically about the difference between and expediency of the concepts of trans-immanence and transcendence. This will require some reference to Taylor's work elsewhere, but I will keep this to a minimum. I realize such a one-sided dialogue may be unfair; I leave that for the reader to determine. Additionally, I decided to take this approach primarily because there is little else about which I feel obliged to comment in light of such a lucid piece.

In calling on a notion of trans-immanence, Taylor explicitly denies that the "unlocking of the world's continual unfolding of itself to itself, and against those structures that would lock it down, lock the world in place" need reference a transcendent God. But trans-immanence, as Nancy has it, is an open immanence, not a closed one.[1] In fact, it is resistance to closure, and thus constructive and surely a viable concept for thinking resistance. Trans-immanence for Taylor, after Nancy, is conceived as "ex-positional through the arts, works to clear passage ways, moving deftly, creatively, to make place(s) and space(s) of world."[2] It "names within Nancy's project the dynamic, ceaselessly flowing sense of the world, liberating world continually into itself, evolving and revolving into even more textured and artfully ex-posited complexity . . . a 'revolt of bodies' toward 'freedom.'"[3] Taylor insists that "within the larger discussions of transcendence and immanence, then, Nancy's 'trans-immanence' is not simply a matter of having done with both . . . Nancy, instead, strikes a neither/nor to transcendence/immanence, recasting both in the discursive milieu of trans-immanence."[4] Art is the supreme expression of trans-immanence, it appears, which is presumably why for Taylor an "artful response" is the catalyst for social movements. Yet communities that own agonistic being and foment in counter-colonial practice are not merely weighed-down victims defending

---

[1] B. C Hutchens, *Jean-Luc Nancy and the Future of Philosophy* (Montreal: McGill-Queen's University Press, 2005), 167.

[2] See the marklewistaylor.net website.

[3] Ibid.

[4] Ibid.

themselves; rather, Taylor intimates that they are communities with moral agency.

Trans-immanence further connotes a dialectic with transcendence, though the latter is not a necessary precondition for thinking the former. At this point one may be left wondering what role, exactly, transcendence has in Taylor's ontology other than as that which, while referenced, is refused and declared a failure. Taylor elsewhere explains that, like Laclau, "Nancy's refusal is a deliberate working amid the ruins of transcendence."[5] Trans-immanence, then, is a crossing, but only to another world "within." While Taylor does not intend for trans-immanence to accent pure immanence, or to think "world" as opposed to "God," his brief account may leave some less than persuaded of this. A synonymous concept to trans-immanence might be "non-reductive immanence," but this hardly equals "neither immanence nor transcendence," as Taylor words it.[6] Trans-immanence remains immanent, and transcendence is still repudiated. Thus, a question arises for me here: Once on a totally immanent plane, despite being able to traverse, slide, or pass through it, does one not suffer from having to choose between saying either too little or too much—too little because human efforts to achieve their ideals are futile, and too much because, when means for striving to achieve these ideals are absolutized, the cost to human life is often immense?

In *Crítica de la Razón Utópica*, Franz Hinkelammert makes a distinction between transcendental imagination and transcendental concepts that may be instructive. Transcendental concepts, for Hinkelammert,

> begin with the objective social relations between subjects and take them to the limits of concepts of institutional perfection. Transcendental imagination, in contrast, begins with the effectively experienced mutual recognition between subjects, [and] transcendentalizes them in a situation of perfection. In the face of the rigidity of the perfect institutions there appears the fluidity of great joy.[7]

Transcendental concepts are conservative by nature, always working from within the limits of the present political apparatus for the

---

[5] Ibid.

[6] Mark L. Taylor, *The Theological and the Political: On the Weight of the World* (Minneapolis: Fortress Press, 2011), 184.

[7] Franz J. Hinkelammert and Juan Antonio Senent de Frutos, *Crítica de la razón utópica* (Bilbao, Spain: Desclee de Brouwer, 2002), 343.

transformation of society. The transcendental imagination, however, is critical of the prevailing structure, because it "places human subjectivity at the core of what is possible, which, in turn, relativizes institutions."[8] Consequently, utopian imagination is like a transcendence *from below*, which believes that the world can be different, and "emerges from alternative concrete experiences, bring[ing] with it what the biblical tradition calls a revelation."[9]

The notion of trans-immanence may be near to this idea of transcendence from below at first glance, but whereas Taylor denies divine transcendence, I find in God's otherness tremendous recourse to both criticism of the carceral state and energy for opposing it. Nevertheless, if Taylor prefers to keep *divine* transcendence within an immanent scope, he can certainly do so, and he is straightforward about his intentions in this regard. Until now, though, this analysis risks conflating the political and theological. While inseparable, for purposes of clarity I propose a distinction between political transcendence, on the one hand, and God's transcendence, on the other. Concerning *political* transcendence, Taylor's employment of trans-immanence may both resonate with and be enhanced by what Rieger, Míguez, and Sung argue in *Beyond Empire,* namely, that transcendence should be humanized, but not immanentized. For Sung in particular, the question is less about *whether* transcendence, but *which,* and how much such transcendence says human beings can achieve for themselves — that is, how realizable their utopia is for a given transcendental horizon. Eschatologically and politically, Sung understands transcendence, as utopia, to be an essential dimension to all human belief and life. According to Sung:

> We cannot think and live without a utopian horizon that provides meaning for our journey and measure and norms for interpreting and judging reality and also the recognition that our utopia, however desirable it may be, is not realizable in its fullness, are fundamental conditions for our reasoning not to be lost in confusion and not to be carried along by the perversions and sacrifices imposed and demanded in the name of the full realization of utopia.[10]

---

[8] Néstor Míguez, Joerq Rieger, and Jung Mo Sung, *Beyond the Spirit of Empire: Theology and Politics in a New Key* (London: SCM Press, 2009), 122.

[9] Ibid., 123.

[10] Ibid., 118.

For theorists Hardt and Negri, as with Nancy, "Empire" — which is closely comparable to Taylor's depiction of American Romanticism and Contractual Liberalism — is described as thoroughly immanent. Empire is the nature of the "soft" power of capital in contrast to the overt dominance or "transcendence" of the nation-state. Sung retorts, however, that Hardt and Negri have misdiagnosed Empire, and it is possible Taylor has done the same with the carceral state. In other words, maybe the specter of the prison system is too pervasive and ideologically "transcendent" itself — albeit a *false* transcendence — to be offset with mere trans-immanence. Maybe a robust and imaginative eschatology could make the prison specter less haunting and expose its futility. But this is still to speak of political transcendence — the historical or horizontal, as it were. I now turn to theological transcendence.

For Néstor Míguez:

> If Jesus the Nazarene is, somehow, the presence of the transcendent in the everyday world, of the universal God who is expressed in peculiarity, of the absolute incarnate in the temporary and limited — that is to say, shown as the material — and, moreover, the creator of the human exhibited on the cross as the dehumanized of the system, this marks one complete break between glory and human wisdom (which reaches its culmination in Empire) and glory and divine knowledge. *But this break is not in the distinction between the transcendent and the immanent, between faith and politics, because the transcendent is included in the immanent, but in its most oppressed way — he became a slave* (emphasis added).[11]

In *The Executed God*, Taylor appreciates as well as anyone the historical, political, and social dimensions of Jesus's ministry and death, which is essential for stirring a counter-carceral Christian theology.[12] The danger of ideological abstraction from the concrete significance of Jesus's death cannot be overstated, as Taylor rightly warns. It is no exaggeration, in my estimation, to assert that, without embodying Jesus's own adversarial resistance to dominative structures, the gospel message itself will be misconstrued. Furthermore, Taylor

---

[11] Ibid., 196–97.

[12] Mark L Taylor, *The Executed God: The Way of the Cross in Lockdown America* (Minneapolis, MN: Fortress Press, 2001).

equally cautions against the establishment of a liberal community of difference and tolerance. Having said this, is it not also true that the greatest power of Jesus's life as a critique of the political and religious establishment is principally derived from the early Philippians' hymn about the incarnation of divine transcendence in the immanence of a human being? To be sure, as Míguez maintains, the transcendent must make itself accessible to the immanent and *from* the immanent. This is why I have employed the terminology of transcendence from below. But the immanent would cease to be immanent if it could transcend itself, which is what Taylor seems to be proposing in the idea of trans-immanence.

If, traditionally, transcendence and immanence only have a binary relationship, and if the objective of credentialed theology is primarily directed toward organizing doctrine, the church, and human life in reference to the transcendent Other, as Taylor supposes, then I join Taylor in abandoning the enterprise. If transcendence inhibits creative, artistic expression and its coming forth from the liminal realm of agonistic politics — that is, from the subalterns who experience and bear most intensely the weight of the world and the full force of socially imposed suffering[13] — then I too want little to do with it. As I see it, though, a notion of transcendence restricted to the immanent plane is not inadequate, but *less* adequate, by comparison, to instill and ultimately sustain the energy and vitality of counter-hegemonic movements. This is true for the incarcerated and their communities, but even more so for those benefiting from privilege who would be hailed (Dussel) to participate in the trials and liberating struggles of those haunted by the specter of the penal state.

As already suggested, rather than making a tired evaluation of what Taylor has so eloquently and promisingly set forth, which I applaud as subversive, incisive, and inspired, I simply hold that a transcendent reference may remain even more potent for critical resistance. Discard its perverse forms, yes, but not what is so central and enlivening to the tradition that has incited great resistance throughout history, even if it has also been coopted and abused. Genuine transcendence is not the cause of Christendom, colonialism, capitalism, and the like. On the contrary, it may be the best source for challenging them.

Most appropriate, then, I submit, is neither the rejection of divine transcendence nor an immanentization of it, but a critique of its distorted expressions — those that reinforce or ossify the status quo

---

[13] Taylor, *The Theological and the Political*, 7.

of power relations and neocolonialism, most notably in the form of mass incarceration. This includes both conservative neoliberal (anti-)utopias and religious ideologies that cease to be liberative. The fundamental problem with such ontologies, I would urge, is not that they appeal to transcendence, but that, as Taylor indicates, they are closed off, totalized, and risk averse. Transcendence doesn't have to mean "outside." A critical transcendence, from the "below" of the crucified, does find its hope in the divine "beyond," but not because this divine is guaranteed to save us from our social apathy or material irresponsibility. Nor is the beyond an invisible hand that reckons necessary sacrifices (capitalism's "creative destruction") of other people's well-being and bodies disposable to serve the interests of the elite few. The "from beyond" of transcendence is precisely what guards against the common human mistake of putting too much stock in what can be accomplished "from here," and by our own power, *within* history. At the same time, the paradox of faith and politics is that radical love and liberating justice for "the wretched of the earth" (Fanon) must be courageously sought in the midst of tragedy and in the face of an uncertain future.

For Christians, the depth dimension of this mission flows from God through Christ, as a power *beyond* history, experienced *in* history, in solidarity *with* history, makes a critique *of* history, giving hope *for* history. Hence, what should be opposed, theologically speaking, is not divine transcendence, but conservative, neoliberal utopias, which is the type of transcendence that has indeed failed and come to ruins. Is the God of the poor and the oppressed a failed transcendental signifier? Maybe so; one can only answer in faith, and admittedly, simple, traditional rejoinders will not do. In short, though, I trust that Christians can live into their faith in such a God as cause for renewed hope and strength to rise up and "sing it hard." For this God, Christians profess, whose character was revealed in a poor, self-sacrificing, executed Hebrew Nazarene, judges the proud and gives grace to the humble.

It was a resurrection eschatology that at least partly empowered Paul and other early Jesus followers to live so boldly for their faith, and with such a counter-narrative to the "lockdown" anti-utopian spirit of Rome. The story of the risen Jesus instilled courage in confrontation with death and suffering. Once more, it seems to me that the problem is not with transcendence per se, but what kind. There are hegemonic and counter-hegemonic theologies of transcendence. Whatever else resurrection means, it is the promise of a future in God for the prisoner. In Sung's concluding words, "Where the reduction of immanence is avoided, there appears the potency of the eschatological claim, of the meaning of justice (Phil. 2. 5–11). To renounce the transcendent is to be left with no standpoint for the radical critique of history."[14]

To stress once more, the claim here is not that trans-immanence is an inept concept as far as it goes. Taylor has shown awareness of the possible efficacy of reference to a transcendent other for critical resistance and does not argue for its deficiency. He simply chooses for reasons mostly unelaborated here to adopt Nancy's ontology instead. Thus, there may well be defensible grounds for such a move, but insofar as these grounds depend on the conspicuous advantage of trans-immanence over a critical and christologically rooted transcendence from below, I consider it a hasty dismissal of what the Christian theological tradition has to offer.

---

[14] Míguez, Rieger, and Sung, *Beyond the Spirit of Empire*, 200.

6

Decolonizing Christianity

Susan Abraham

The most compelling issue for theology today is the colonial legacy
of theology. In the disciplines of religious studies and theology the
colonial framework in which the discourse and the colonial legacy
of contemporary theology operates has come under scrutiny for its
entanglement and continued engagement with colonial and neocolonial agendas. In religious studies, for example, a number of critical
analyses point to the manner in which religion itself, as a category,
has been aligned with the making of national identities and with
the exercise of colonial power. Religion, therefore, cannot be studied
as an inert belief system. Religion coexists with other discourses in
social spaces marked by power. This means that religion cannot be
perceived or studied apart from the postcolonial reality of nation. In
the study of theology, which one might (mistakenly) think is justified
in understanding itself as the study of a (largely) inert belief system,
the emphasis has shifted to a practical politics of spirituality and
liberation. Here, contemporary systematic theologians seek to address the relation between European colonialism and the discourse
of theology. Theology, as has been consistently argued, arises in
contexts. Theologians such as Kwok Pui Lan, Marcella Althaus-Reid,
Ivone Gebara, R. S. Sugirtharajah, Gloria Anzaldua, among a host of
newer theological voices, engage the relationship between Europe
and Christian theology in terms of identity critiques, political theology and spirituality, the entangled relationship between *secularism*
and *religion*, and strategies to combat economic, political, cultural
and social violence against women, children, the poor, and the environment. These postcolonial theological voices point to the ways
in which Christian theology in the West, with its emphasis on beliefs

and truth, has cast not only the category of religion in a particular way, but also presented theology as a discourse that is resistant to contemporary concerns of political liberation.

The historical context of colonization and decolonization in various parts of the world, which largely occurred in the twentieth century, has been followed by academic reflections collected under the broad umbrella of postcolonial theory. The aim of postcolonial *theory* is to decolonize Western knowledge. That is, it operates as an ongoing major critical discourse within the Western academic division of the humanities. One might think that decolonization happened automatically when various parts of the world emerged from modern European colonial rule. However, decolonization does not mean the simple uncoupling of colonizer and colonized. In this view, to decolonize is to unlink the presumed continuity between European Christianity and its forms in the colonies. Both secularists and traditionalists can make this mistake. For example, secularist academics often decry Christianity and Christian missionaries as being hopelessly embroiled in the imperializing moves of European political powers without adequately nuancing the history of European politics and its intertwining with church power. Simultaneously, secularists also fail to track the creative moves made by missionaries in the field who were taught to expect "savages" and "barbarians" that they had to convert to Christianity. Once they arrived, however, many found complex societies that had finely honed understandings of good and evil and visions of what the good life might mean. Traditionalists, on the other hand, given to a particular politics of truth and authority, stress the provenance of the modern spread of Christianity from the global West as a way to counteract domestic marginalization, but also as forms of elite belonging to "official" Christianity. Decolonization strategies include the patient tracking of the tactics engaged in by communities of Christians in the whole complex of social and political power.

In contemporary postcolonial theory decolonization is a complex activity spurred by varieties of political, cultural, and critical interventions in a number of disciplines. Even though this critical discourse has given rise to much specialized writing in the academy, any attempt to define it remains difficult. It has no organized methodology or even an originating moment, since academic postcolonial theory ranges far beyond the historical legacy of the modern European colonial encounter. As a number of postcolonial theorists have indicated, postcolonial theory is also complicated by its twin methodological convictions — that of Marxism, on the one hand, and poststructuralism and postmodernism, on the other. Here of course, decolonizing postcolonial theology finds easy alliances with liberation theologies in Latin America, Asia, and Africa. Since the force of colonization was exerted differently in each part of the globe, a history of class struggle under past and contemporary colonialism engages not only with Europe but with domestic regimes in collusion with economic organizations and military superpowers. While poststructuralism and postmodernism may seem to be more relevant to Western academic concerns, the reflexivity of linguistic forms, the nature of dogmatic truth, and the authority of scriptural interpretation are now expressed in many nonacademic venues. Chief among these concerns is the penchant of official Christianities to interpret scripture and dogma in ways that continue to exploit, marginalize, and perform violence on women. Postcolonial theory is also postmodern because it is a form of contra-Western-modern discourse. The emphasis here is not simply in terms of language and performative analyses; as a form of contra-Western modernity, it identifies other forms of modernity as well as resistance strategies on the part of traditionalisms that coexist with Western modernity across the globe.

In a similar vein, for postcolonial Christian *theology*, the question of how to decolonize theology leads to critical and constructive engagement across methodological and political commitments. For example, some postcolonial theologians engage in a materialist critique of postcolonial contexts by way of race, class, gender, and sexuality analyses. Others are more concerned with the manner in which certain theological ideas such as freedom, liberation, and religious identity and belonging are constructed in a cultural frame. Another approach has been to constructively rethink the grammar of theology. This leads to questions such as the following: What has been the effect of the symbols that operate in the theological framework, such as God, Christ, human being, and church? Do they or can they function in a manner that is non-oppressive and non-imperialist?

In an earlier phase of decolonizing theology, the category "culture" simply meant the sense in which cultural location modified theology. Proposals for African American, Latin American, Asian, and African theology highlighted ways in which cultural particularity challenged Western forms of theology that spoke from a universalizing position. The idea that culture has a role to play in theological thinking is not itself a new idea. Doing theology using cultural analysis and cultural criticism has been part of varied forms of theology such as political theology; correlation theologies;

ethnographic theologies; and feminist, womanist, *mujerista,* and *min-jung* theologies. In the past decade a number of theological studies have reflected on the significance of culture as important for theology and pressed the argument that theology itself as a genre ought to be seen as a mode of cultural production. In other words, Western theology that persisted without reflecting on its own cultural matrix was shown to be rather provincial in its language, its philosophical and political orientations, and its understanding of power.

The complexity of the category culture, however, has not always been apparent. This has limited the critical impact of some third-world theologies and impaired our understanding of the manner in which a colonial legacy continues to operate in Western and academic theology. R. S. Sugirtharajah, in *Postcolonial Reconfigurations: An Alternative Way of Reading the Bible and Doing Theology,* argues that third-world theologies, arising in postcolonial contexts, are basically "experiential discourses" that reflect the impoverished condition of people. He also points out that the perception that third-world theologies only deal with "experience" ultimately compromised their importance in the eyes of Western academic theology, which perceived in them a lack of rational argumentation. That is, third-world theologies were understood to problematically present experience in opposition to reason. How, then, can postcolonial theologies make clear the *analytical* framework in which "experience" complicates the traditional formulations of theological foci such as God, Christ, human being, and church function as a set of symbols in a system that functions together with other symbols of power and domination? Sugirtharajah, therefore, provides us with an important warning, that is, not to draw simplistic correlations between human experience and theological ideas.

Unfortunately, many so-called third-world theologies and experience-based theologies have fallen into this trap, simplistically correlating experience and theological language, leading to what has been decried as "identity politics" in theology. Identity politics, arising from the uncritical use of cultural identity categories such as Asian or black, do not necessarily decolonize theological knowledge. Instead, by aggressively presenting themselves as "marginal" to academic theological discourse, these forms of identity-based theologies functioned to reinscribe highly problematic relations between the so-called center and the margin. Furthermore, they rarely acknowledged the immense pluralism that blanket names such as *Asian* (among other such names) hide.

So how do postcolonial theologians take account of these pitfalls in the attempt to decolonize theology? Here, I present two points of exploration. The first issue is that of identity and experience; this issue has been complicated in different ways by secular postcolonial theory and by postcolonial theology. The second issue deals closely with postcolonial writing and reading as ethical practices that attempt to decolonize knowledge. Postcolonial theology does not result in easy strategies for decolonizing theology, implicated as it is in the colonial and civilizing mission; for this very reason, however, grappling with such strategies is important.

Negotiated Identities and Pluralized Experience

In ordinary parlance, *identity* refers to a unified and cohesive name for oneself, one's community, or one's nation. For many of us the identities of gender and race, for example, are self-explanatory and coherent. The problem with this assumption, however, stems from the recognition that all identity categories have been shown to circulate in a cultural context marked by power differentials that value different identities differently. For postcolonial theology the quadruple issues of race, class, gender, and sexuality form a constellation of oppressive strategies that shore up colonial forms of Christianity. Identity politics, whether played out in the Western academy or in nationalistic contexts around the world, reified modern forms of identity as if there were no context to their own provenance.

In India, for example, the experience of narrating the colonial encounter and identity as it was forged in the colonial encounter began with the anticolonial and national rehabilitation experiences of resistance in the nineteenth century.[1] These experiences created ambivalence: while the anticolonialists raided the cultural and philosophical heritage of their past to counter colonialism, they also discovered to their horror "that the indigenous heritage they so eagerly turned to contained several contaminated aspects, customs and practices such as untouchability, caste distinctions, polygamy, female circumcision, and widow-burning."[2] The ambivalence, however, enabled the development of what can be legitimately called third-world hermeneutics, a methodology that borrowed methodological

---

[1] R. S. Sugirtharajah, *Postcolonial Reconfigurations: An Alternative Way of Reading the Bible and Doing Theology* (London: SCM Press, 2003), 1.
[2] Ibid.

insights from the Europeans while inflecting aspects of indigenous culture and everyday experience. The consequent theology came to emphasize experience and identity-based hermeneutics. One can argue that this form of identity-based strategies has a limited but necessary value, perhaps as an initial phase of resistance. Gayatri Chakravorty Spivak calls such strategies "strategic essentialism."[3]

Like other third-world theologies, postcolonial theology from India started with the feelings and pain of people confronting the historical trauma of yet another colonial power. European theologies obviously were and are not attuned to this form of trauma. Hence, experiential theology challenges the idea that theology is universalizable. Yet, while the experience of colonialism changes the contours of theology, the foundation of theology—its articulation and belief in God—does not change. As Sugirthararajah's epigraph to Part II articulates, theology remains the same whether done at 120°F or at 70°F.[4] What does *not* change is the object of theology and the theological imagination—God. What does change is the *theologian*.

The postcolonial theorist with whom the ideas of negotiated identity, hybridity, and diaspora have been most associated is Homi Bhabha. In terms of Bhabha's work, one could enter almost anywhere and perceive his concern with complicating identity, particularly in view of the fact that the material consequence of postcolonial history was the creation of "independent" and secular nation-states. Therefore, national identity in our time arises out of a negotiated reality with the colonial power and interpretations of the cultural legacy of the new nation. For Bhabha, and a host of others, speaking of culture in terms of national identity is *the* problem to be overturned in a postcolonial academy. Braiding together poststructuralism, psychoanalysis, cultural theory, and Marxism, Bhabha argues that the postcolonial subject is best understood in a framework of temporality rather than spatiality. That is, identity is to be thought of as a signifier that circulates in a particular *time* period instead of being reified in terms of the clear-cut *space* of the nation.

The goal of mobilizing the category culture is not merely to bring forth the "free play of polarities and pluralities" in the space of

---

[3] Gayatri Chakravorty Spivak, *Outside in the Teaching Machine* (New York: Routledge, 1993), 3; for a full discussion, see 1–23.

[4] See Klaus Klostermaier, epigraph, in ibid., 117. "Theology done at 120°F in the shade seems, after all, different from theology at 70°F. Theology accompanied by tough chapattis and smoky tea seems different from theology with roast chicken and a glass of good wine. Now who is really different, *théos* or theologian?" (*Hindu and Christian in Vrindaban* [London: SCM, 1970], 40).

the nation.[5] Rather, it is to bring forth a "jarring of meanings and values" in the process of cultural interpretation. This is a subtle but exceedingly important point that Bhabha introduces into the study of culture and one of critical importance for theology. When culture becomes a part of theological thinking, what surfaces is not some exotic identity category that advances experience as cohesive and unified. Rather, the whole enterprise of thinking theologically undergoes a transformation as perplexing interventions performed by culturally significant others changes the "scenario of articulation."[6] Consider, for example, the recent work of constructive theologian Marion Grau, whose reflections on missionary activity in the colonial context of South Africa have much relevance for postcolonial practical theology. Here we see that negotiated identities and pluralized experience change the very articulation of theological ideas.

Marion Grau's book *Rethinking Mission in the Postcolony: Salvation, Society, and Subversion* presents a historical and theological analysis through the matrix of cultural negotiation as presented in Bhabha's theories of identity, hybridity, and diaspora.[7] Mission is a theological area that is of great interest to postcolonial theologians, particularly in the wake of secularized and Western critiques of the imperializing missions of Christianity. Much historical work has been done to overturn such a view of mission without erasing the reality of the colonial violence in which at times Christian missions participated. However, in a theological exploration of the issues surrounding mission, Grau argues that mission practices demonstrate the same kind of ambivalence about identity that Bhabha charts, and furthermore, that missions' scenario of articulation is far more complex than merely the experience of power in terms of colonizer over colonized.

That is, the category culture is a vast field of networked relations in which everyone, not just the missionary and his hapless convert, is operating. A postcolonial theology of mission must take cognizance of the complexity of mission history and point out, first of all, that flat descriptors of national identity—such as *fifteenth–century Portugal* or *the British Navy*—are fundamentally metaphors. These metaphors ought to signal to the porosity of intercultural encounters. For example, more than half of the British Navy was not British, and

---

[5] Homi Bhabha, "DissemiNation," in *The Location of Culture* (New York: Routledge, 1994), 162.

[6] Ibid.

[7] Marion Grau, *Rethinking Mission in the Postcolony: Salvation, Society, and Subversion* (New York: T & T Clark, 2011).

Napoleon's "French" army included Poles and Germans.[8] When this is taken into account, we begin to see that theological ideas such as conversion necessarily meant conversion to a religio-cultural identity, already hybrid, and conversion did not happen only to the convert. Both religious and cultural systems are a two-way "commerce," as Grau argues and traces in the historical archive of the Anglican Colenso Mission in South Africa.

In a fascinating exploration of the Zulu, the Colensos, and the hermeneutics of salvation, Grau presents the contours of a "polydox" theology of mission, tracking the manner in which identity in the colonial encounter remains just one signifier amid a series of colonial interventions. Here, conversion to Christianity cannot be seen apart from the sociopolitical and economic context in which Christian identity operates. Conversion to Christianity, therefore, is grounded in economic and cultural experiences. Missionary institutions attracted "physically or socially orphaned persons, the disenfranchised, women, and persons of lower class or status" by offering what Grau goes on to call "an opening in the density of established relationality."[9] That is, missions often allowed the lower strata of society to perform interventions on their own behalf to overturn the rigid stratifications of their societies.

Thus, missionaries were never the sole agents in the colonial encounter. Colonized people, by engaging in resistance and negotiation and using missionary institutions to advance in domestic contexts, challenged patriarchal, social, cultural, and theological norms. For example, Grau points to Tsitsi Dangarembga's novel *Nervous Conditions*, in which the protagonist Tambu's motivation for conversion includes her hunger for education; the urgent need to transcend the patriarchal and chauvinist world of village and family; and her preference for the cultural, economic, and social privileges of the colonial cultural world.[10]

The manner that scripture arrives in the missionary context also demonstrates complex negotiations among the message, the messenger, and the medium of the message. In the section "Translating God: What Is the Message?" Grau points out that translating the Bible into African tongues functioned to relativize the grip the missionaries had on the Bible. Such a phenomenon is also charted

---

[8] Ibid., 10.
[9] Ibid., 162, 163.
[10] Ibid., 167.

by Bhabha in his chapter "Signs Taken for Wonders: Questions of Ambivalence and Authority Under a Tree Outside Delhi, May 1817."[11] There, Bhabha demonstrates, albeit from a non-theological and secular standpoint, the surprising forms of agency circulating in the colonial encounter that arise because of the Bible being translated into vernacular languages. Similarly, Grau asserts that one cannot evade the "politics of translation" in which the translators "inscribe the incarnate faith of those who communicate the faith as much as they transmit faith in an incarnate God. Such an incarnate faith becomes reincarnated when its flesh moves and relocates."[12]

In decolonizing contemporary Christian theologies of mission Grau demonstrates a twofold task. On the one hand, decolonizing Christianity does not mean that Christian theologians simply capitulate to the demands of secular studies of religion, which often simplistically argue that mission theology went hand in hand with imperial Christianity. In fact, the capacity to rethink colonial encounters and to trace how agency was enacted in surprising and novel ways complicates the position not only of theologians, but also of secular thinkers of postcolonial theory such as Homi Bhabha.

On the other hand, Grau's book is a provocative and thoughtful suggestion to think anew about mission theology. Mission, after all, is a concrete and formative practice of Christian traditions. Its colonial heritage, however, has given progressive theologians pause and has made it difficult for many to think of mission theology in language other than the imperial language of exclusivist Christianity. This is all the more problematic because conversion, understood as the transformation of identity, is a flashpoint for religious violence around the globe today.

Following the implications of this, constructive theologies of mission can begin to think of "mutual mission"[13] in which Christian belonging, and therefore identity, cannot be uniformly "orthodox." In a milieu of shared experiences, conversion is a mutual experience of transformation and trust of human relations. This idea is in no way meant to assert that the colonial encounter was not marked by the dehumanizing violence of imperial Christianity. On the contrary, in the face of that reality Grau underscores that a theology of mission must emphasize relationality at the heart of the identity negotiations

---

[11] Bhabha, *The Location of Culture*, 102–22.
[12] Grau, *Rethinking Mission in the Postcolony*, 181.
[13] Ibid., 280.

discussed in this section—relationality between the divine and the human as well as that among human beings as the basis of mutual conversion and transformation.

The Practice of Postcolonial Theological Writing and Reflection

Without a doubt, the missionary and colonial context of European modernity was marked by the circulation of texts and discourses that disciplined lines of authority and legitimacy. Perhaps one of postcolonial theory's strongest contributions to the decolonization of knowledge in the academy can be located in its critique of texts and discourse. This strand of postcolonial theory comes by way of post-structuralism, which is a radicalization of structuralism presented by the Swiss linguist Ferdinand de Saussure. *Poststructuralism* may be defined as a transdisciplinary critical examination of how we represent the world through language and ways of thinking. Thus, it takes into account the central problem at the heart of knowledge production and intellectual practice. When reflecting on the most compelling questions for theology today, the academic production of theological knowledge has to be brought to crisis in light of the critiques of postcolonial poststructuralism.

The ideological frame in which colonial and imperial power circulates can be seen in the control employed over language. Bill Ashcroft, Gareth Griffiths, and Helen Tiffin, in their early analysis of the theory and practice of postcolonial literatures, argue that one of the main features of imperial oppression is control over education and language.[14] Language is how hierarchical power, with its structures and arguments about truth, order, and reality are circulated, sustained, and used to guarantee control over other mechanisms of disciplining life. How is authority established in and through language? In the colonial context it is clear that language is used in a way that consolidates imperial power. Nevertheless, the idea that language is the site of ideological persuasion is not an unfamiliar idea to theology.

The debate over texts—the reading as well as the writing—has been extensively studied by theologians committed to writing theologically in the context of pluralism. For example, in his essay

---

[14] Bill Ashcroft, Gareth Griffiths, and Helen Tiffin, *The Empire Writes Back: Theory and Practice in Postcolonial Literatures* (London: Routledge, 1989), 7. The epigraph to the book attributes the phrase "The Empire Writes back" to Salman Rushdie.

"Writing," David Tracy points out that written texts, called scripture, in religious contexts have a particular kind of role. That is, they have a normative stance vis-à-vis other texts. However, his analysis represents a form of postcolonial response from within the Western enclave. In the context of modern understandings of historical critical and hermeneutical methods, the very notion of what it means to assert normativity is in question. In the essay Tracy is primarily concerned to present a hermeneutics of writing where "the greatest puzzle and complexity lie not in traditional Christian theological debates on 'scripture alone' vs. 'scripture and tradition,' but rather in the Christian self-understanding of the hermeneutical relationship of the presence-oriented category 'Word' to Scripture as *written* text, and thereby, to writing."[15] In other words, the Christian understanding of scripture has to do with an event, an event of divine self-manifestation in the Word, which is Jesus Christ, an argument that is directed to the loss of a sense of sacredness in the West with regard to scripture. Tracy is attempting here to overturn the secular "linguistic turn" in religious studies, which examines religious and theological language for the ways they create and sustain imperial power. In this essay, however, he is clearly attempting to challenge the secularized analysis of language by asserting that scriptural language as normative language can only be analyzed in terms of its referents. In other words, Tracy is explicitly arguing against the deconstructive method inaugurated by postcolonial and poststructuralist methods. However, this does not mean that he is interested in a rigid understanding of the "truth" of text. Thus, deconstruction need not be the only strategy to unearth the imperial and colonial legacies of sacred texts. Of course, his argument does not have the kind of political edge that postcolonial theologians seek in their writing and reading.

In an argument such as Tracy's, the Christian idea of "event" underscores the gratuitous and gracious nature of divine revelation in the "Word-as-Word-event" and is a happening of language itself that is not under the control of the subject. Tracy here is undercutting one of the most entrenched ideas of modernity — that the autonomous subject is in control of meaning-making when reading or writing. The act of writing, therefore, reveals a capacity for excess beyond human control, which has been left largely untheorized by those who are not convinced of the linguistic turn. While it is true

---

[15] David Tracy, "Writing," in *Critical Terms for Religious Studies*, ed. Mark C. Taylor (Chicago: The University of Chicago Press, 1998), 385.

that Tracy is making room here for divine action and agency, post-colonial theorists and theologians will demur that room ought to be made also for the differently construed human other. That is, Tracy is still invested in a modern (and Western) focus on meaning, while postcolonial theorists are arguing against the omission of the subjugated participant of reading or writing. He spends no time analyzing the authorized reader and writer of scripture, such as Grau demonstrated in her analysis of missionary dynamics. What is clear in such a view of theological writing is that writing is but one modality in which the principal ideas of a religious tradition may be understood. Tracy presents a *theological* argument in which theological language is a practice of and by the Christian practitioner. Would such a view of language be inimical to secular postcolonial analyses of language, which may not argue for the *sui generis* character of theology to make the claim that language is a site of revelation?

Here I turn to one of the more subtle thinkers and performers of postcolonial writing, Trinh T. Minh-ha, who has influenced a generation of thinkers in postcolonial religious and theological thought. Postcolonial theology, in this vein, is not a straightforward concern for the Christian church and its publics in postcolonial contexts. Postcolonial theology, instead, is a constructive enterprise aiming to think theologically using the many critical tools of postcolonial theory. An exploration of Trinh's work provides us with a starting point to think of how postcolonial thinkers may use postcolonial theory to think theologically. Trinh herself is not a theologian. She is a writer, filmmaker, and composer, but her reflections on writing to decolonize have influenced many who want to think of the material reality of religion and not just a belief system.

Trinh's most often quoted work in postcolonial studies of religion and theology is *Woman, Native, Other: Writing Postcoloniality and Feminism*. Here, writing is put forward as a project to examine postcolonial processes of displacement, cultural hybridization, decentered realities, fragmented and multiple selves, marginal voices, and languages that intervene and rupture. These are themes, as we have seen, that operate across postcolonial writing and thinking. Consider some lines of poetry penned by Trinh that serve as the epigraph to her chapter entitled "Commitment from the Mirror-Writing Box":

i was made to believe
we who write also dance
yet no dancer writes
(the way we write)

no writer ever dances
(the way they dance)
while writing we bend
and bend over
stoop sit and squat
and can neither stand erect
nor lie flat on our back
whoever pretends to deed
walks skip run while writing
must be flying free
as free as a cage-bird
seeing not lines as lines
bars as bars
nor any prison-yard[16]

Here she explains in her poetic political writing that the act of writing is a "triple bind" for postcolonial gendered subjects: "we are (therefore) triply jeopardized — as a writer, as a woman and as a woman of color."[17] In such a view, writing must be akin to a mirror, a mirror that is able to show reflections, albeit the reflections of other mirrors.[18] Moreover, writing as a mirror demonstrates that no one can own the image thus produced. When a woman writes, she must assiduously avoid repeating the "priest-God" scheme in which language as mastery and knowledge functions as "truth."

Writing cannot be the mere description of the "sovereignty" of the author.[19] Postcolonial writing has to avoid such "euphoric narcissistic accounts of yourself and your own kind."[20] Writing is not a projection of the sovereign and isolated self but the shared manner in which we read other texts. In making such a subtle point, Trinh argues that the "me" of writing must disappear to make room for the "I" of reading and writing. Writing and reading is not about "me." Trinh here is undercutting the kind of self-centered identity politics that spoke for liberation in postmodernity. It is important to note here that Trinh, similar to Tracy, is performing an intervention that destabilizes the presumed subject center of reading and writing, but in another way than Tracy, for a different political end. She is

---

[16] Trinh T. Minh-Ha, *Woman, Native, Other: Writing Postcoloniality and Feminism* (Bloomington: Indiana University Press, 1989), 5.

[17] Ibid., 28.

[18] Ibid., 22.

[19] Ibid., 29.

[20] Ibid., 28.

more invested in critiquing the normative Western subject than in affirming the truth of text. In so doing, she provides a strategy to decolonize truth and authority in reading and writing by destabilizing the expectation of an authorized reader or writer.

For Trinh, it is not postcolonial heroic identity that must feature in postcolonial writing. It is rather a manner of deconstructing language and its power frameworks so that the elusive "I" of gendered postcolonial subjectivity may find the room to speak and to be heard. Such a form of subjectivity, however, is more about holistic surrender to one's work than its mastery — our work writes itself through our bodies. Similar to Tracy's argument, that meaning can only be produced in encounter; here, meaning is produced by the unsaying body that presents a more than linguistic meaning in the writing. Only such an embodied use of language, always anterior to the writer,[21] makes of writing a form of nurturing or *nourricriture*.[22] Thus is writing able to "[connote] material, a linguistic flesh."[23] Only in this way can postcolonial thinkers write the body. Body writing does not mean that one raises problematic race optics or gendered roles as signifying the difference that postcoloniality underscores. Instead, the attempt to decolonize the written body means that the body surrenders to the work of nourishing the world through its incarnating words.

Subverting the Colonial Legacy of Theology

Each of these thinkers of the practice of reading and writing makes very particular arguments that touch upon the concerns and the spirit of postcolonial theology. As was asserted earlier, there is no such thing as postcolonial theology if this is read merely as an identity category. Postcolonial theology has to decolonize actively. Therefore, it is a form of political theology. Decolonizing theology means to investigate its historical connections with modern colonialism and its continued collusion with modern forms of neocolonialism spurred by both secular and traditionalist interests. Postcolonial writing is not heroic writing about unique experiences or even unique consciousness, and it avoids victimology. It is reading and writing in order to make room for the humbling surprise of revelation, both of the divine and of the human being. In postcolonial

---

[21] Ibid., 36.
[22] Ibid., 38.
[23] Ibid.

theology's disavowal of heroism and unique privilege, however, it seeks to undo the damage of Western modernity and the timely appearance of the marginalized subject as a character in heroic writing. However, in calling to mind the embodied writer who incarnates herself in her writing, a differently construed writer/reader emerges—one that brings to crisis self-enclosed ideas of truth and authority.

For postcolonial practical and political Christianity a theology of mission must be able to reflect the complex reality of continuing global relations. Unlike the easy dismissal of liberal and secular thinkers critical of Christian mission, a postcolonial theology of mission has to be multiply engaged with history, culture, and national and international realities. A theology of mutual mission, in which the asymmetrical relationship between Christian missionary and the recipients of missionary work is transformed, is the critical and constructive work of decolonizing theology. One strand of interest that ought to inform a contemporary theology of mission is to engage the context of interfaith dialogue, particularly as it pertains to national interests. Theologies of mission cannot but take such a context of complex negotiations into account when constructing contemporary theologies of mission that explicitly seek to decolonize. In both cases attention to critical theories of subjectivity, identity, and epistemology are matched by fluency in economic, political, and cultural theories. Theology can no longer remain in a ghetto of speakers of an assented-to language game in which truth and authority are never brought to crisis. Theology, like all human enterprises, jostles for a place in a social and political context with multiple accounts of truth and authority, and a comparative frame for adjudicating these multiple claims creates the conditions for decolonizing. My argument for the most compelling issue for theology today, the colonial legacy of theology, rests on the conviction that theology's potential to liberate rests on the *tradition's* potential to liberate from within. After all, the incarnate, living God calls us to freedom precisely in our human condition enfolded within a divine horizon, one that we may not "know" but that is always beckoning. This ancient legacy of theology remains the best corrective to imperializing forms of theology that seem unable to shed their colonial trappings.

A Response to Susan Abraham

Speaking of *That Without Which Not*

MARLENE BLOCK

Susan Abraham challenges us to confront the ways in which theology has been and still is immersed in, determined by, and complicit with colonial and neocolonial agendas. The most compelling issue in theology today, she asserts, is the colonial legacy of theology. I agree that the decolonization of theology is a task that is vitally important to contemporary theology, but as I studied Abraham's suggestions for doing so, I began to realize that it is not only the case that theology needs to be decolonized, but also that postcolonial theory can be enriched and perhaps even corrected in certain ways through the application of a clearly articulated theological vision. While I sense that Abraham shares this interest as well, I believe that in her essay the theological perspective is subordinated to other, non-theological perspectives, or it is at least somewhat muted in its expression. There is good reason for this. A key point that theology needs to grasp is that it is embedded in particular contexts, just as are all disciplines and all human activities. Nevertheless, I found myself wondering what it is specifically that theology brings to the table, so to speak. Can we envision a theology that is sensitive to the issues raised by postcolonial theory but that remains distinctly theological?

In a general sense Abraham's work here can be seen as an effort to deepen and correct theology by putting it in dialogue with that which is *other* than theology. One can speak of the interaction among different disciplines, different discourses, or different fields, but I note how quickly the imagery we use becomes territorial, and this is a problem. It is clear that at the level of the study of disciplines, we face some of the same problems with the construction of and negotiation of identities that we find in areas of life writ larger.

There is not simply *theology*—there are theologies. Yet in relation to non-theological disciplines within the academy, theology sometimes takes on a more homogeneous appearance, despite the myriad ways in which we are in fact fragmented and multiple. It would be difficult to deny that the status of theology within and also beyond the academy is a highly fraught and highly problematic one. This may be due to theology's inextricable link to something outside the academy called church—a link that is often falsely seen as necessarily constricting or compromising theology's view. We may disagree on what we desire for theology, or on what we think theology is, but I think all can agree that theology, when it exists at all in the academy, does so in a very strained and precarious way. This is not to deny that there are many *within* the academy and *outside* of theology who are quite willing to utilize theological ideas, or who are willing to embrace a kind of quasi- or post-theological vision, or who perhaps deploy theological notions without even being aware of their theological provenance. But that is different from embracing theology as such or speaking from a theological standpoint. The first question that I want to pose has to do with the possible role of a decolonized theology within the academy. Will a decolonized theology have an easier time of it, so to speak? A second question following quickly on the first is this: must a decolonized theology let go of tendencies, desires, concepts, and methods that were traditionally seen as being essential to it *as theology*? Can we perhaps also say that there is something within theology that would have led theology to become decolonized or would have led theology to recognize the value of becoming decolonized in Abraham's sense *on its own,* if only it had not lost its way? I think Abraham would agree that there is; she clearly states at the end of her essay that her argument "rests on the conviction that theology's potential to liberate rests on the *tradition's* potential to liberate from within."

Abraham notes that theologians have appropriated and utilized the concept of culture in their thinking, although often uncritically. She notes that in view of this uncritical appropriation, the postcolonial rereading of the concept of culture is of particularly "critical importance" to theology. Culture, in the postcolonial reading, is not an exoticized identity category that can be given plural form as so many other cultures. Rather, she points out, "the goal of mobilizing the category culture is . . . to bring forth a 'jarring of meanings and values' [Bhabha's phrase]." Is there not something in theology already that brings forth just such a jarring of meanings and values, perhaps even a more radical jarring of meanings and values, but which theology has at times lost sight of within itself? Here I would refer, for example, to one of the central concerns in many traditional theologies that insist upon the distinction between *religion* and *theology* and which seek to critique the concept of religion from the standpoint of something called revelation. While the impetus for such critiques of religion and of culture from a theological standpoint is very different from that which motivates the anthropological and postcolonial critiques of the concept of religion, we can nevertheless detect a similarity and perhaps even a kind of kinship in the *theological* destabilization of the category religion.

In the section of her essay titled "Negotiated Identities and Pluralized Experience," Abraham makes clear that postcolonial theory is a rereading *in light of* and *with the aim of*; that is, it is a rereading *in light of* postcolonial concerns such as identity, hybridity, and diaspora, and *with the aim of* heightening awareness of the ways in which our practices, disciplinary and otherwise, perpetuate or have reinscribed oppressive relations, the task then being to find a way out of these oppressive forms. In this, one can easily see the critical and liberationist inspiration of a decolonized theology. This leads me to pose this question: in what specific ways is a postcolonial, decolonized theology divergent from or convergent with liberation theologies? My sense is that there is an important difference, and it might have to do with the way in which and the extent to which non-theological disciplines are allowed to have their say to theology. In any case, one can easily see that it is possible for theology to pursue the same aim of heightening our awareness of the ways in which our practices perpetuate or even foster oppressive relations, while at the same time reading and rereading the world in a different, theological light.

I find Abraham's discussion of the work of Marion Grau to be particularly suggestive in this connection. Theology has a problematic status in certain quarters, as I noted above, but far more problematic is the position of the more specific *theology of mission*. To those for whom theology is objectionable, theology of mission is even more so. There are some important historical reasons for this, but Grau's work establishes that the status of mission theology is in part the result of a lack of knowledge and understanding of the complexities of actual mission encounters. Mission is often seen simplistically as the exercise of the power of the core or center upon the peoples of the periphery. As Abraham shows, Grau's work destabilizes this prejudicial view through her postcolonial analysis, which is at once postcolonial *and* theological, and which sees mission not as carrying us to the *periphery* of Christianity but into the very *heart* of it. She does this without at the same time denying the injustices that have taken place in the *name* of Christianity. I believe Grau is able to accomplish this because her work is at once theoretical—grounded in the study of historical and ethnographic particulars—and yet spoken with a truly theological voice—but not one for whom all of these non-theological disciplines are just so much matter to be subordinated to theological form. Rather, she aims to allow them to transform the theological imagination in a much more radical way perhaps than can be readily seen in liberation theologies. Relationality is at the heart of her theology of mission, just as it is at the heart of questions of identity negotiation and destabilization in the discourse of postcolonial theory. Yet, as Abraham observes, for Grau this relationality includes not only that between human beings, but also "relationality between the divine and the human as well."

At the heart of Abraham's argument is a general issue, namely, the undeniable and unavoidable necessity of recognizing the fact that theology, as every human endeavor, exists in a specific context, and that an important part of the task of every theologian must be to attend to this context, especially since theology may be determined by and even be silently complicit with the forces that arise from this context and that work against theology's conscious aims and ultimate intents. With respect to this issue theology is no different from other disciplines. My struggle here is to answer the following question: given the situatedness of theology in context—a condition that theology shares with every human endeavor—what is distinctive about theology? What can it bring that is distinctly theological in content or method? As I studied Abraham's essay, I felt the need to walk a "tightrope," wanting to absorb fully the important lessons and insights of postcolonial theory while at the same time remaining theological in my orientation and not becoming post-theological, anti-theological, or confusedly theological. And so I asked, is there something—some method, some aspect, some orientation, some reality, or some referent—*that without which not*? That is, is there something without which there *is* no theology as such or no theology worthy of the name? Can we locate *that without which not* without falling into an overly facile stipulative articulation of what theology is or ought to be? I have the sense that in postcolonial theory everything is in motion, everything is shifting, and I believe in a sense that that is the truth of our human situation. And yet I still find myself looking for a ground that isn't constantly in motion beneath my feet. I recognize that this may be a seeking in vain.

It is helpful to look more closely at what I consider to be the central concept underlying this discussion, the notion of context, which is not a simple one. One of the most promising contributions of postcolonial theory to theology, in my view, resides in the extent to which this theory complicates our understanding of context and contextualization, showing the myriad ways in which seemingly bounded and self-contained identities are crisscrossed in complex ways by many and often disparate kinds of relations. Context is not to be thought of in spatial terms or as a kind of stage that we simply walk onto or as inert matter or background that simply surrounds what stands clearly bounded in the foreground for us. Context is much more dynamic, much more fluid, much less tractable, and in its influence at times, much more insidious than this. This at least is the conclusion I draw from Abraham's discussion of postcolonial theory. Abraham draws attention to the fact that there has been a tendency in theology not only to ignore context and its complexities, but also a tendency to actively *decontextualize* theological truths, specifically by projecting them as belief systems that can be viewed as independent of context, as absolutized, or as fixed. Strategies of decontextualization have the effect of simplifying, essentializing, and abstracting from the particulars of living webs of relations. She also refers to a specifically theological notion of context without describing it in these terms. She asserts that "the incarnate, living God calls us to freedom precisely in our human condition enfolded within a divine horizon, one that we may not 'know' but one that is always beckoning." I suggest that this "divine horizon" is an ultimate theological expression of context. We might rightly ask whether to speak of an "ultimate" context or a "divine horizon" is really only a roundabout way of invoking an illusory independence from context or, again, to provide a rationale for decontextualizing. In this connection Abraham's qualification of this horizon is exceedingly important. She notes that the "divine horizon" is one that "we may not 'know' but one that is always beckoning." I think it is useful to think of the divine horizon as an ultimate *context*, because in doing so we can establish a link or possible connection and common ground with other non-theological discourses for which context is a central theme or problem. It is, however, absolutely crucial that we listen carefully to Abraham's assertion about this divine horizon, namely, that we can't know it or our embeddedness in it in the same way we know contexts that we treat as being nearer to hand. There is a certain and necessary theological "not knowing" that marks our relation to this ultimate horizon, even as we feel its pull.

In Abraham's theological statement we find a clue to the positive task that theology must set for itself. If we are embedded in contexts that make it difficult for us to realize or even hear God's call to freedom for all people, and if our intellectual practices lead us to decontextualize and absolutize in ways that blind us to the manner in which we obstruct others' ability to hear and answer this call, then it is clear that theology must work to discover the particularities of our embeddedness in structures of oppression and must critically confront decontextualization as a strategy that is potentially oppressive. But, of course, it is not enough simply and critically to examine practices and strategies of decontextualization, nor is it enough to analyze and theorize about theology's contextualization. These are important and necessary tasks but not sufficient to achieve the theological aim. In fact, one could argue that other disciplines are much better situated to conduct such analyses. Contexts are not simply given and there to be studied; they have a dynamic aspect and can be created. It remains theology's task to create *new* contexts, that is, to *recontextualize* itself. This is perhaps another positive way of stating Abraham's assertion that theology must be decolonized. Theologians must creatively seek new ways, new practices, and new life in the old ways and practices that will enable them to hear and to realize what Abraham calls elsewhere God's call to freedom. And this freedom must be understood concretely as a call to freedom for all peoples.[1]

Abraham's essay has led me to wonder about the potential resources within theology that will enable it to reorient itself in such a way as to respond to the important issues raised by postcolonial theory, while at the same time continuing to speak with a distinctive theological voice. A tension remains here. And so in conclusion I ask the question again, what is theology, what is its task? What *must* it do if it is to remain theology? Karl Rahner gives a deceptively simple answer to this question.[2] He was concerned with the role of theology in relation to the other disciplines within the academy, and he was asking with some sense of urgency or perhaps even irritation, is there something that theology *must* do? He answered that theology

---

[1] For a discussion of this notion of freedom and for her more extensive treatment of the intersection of theology and postcolonial theory, see Susan Abraham, *Identity, Ethics, and Nonviolence in Postcolonial Theory: A Rahnerian Theological Assessment* (New York: Palgrave, 2007). I learned much from her discussion in this work of Rahner's theology and postcolonial theory.

[2] Karl Rahner, "Theology Today," in *Theological Investigations*, vol. 21, *Science and Christian Faith* (New York: Crossroad, 1983), 56–69.

must speak about God as such. This is a deceptively simple answer to a very difficult question. It is deceptively simple because one might be tempted to conclude that identifying theology's task is a simple matter of analyzing the derivation of the term *theology*, and by so doing locating its subject matter. But Rahner notes that theology has no subject matter in the same sense as do other disciplines. Nevertheless, theology must speak about God. And so Rahner claims a certain specific discourse is characteristic of theology, yet it is not the discourse *as discourse* that is the theologian's subject. Rahner insists that theology must speak about God, and not just about *speaking about speaking* about God, or speaking about whether we *can* speak about God. Theologians must speak about God *as such*, and if they fail to do so, then theology will no longer exist, and worse, it will have died by its own hand. The affirmation of the necessity of this task is perhaps a simple and straightforward one, yet the nature of the task that confronts us is not. When we speak about God as such, we speak (Rahner says paradoxically) about the holy, *unutterable* Mystery. We are saying what can't be said—but yet we must attempt to say it. The theologian does not speak of a god that we fully grasp (that would be an idol), nor does the theologian speak of a god we can use as a tool to hammer away at those who do not share *our* view of God. We can't use God to draw lines or to create smooth borders. With this kind of speaking, theology becomes (in Rahner's view) the *guardian* of pluralism within the academy and the voice of a *radical* relativism, but a relativism that is radical only because it is a *holy* relativism. Theology becomes the vociferous opponent of the attempt to absolutize any immanent experience or any immanent value. Theology becomes, in his word, a "troublemaker" in the academy. In relation to this notion of God as such, God as holy and ineffable mystery, every apparently fixed boundary and static identity is shown to be in flux, in motion, and ultimately, in passing. Thus it seems that it is only in relation to this notion of God as such, and in its speaking boldly of God as such, that theology can hope to be radically decolonized. Theology exists and has something to say only insofar as and only so long as it speaks of *that without which not*.

7

Faith and Ecofeminism

*Religion and the Liberation of Women
and the Earth from Oppression*

ROSEMARY RADFORD RUETHER

Ecology and feminism or ecofeminism are topics that are among the most compelling issues in contemporary theology. Both of these topics have long been neglected in Christian theology. Christianity has implicitly or explicitly justified the inferiorization of women in its theological and practical tradition, even though its founding scripture underlined the equality of women and women in Christ. This issue began to be addressed systematically only in the second half of the twentieth century. Similarly, although Genesis declares that all things which God created are "very good," the church stood by while nature was polluted and destroyed. Redressing these mistakes in Christian thought and practice are crucial issues in the reform and renewal of Christian theology today.

Respect for both women and for ecology pose profound challenges to classical Christian theology and indeed all the classical religions shaped by the worldview of patriarchy. This essay focuses on Christianity, with its roots in the worldviews of the Ancient Near East and the Greco-Roman worlds. How are these two themes interconnected? This question is addressed by the term *ecofeminism.*

An earlier version of this essay was published as "Ecofeminism: Challenge to Theology," in *Christianity and Ecology: Seeking the Well-Being of Earth and Humans,* ed. Rosemary Radford Ruether and Dieter Hessel, 97–112 (Cambridge, MA: Harvard University Press, 2000). It has been updated for this volume.

Ecofeminism or ecological feminism examines the interconnections between the domination of women and the domination of nature. It aims at strategies and worldviews to liberate or heal these interconnected dominations by better understanding of their aetiology and enforcement.

There are two levels on which this relation between sexism and ecological exploitation can be made: the cultural-symbolic level and the socioeconomic level. My assumption is that the first is an ideological superstructure that reflects and ratifies the second; that is, social patterns developed, deeply rooted in the distortion of gender relations with the rise of patriarchal slavocracies in the Ancient Near East, that inferiorized women as a gender group. The system of domination of women itself was rooted in a larger patriarchal hierarchical system of priestly and warrior-king control over land, animals, and slaves as property, to monopolize wealth, power, and knowledge.

As this system of domination was shaped socially, ideological tools were constructed to ratify it as a reflection of the "nature of things" and the "will of God/the gods." Law codes were developed to define these relations of power of dominant men over women, slaves, animals, and land as property.[1] These law codes were depicted as handed down to an inspired lawgiver by God/the gods. Creation stories were spun to depict this hierarchical social order as itself a reflection of the cosmic order.

In the Ancient Near East and classical Athens several creation stories were constructed to ratify this design of society. In the Babylonian creation story, which goes back to the third millennium BCE, the story of cosmogony is told as a theogony of the gods that culminates in an intergenerational conflict between the old earth mother, Tiamat, and her great-grandson, Marduk. A mother-dominated old world of primal energies is set against a new world order of city-states championed by Marduk.[2]

Marduk is seen as conquering chaos and creating cosmos by conquering the primal mother, treading her body underfoot and splitting it in half, using one half to fashion the starry firmament above and the other half the earth below. Her subordinate male consort is then slain and from his blood, mixed with the earth, are fashioned

---

[1] For these relations of patriarchal domination in Ancient Near Eastern and Greek law codes, see Rosemary Radford Ruether, *Gaia and God: An Ecofeminist Theology of Earth Healing* (San Francisco: HarperSanFrancisco, 1992), 174–80.

[2] See "The Creation Epic," in *Religion in the Ancient Near East*, ed. Isaac Mendelson, 17–46 (New York: Liberal Arts Press, 1955).

human beings to be the slaves of the gods so the gods can be at lei-
sure. The elemental mother is turned into "matter," which can then
be used to shape a hierarchical cosmos. The creation of humans as
slaves to the gods within this cosmos defines primary social relations
as that of masters over slaves.

In both the Hebrew and the Greek creation stories this primal
battle against the mother that suggested an earlier alternative
world is concealed. These stories begin with the presupposition
of patriarchal dualism as the foundational nature of things. For
the Greek philosophical story, told by Plato, the primal dualism of
mind divided from matter was the first state of things. On the one
side stood Mind, containing the archetypal ideas; on the other side,
unformed matter, the receptacle or "nurse" of things to be. Between
the two stands disembodied male agency as the divine architect or
Creator, who shapes matter into a cosmos by fashioning it after the
intellectual blueprint of the divine ideas.[3]

The Creator shapes a circular and hierarchically ordered cosmos
with the fixed stars and the realm of the gods at the outer edge, the
earth at the bottom, and the planetary spheres ranged in between.
He then fashions the world soul to set this cosmos in motion. Taking the residue of the world soul he cuts it into individual souls and
places them in the stars. There they have a pre-incarnational vision
of the eternal ideas. Then they are encased in bodies, fashioned by
the planetary gods, and put on earth.

The task of the soul is to control the passions that arise from the
body and to cultivate the intellect. If the soul succeeds in this task,
it will doff the body at death and return to its native star, there to
live "a blessed and congenial existence." But if it fails to control
the body, it will enter a cycle of reincarnation, entering the bodies
of lower beings, women, lower social classes, and animals.[4] The
fall into an animal is terminal for the soul, but from lower forms
of humans—women and lower classes—the soul can rise through
successive incarnations into the highest state, the elite Greek male,
and be liberated into disembodied bliss.

Although Christianity would shed the ideas of the preexistence
and reincarnation of the soul, it followed key presuppositions of

---

[3] Plato, *Timaeus* (49), from *The Dialogues of Plato*, vol. 2, ed. Benjamin Jowett
(New York: Random House, 1937), 29.
[4] Plato, *Timaeus* (42), in Jowett, *The Dialogues of Plato*, 23; also Plato's *Phae-
drus*, where he adds the idea that the fallen soul will enter into various upper-
class or lower-class people depending on the extent of its fall into the passions
(Jowett, *Dialogues of Plato*, 248).

Plato's cosmology, reading the Genesis story through the lens of the *Timaeus*.[5] It continued the presuppositions that the soul is an ontological substance separable from the body, living in an alienated state on earth, whose true home lies in heaven. It attempted to combine the Platonic eschatology of the soul's return to the stars with the radically different Hebrew eschatology of the resurrected body on a millennial earth, by imagining a "spiritual body" stripped of its mortal components that would clothe the soul in its final heavenly state.[6]

Like Plato, Christianity imaged the soul in relation to the body as male controlling power over female-identified body and passions that are to be controlled. Although women are conceded also to possess a redeemable soul in God's image, the classical Christian theological tradition sees this soul as non-gendered. A genderless soul that can be redeemed through baptism into Christ is distinguished from women as female, who are seen as inherently closer to the sin-prone bodily tendencies.

This lower nature demands that women be subordinated and kept under control by men, but it also means that women are prone to insubordination and subversion of male rational control. It is through this female tendency that the male was seduced into sin in the beginning and paradise lost, ushering humanity into a fallen world.

In this story of original paradise, sin, and fall Christianity drew on a very different cosmology and earth story from the Hebrews. The Genesis story posits a patriarchal God who shapes an original chaotic matter into cosmos through his word-command during a six-day work week, culminating in sabbatical rest. The human, created male and female on the sixth day and given the command to rule over the earth and its plants and animals, is not created as a slave but as a royal servant or administrator of the earth as representative of God or "in God's image" (Gn 1:26–27).

There is no explicit mandate for the domination of some humans over others, as male over female, or master over slave, in the Hebrew story. This allowed the Genesis story to be used as a potent basis for an egalitarian view of all humans as equal in God's image in later Christian movements that sought to dismantle slavery and sexism. But this later Christian usage of Genesis 1 overlooks what was implicit in

[5] See Origen, *On First Principles* II, 2, 2 (New York: Harper and Row, 1966), 81–82; see also Radford Ruether, *Gaia and God*, 133.

[6] Gregory Nyssa describes the risen body as stripping off all that has made it mortal; see his "On the Soul and the Resurrection," in *Nicene and Post-Nicene Fathers*, 2nd series, vol. 5 (New York: Parker, 1893), 464–65.

the Hebrew story and explicit in Hebrew law and exegesis. Adam is a generic human who is assumed to be embodied by the male patriarchal class who represent dependent humans, women, slaves, and children and who rule over God's creation.[7]

Moreover, in Genesis 2 – 3, as if to make the gender assumptions explicit, the male is identified with the original male human being out of which the female is created by the male God and handed over to him as his wife-servant. Contrary to modern feminist apologetics, this is not an egalitarian relationship but one in which the male is the normative human and the female a derivative auxiliary.[8] Moreover, this derivative female is then described as initiating disobedience to God's command and thus causing the pair to be thrown out of paradise to live an oppressive existence. He is punished by hard labor, while she is punished by painful childbearing and subjugation to her husband.

Although the present fallen world is sunk in sin, Hebrew thought looks forward to a future time when paradise will be restored. When humans (Israel's patriarchal class) turn and obey God, God will restore them to an idyllic world where there will be no violence between man and man, alienation between man and nature will be overcome, and harmonic relations will reign on a peaceful and prosperous earth. Originally this Hebrew future hope for a future paradise was earth and mortality bound. It assumed that redeemed humans would live a long, healthy, but mortal life on a peaceful and bountiful but mortal earth.[9]

Later contact with Persian eschatology and Platonism would reshape Hebrew futurism into apocalyptic scenarios in which the dead of past generations rise, are judged by a messianic king, and the whole earth transformed into immortal conditions. It is this apocalyptic eschatology that is received by the Christian movement and fused with elements of Platonic cosmology to create the classic Christian story of creation, fall, and redemption.

Since Christianity dropped the ideas of the soul's preexistence and reincarnation, it also lost the explanation for women's inferiority

---

[7] See Phyllis Bird, "'Male and Female He Created Them': Gen 1:27b in the Context of the Priestly Account of Creation," in *Image of God and Gender Models in the Judaeo-Christian Tradition*, ed. Kari Borresen, 11–34 (Minneapolis, MN: Fortress Press, 1994).

[8] See Phyllis Trible, "Depatriarchalizing in Biblical Interpretation," in *Journal of the American Academy of Religion* 41/1 (March 1973): 30–48.

[9] See Rachel Zohar Dulin, "Old Age in the Hebrew Scriptures," PhD thesis (Chicago: Northwestern University, 1982).

based on the view that women are born through the failure of souls in past male incarnations to control their bodily passions. Some early Christian movements suggested a subversive liberation in Christ, from all relations of subjugation, women to men, slaves to masters, subjugated to ruling nations. The original equality prior to sexual differentiation is seen as restored, drawing on the Galatians text, "There is no longer Jew or Greek, there is no longer slave or free, there is no longer male and female; for all of you are one in Christ Jesus" (Gal 3:28).[10]

But as Christianity was institutionalized in the patriarchal family and political order, it moved quickly to suppress these radical interpretations of redemption in Christ. Although equal access to heavenly redemption was conceded to women, this future hope was not allowed to subvert patriarchal relations on earth in the newly forming Christian church and society. This is already expressed in the post-Pauline dicta in 1 Timothy, which declare that women were created second and sinned first and therefore are to keep silence and to have no authority over men in the Christian community (1 Tim 2:11–15).[11]

Augustine, in his commentaries on Genesis in the late fourth and early fifth centuries, would shape the theological rationale for women's subordination that would be followed by the dominant line of Christian theologians through the Reformation. For Augustine, woman, although given a non-gendered soul by the creator that enables her to be redeemed, was created in her female nature to be subordinate to the male in the sexual-social roles of wife and child-bearer. For Augustine, femaleness itself represents the inferior bodily nature, while the male represents the intellect, which is to rule over both his body and hers. He is the collective Adam made in God's image, while woman as woman does not possess the image of God in herself but images the subordinate body. She is "in the image of God" only when taken together with the male "who is her head."[12]

Moreover, for Augustine, due to her inferior and more sin-prone nature, Eve initiated disobedience to God. The male, in assenting to her prompting, thus conceded to his lower self. Only thus does

---

[10] See Rosemary R. Ruether, *Women and Redemption: A Theological History* (Minneapolis, MN: Fortress Press, 1998), chap 1.

[11] See Dennis R. MacDonald, *The Legend and the Apostle: The Battle for Paul in Story and Canon* (Philadelphia: Westminister Press, 1983).

[12] Augustine, *De Trinitate* 10,10,7. See Radford Ruether, *Women and Redemption*, chap. 2.

the whole human fall into sin.[13] Although humans as a whole are punished by a loss of original immortality that was the gift of union with God and have lost the free will that allowed them to choose God over their sinful self-will, women are punished for their special fault by coercive subjugation.[14]

For Augustine, woman was created subordinate and is now in a state of forced subjugation to punish her for her original insubordination and to keep her in her place. Redemption does not liberate her from this subordination. Rather, through voluntary acceptance of it, she makes herself obedient to God and a fit subject of heavenly bliss. Then, finally, there will be no hierarchy of male over female, but all the blessed will live in gloriously spiritualized bodies freed from sin and death.

These patriarchal patterns that fused Hebrew and Greek thought reigned in Christian cosmology, anthropology, Christology, and soteriology until modern times, being taken up and renewed by the mainline Reformers, Luther and Calvin. In the sixteenth and seventeeth centuries a few maverick feminist humanists and the Quakers challenged the doctrine of male domination as order of nature and punishment due women for their priority in sin. They picked up suppressed early Christian themes of radical egalitarianism and argued that all humans were made equal in the original creation.[15]

For these thinkers, the domination of women, as well as other forms of domination, such as slavery, came about through sin—not women's sin, but the sin of dominant males who distorted the original harmony by usurping power over others. Christ came to overcome all such dominations and to restore the equality of women and men, but male church leaders have distorted the gospel into new rationales for sexism. Redemption means not just a promise of spiritual equality in heaven but a social struggle to overcome unjust domination of men over women, masters over slaves, here on earth.

This theology of original and redeemed equality over against patriarchal slavocracy was picked up and developed by the abolitionist feminists of the nineteenth century, such as the Grimké sisters and

---

[13] Augustine, *City of God* 14:11.

[14] Augustine, *On Genesis Against the Manichaeans* II.19, in *The Fathers of the Church*, vol. 84, ed. Roland J. Teske (Washington, DC: Catholic University of America Press, 1991). See also Radford Ruether, *Women and Redemption*, chap. 2.

[15] Particularly the tract of Agrippa von Nettesheim (1509), *De Nobilitate et Praecellentia foeminei Sexus*, ed. Charles Bene (Geneva: Droz, 1990); see also Radford Ruether, *Women and Redemption*, chap. 4.

Lucretia Mott. In the pithy words of Sarah Grimké, writing in 1837, "All I ask of my brethren is, that they take their feet from off our necks and permit us to stand upright on the ground which God designed us to occupy."[16] Sarah Grimké had no doubt that that ground was one of an autonomous human being created to be man's peer and equal partner, not his subordinate.

This anthropology of original and restored equality was rediscovered by modern feminist theology and has been the basis for a critique of patriarchal anthropology in recent decades. But the nineteenth-century feminists did not question an anthropocentric worldview in which man and woman together were created to dominate and rule over the nonhuman creation. It is only with the deepening of feminist theology in ecofeminism that there has been a questioning of patriarchal cosmology and a recognition of the need to grapple with the whole structure of the Christian story, not just with gender relations, in its anthropology.

When I speak about the challenge of ecofeminism to theology, it is in the context of radicalization that takes place as ecological consciousness is incorporated into feminist theology. One then realizes the need to question and reconstruct the cosmological framework out of which the Christian worldview grew from its ancient roots in the Hebrew and Greek worlds. A full treatment of the implications of these deeper questions is still very much in process. One awaits a full presentation of what an ecofeminist theology would look like. Here I attempt only a few suggestions about how the self, sin and redemption, God, cosmology, and eschatology are being rethought by ecofeminist theology.

I begin with a view of the self in ecofeminist theology as the starting point for a challenge to the Platonic construct of soul and body, which still reigns officially in Christian thought. The basic assumption of ecofeminist theology is that the dualism of soul and body must be overcome, as well as the assumptions of the priority and controlling role of male-identified mind over female-identified body. This anthropology is at the heart of the distortion in Western thought of our relation to ourselves, as well as to our fellow earth creatures and the cosmos as a whole.

Humans are latecomers to the planet. The plants and animals existed billions of years before us. We are descendants of the long

---

[16] Sarah Grimké, "Letters on the Equality of the Sexes and the Condition of Women" (1837), in *Feminism: The Essential Historical Writings*, ed. Miriam Schneir (New York: Vintage, 1992), 38.

evolution of increasingly complex life forms on earth. Our consciousness does not set us radically apart from the rest of the life forms on earth but is part of a continuity of matter-energy dynamics that bursts into life, awareness of life, and self-reflecting consciousness in organisms with progressively more complex brains. We were not created to dominate and rule the earth, for it governed itself well and better for millions of years when we did not exist or existed as a non-dominant mammal.

Only in very recent earth history, in the last few thousand years, has Homo sapiens emerged as an increasingly dominant species, using its special gifts for thinking and organizing to control and exploit the majority of humans and the nonhuman earth community. Stewardship, then, is not a primal command, but an ex post facto effort of dominant males to correct abuse and become better managers of what they have presumed to be their patrimony, namely, ownership of the rest of the world.

We need to recognize that our self-reflective consciousness is not a separable ontological substance but our experience of our own interiority, which is integral to our brain-body and dies with it. We are finite sparks of self-conscious life who arose from earth and return to it at death. Our consciousness did not fall from a heaven outside the earth and will not escape outside of it into an eternal life. Our destiny and calling is of and for this earth, our only and true home. Immortality does not lie in the preservation of our individual consciousness as a separate substance but in the miracle and mystery of endlessly recycled matter-energy out of which we arose and into which we return. To better translate the Ash Wednesday proclamation, "we are earth; to earth we shall return."

This means we need to use our special capacities for thought, not to imagine ourselves as ruling over others, superior to them, and escaping our common mortality, but rather to celebrate the wonder of the whole cosmic process and to be the place where this cosmic process comes to celebrative consciousness. We also need to use our capacities to think and understand these processes to find how to harmonize our lives with the life of the whole earth community. This demands a spirituality and ethic of mutual limitation and nurture of reciprocal life giving, the very opposite of the spirituality of separation and domination.

This ecological consciousness of self calls for a very different understanding of the nature of evil and its remedies. We need to give up the presuppositions of an original paradise when there was no evil and a future paradise when evil and death are overcome.

Rather, we need to look more closely at the aetiology of our particular distortion of our relation to one another and to the earth through
myths of separation and domination. Here I find myself particularly
instructed by Brazilian ecofeminist theologian Ivone Gebara.

In Gebara's view, natural evil, in the sense of finitude and tragedy,
have always been with us and all life forms on earth and will always
be so. The primal sin is not a disobedience that caused us to fall into
a mortality to which we were not originally subjected. Rather, the
primal sin lies in the effort to escape from mortality, finitude, and
vulnerability. The desire to escape from mortality may have long
been a part of human awareness of the fear of death, but it took organized, pernicious forms with the rise of powerful males who sought
to monopolize power over other humans, land, and animals. For
them, the ultimate power over others was to rise superior to death
itself, to organize their power to assure themselves of an invulnerability to that finitude that is the common lot of earth creatures.[17]

This very effort to secure their own invulnerability from want and
death impelled an endless process of seeking to amass power at the
expense of the rest of humans and the earth. Thus these dominant
men, seeking ultimate salvation from vulnerability, constructed
systems of abuse and exploitation of other humans and the earth in
order to amass overweening wealth and power. Women became the
particular targets of this flight from vulnerability because they represent men's finite origins and the realities of earth-bound pain and
limits. To rule over and to flee from women, the body, and the earth
was to seek to conquer and flee from one's own denied finitude.

For Gebara, it is this impulse to dominate and exploit in order to
conquer want, imagining oneself to have transcended finite limitations, that has created the system of distortion that heaps excessive
want and untimely death on the majority of humans and other
earth creatures. This system of exploitation threatens to undo the
processes that maintain the lifecycle of all earth beings in relation
to one another, crafted by the earth over billions of years. It is this
system of domination and distortion that is sin, or culpable evil, as
distinct from tragedy and death which are natural and inevitable.

This understanding of the aetiology of sin and the fall into domination also dictates how Gebara understands salvation. Just as we
must give up the original paradise when there was no tragedy or
death, so we must give up the future paradise when tragedy and

---

[17] Ivone Gebara, *Teología a Ritmo de Mujer* (Madrid: San Pablo, 1995), 146–56.
See also Radford Ruether, *Women and Redemption*, chap. 8.

death are overcome.[18] We need to recognize that these myths of immortal and perfect beginnings and ends not only falsify our real possibilities but are themselves the projection of the escape from vulnerability that is at the heart of sin.

The real salvation that is available to us is of much more modest dimensions, and yet nevertheless of world historic and global proportions. We need to dismantle the system of distortion that gives a privileged class overweening wealth and power at the expense of most humans and that is destroying the life-sustaining balances of the earth. In so doing we will not expect a paradise free from tragedy and death, but rather a community of mutual life giving where we can hold one another in the celebrative as well as the tragic moments of our common life as earth creatures.

This more modest redemptive hope was summed up in the conclusion of the women's creed written by Robin Morgan for the Women's Conference in Bejing, China, in September 1995:

> Bread. A clean sky. Active peace. A woman's voice singing somewhere. The army disbanded. The harvest abundant. The wound healed. The child wanted. The prisoner freed. The body's integrity honored. The lover returned. . . . Labor equal, fair and valued. No hand raised in any gesture but greeting. Secure interiors — of heart, home and land — so firm as to make secure borders irrelevant at last.[19]

This is the vision of an ecological hope freed from false escapism and content to make common joys abundant and available to us all in the midst of those tragedies of limits, failures, and accidents that also should be equally shared, rather than heaped upon some in excess so a privileged few may imagine themselves immortal.

The dismantling of an escapist self and salvation history that is the root of human sin and *han* (victimization of others and the pain of victimization)[20] also demands a dismantling of the view of cosmology, God, and Christ that has sustained this distortion. Instead of

---

[18] Gebara, *Teología a Ritmo de Mujer*, 146–56.

[19] This creed was sent to me by Catherine Keller of Drew Theological Seminary in Madison, New Jersey.

[20] The term *han* comes from Korean *minjung* theology, which discusses the experience of victimization. For a theology that interconnects the Western Christian emphasis on sin with the *minjung* emphasis on *han*, see Andrew Sung Park, *The Wounded Heart of God: The Asian Concept of Han and the Christian Doctrine of Sin* (Nashville, TN: Abingdon Press, 1993).

modeling God after male-ruling-class consciousness, outside of and
ruling over nature as its controlling immortal projection, God in ecofeminist spirituality is the immanent source of life and the renewal
of life that sustains the whole planetary and cosmic community. God
is neither male nor anthropomorphic. God is the font from which
the variety of particular beings "co-arise" in each generation, the
matrix that sustains their life-giving interdependency, and also the
judging and renewing insurgency of life that enable us to overcome
the distortions that threaten healthy relations.

This understanding of God is leading several ecofeminist theologians to reconstruct the understanding of the Trinity as the sustaining matrix of immanent relationality. Ivone Gebara sees the Trinity
not as a separate, self-enclosed relation of two divine males with
each other, mediated by the Spirit, but rather as the symbolic expression of the basic dynamic of life itself as a process of vital interrelational creativity. Life as interrelational creativity exists on every
level of reality. As cosmos, it reveals itself as the whole process of
cosmic unfolding and interrelation of planets and galaxies. As earth,
it shows us the dynamic interrelational process of life unfolding in
the biosphere.[21]

Each species exhibits many differences, including human beings
with their many races and cultures. We should celebrate this diversity of humanness and affirm our interrelation with one another in
one community on earth. Likewise, both interpersonal society and
the person exist as a creative dynamic of expanding plurality and
new interrelationality, of unity and diversity in interaction. The
trinitarian dynamic of life is both creational and salvational; it both
creates new life and seeks to correct distorted relations and reestab-
lish life-giving, loving relationality. The name of the trinitarian God
as sustaining, redeeming matrix of cosmic, planetary, social, and
personal life is Sophia: Holy Wisdom.

In the context of this understanding of the ecological self, good
and evil, and the trinitarian God, what does it mean to speak of Jesus
as Christ? Can we still affirm this one historical figure as the unique
incarnation of God's creating Logos, even reinterpreted as Sophia?
In what way is he both Sophia and Messiah? Gebara questions the
messianic myth of a heroic warrior who will deliver victims from
oppression, punish the oppressors, and create an ideal earth freed

    [21] Ivone Gebara, "The Trinity and Human Experience," in *Women Healing
Earth: Third World Women on Ecology, Feminism and Religion*, ed. Rosemary Radford Ruether, 13–23 (Maryknoll, NY: Orbis Books, 1996).

from sin and want. She sees this myth as the counterpart, arising from victims, of the desire to escape from finitude, but now coupled with the thirst for revenge upon those who have secured their own privilege at the expense of others. Messianic myths, as revenge scenarios of victims, do not break, but they reproduce the cycle of violence and create new victims and new victimizers.

Jesus, for Gebara, is a very different prophetic figure who sought to break through the cycle of violence. Taking the side of the victims, he also called those in power to repent and enter into a new community of mutual service. The dominant system could not tolerate his message and killed him to silence his counter vision. But his followers also betrayed him by turning his call to a community of shared love into a new messianism, making him into the warrior imperial Savior that would secure the Christian system of dominating power.[22]

Thus, to ask how Jesus is the Christ, one must overturn the messianic myth. Jesus instead stands as an anti-messiah calling us to rediscover the community of equals that appears when the system of sin and *han,* of victimizers and victims, of rich and poor, is dismantled. We enter, then, not a community of immortal blessedness freed from finitude and limits, but a community of shared joys and sorrows as earth creatures, Pharisees and prostitutes, the lame and the blind, women and men on the edges of the dominant system breaking bread together.

Likewise, if Jesus reveals God, the God he reveals is not the split off, dominating Logos of immortalized male sovereignty, but the Holy Wisdom of mutual self-giving and life-sustaining love. He embodies the Holy Wisdom that creates and renews the creation, not as its exclusive and unique representative, but rather as a paradigm of her presence, one among many other sisters and brothers, to recall us to our true selves and relations from the madness of escapism and domination. These are the "temptations" from which we ask to be delivered, even as we pray for those conditions of daily bread and mutual forgiveness that recreate God's will done on earth.

Gebara's understanding of the immanent trinitarian God of life's dynamic relationality places revelation in our experience of nature. We read (and critique) our historical scriptures in the light of the book of nature. All life from the evolution of the galaxies to the dynamics of the self manifest the presence of God as sustaining Wisdom of creation. But this does not mean a blissful world of idyllic

---

[22] Gebara, *Teología a Ritmo de Mujer,* 146–56.

conditions. Nature reveals how life sustains its precarious balances by painful and tragic means. Lion and lamb do not lie down together but keep one another's populations in sustainable limits by a bloody process of eating and being eaten.

We are tempted in speaking of nature as revelatory to see nature through paradisal lens, ignoring its violent and tragic face. We imagine it as Eden only by removing ourselves from it and viewing it through the plate-glass window of our momentary havens of invulnerability, purchased at the expense of many other humans. But a tornado can shatter this glass and sweep away this shelter at any moment.

Two revelatory words come, from nature and from history, that are not easy to reconcile. Some in Christian thought even saw them as revealing different gods opposed to one another. I call these two words the call to sustainability and the call to preferential option for the poor. When I garden, I would be foolish to make a preferential option for the weak and the diseased. I need to root out the excess growth of many plants so that a few, the healthiest, can grow well. In like manner, as Jay McDaniel agonized, nature gives the pelican two eggs so that one will survive, but if the first hatches well, the second will be pecked to death and thrown from the nest.[23] This cruelty is necessary for a sustainable population of pelicans or tomatoes. Sentimentality for the second pelican or the excess plants would be misplaced.

Likewise, humans need to limit their own species proliferation at the expense of the other species of earth as much as possible by decisions not to conceive rather than to abort. But to deny the need for birth limitation in the name of life is no favor to children. It means that thousands die each day of malnutrition soon after birth. To refuse to limit ourselves rationally means that these limits will be imposed cruelly and violently.

A different call comes from our history of sin and *han*, arising as a protest against the distortion of relations between humans and between humans and other creatures into overweening wealth for a few and impoverishment for the many. This pattern is not, contrary to social Darwinism, an expression of a natural ethic of the survival of the fittest, for nature does not favor the large carnivore, precariously perched at the top of the food chain, over all the creatures on which it depends, but seeks dynamic balance through a combination

---

[23] Jay McDaniel, *Of God and Pelicans: A Theology of Reverence for Life* (Louisville, KY: Westminister/John Knox Press, 1989), 19–21.

of mutual limits and cooperation. The scurrying insects that compost the forest are far more important to its well-being than the lion.

The preferential option for the poor seeks to correct the destructive option for the rich at the expense of the well-being of the whole community of life. The ethic of the preferential option for the poor calls us to feed and nurture the child of the poor dying from malnutrition and unclean water and rectify the conditions that are causing this untimely death, while the ethic of sustainability calls us to help the mother of this child limit her childbearing.

The two ethics often stand in tragic tension, but they should not be allowed to fall into irreconcilable dualism: into a war-god of victory of the strong over the weak, on the one hand, and, on the other, a God of compassion for the weak distorted into a defense of fetuses against women. We need to seek the right balance between justice and sustainability. The challenge of ecological theology and ethics is to knit together, in the light of both earth knowledge and the crisis of human history, a vision of divine presence that both underlies and sustains natural processes and also struggles against the excesses of the powerful and reaches out to the victimized to create communities of mutual flourishing.

A Response to Rosemary Radford Ruether

Hope in the Face of Limitation

Kirsten Gerdes

As I write this, there are numbers of recent—seemingly unrelated—
events in the United States that should be cause for concern among
anyone interested in issues of theological ethics, ecofeminism, critical race studies, and ecology. For instance, the cost of oil is rising,
which affects so much of our oil-dependent infrastructure, from
transportation to agriculture to manufacturing. In April 2012, pho-
tos surfaced of US soldiers posing with dismembered Afghans. A
few weeks later national security leaks at the White House released
information revealing that President Obama has a secret "kill list"
of known terrorists, which reserves the ultimate decision to kill or to
capture to him alone.[1] In March 2012, Michelle Duggar, the mother
on the reality television show "Nineteen Kids and Counting," made
comments rejecting overpopulation and its ecological implications
as a myth. Of course, there are also the growing restrictions on
women's legal access to reproductive health in the United States,
whether regarding access to birth control on private employers'
health insurance plans or abortion, with new laws attempting to be
passed in places like Arizona—where the state passed a law in 2012
declaring that gestational age of a fetus legally begins two weeks
before conception—and Oklahoma—whose Senate passed a bill in

---

[1] Of note regarding the release of this information is that many who are
most vocal against it are more concerned with the security breach itself, or
the speculation that the leaks are a political move in an election year in order
to make President Obama appear as a strong leader, than they are with what
should be an alarming reserve of power exercised in secret by a democratically
elected president.

2012 to make zygotes legal persons.[2] At root, these events are bound together by an ideology of domination that ecofeminist theologians like Rosemary Radford Ruether seek to expose and eradicate.

In her essay Radford Ruether insightfully outlines the importance of ecofeminist theology as a compelling theological issue. She uses a feminist lens to analyze a predominantly patriarchal Christian history, both in its theology and its practice. Pointing out that this patriarchy has been used to justify widespread violence and oppression of creation—human and nonhuman alike—Radford Ruether calls for a renewed ethic of both preferential option for the poor and sustainability in order to address contemporary (and anticipated) needs in society. Although I agree that the ethics she proposes are, indeed, the direction contemporary ecofeminism should move, a more concrete picture of how these ethics might be employed legally, politically, and theologically in real communities, as well as ecofeminism's wider inclusion of the critique of the intersection of oppressions—not just gendered, but racial and class based as well—are required to address adequately and "hope fully" the issues facing contemporary theology.

The story Radford Ruether outlines begins with the creation myths that were borrowed from the Babylonian and Greek myths and then reinterpreted in the Hebrew Bible and the New Testament. Although the Babylonian myth rested on a primary matriarchy perceived as chaos that is overturned for a patriarchal cosmos, the Greek and Hebrew creation myths covered over the defeat of a primordial, primal mother and replaced it with a presupposed patriarchy. Additionally, Christianity's incorporation of a Platonic dualism that privileges the transcendent over the immanent—the soul over the body—and connects the male as original with the soul and the female as derivative with the body, renders the establishment of a 'divinely' ordained patriarchy complete.

Radford Ruether argues that this Christian theology of creation is inextricably related to a Christology that is presented as an escapist redemption—through Christ, one receives a spiritual salvation that would eventually lead to the transcendence of this earthly realm for a perfect, eternal heavenly realm. Radford Ruether informs us that any subversively feminist interpretations of salvation as liberation from

---

[2] Arizona's House Bill 2036 was ruled unconstitutional by the 9th US Circuit Court of Appeals in May 2013, overturning the decision of a federal judge to uphold the law in July 2012. As of January 2014, the US Supreme Court declined to hear Arizona's appeal to reinstate the law. Oklahoma's personhood bill was ruled unconstitutional by the Oklahoma Supreme Court in April 2012.

the established patriarchal order were excluded by the developing Christian orthodoxy, codified in Augustine's writings on creation and women in particular. But that thread of liberatory thought is picked up by later movements of individuals seeking to question the established hierarchies. Radford Ruether paints a picture of a continuity between earlier proto-feminist Christians pulling on this thread to unravel patriarchy's hold on social institutions and the growing movement of individuals in the late twentieth and early twenty-first centuries who see the aims of feminism and ecology as inherently linked ideologically. They do so through a rejection of two concepts that contribute to an "impulse to dominate and exploit in order to conquer want," namely, a mind-body dualism and the idea of the self as separate substance.

She relies on Ivone Gebara's reinterpretation of salvation, which is a dismissal of an escapist eschatology that is at the heart of sin. What results is the means by which we can attempt to eradicate the systems of oppression and begin to see ourselves as interrelated with the cosmos; it requires a radical reinterpretation of the traditional trinitarian doctrine, particularly Christology. Radford Ruether asserts that reorienting our views in this way brings two ethics into a necessary tension: the call to sustainability and the preferential option for the poor. The former asks us to limit ourselves, while the latter asks us to give of ourselves, and it is the work of theology to bring the two disparate ethics together.

I agree with Radford Ruether's approach of starting at the beginning, for lack of a better word, with creation theology. Her reference to Gebara's revisioning of primal sin as the attempt to escape from mortality resonates with process theologian Catherine Keller's call in *Face of the Deep* to reject a *creatio ex nihilo* in favor of a creation out of the chaos of the deep. Keller writes:

> To a theology of becoming, this radical genesis *divines* the potentiality of the tehom [the Abyss]. Its creativity does not create by itself. By itself it *makes* no difference. . . . The great cosmic decision has been traditionally, with justice, named *the creation*; its agency, *the creator*. That which divines the possible also limits the infinite to its multiplying finitudes. . . . It makes it not from nothing but from everything—from the unruly multiple.[3]

---

[3] Catherine Keller, *Face of the Deep: A Theology of Becoming* (London: Routledge, 2003), 180.

Thus, not only is humanity connected to the rest of creation in its mortality, as Gebara and Radford Ruether imply, but also through the "plurisingularity," as Keller refers to it, of creation. Instead of viewing the immanent world as derivative of a prior perfect world or of a heavenly realm, this tehomic perspective suggests that relation is primary through the primal chaos. Instead of grasping for a future immortality, it recognizes its origins as infinite. In fact, this tehomic perspective images for us a plurisingular God that creates through limitation—in Keller's words, it is a God that "limits the infinite to its multiplying finitudes." Perhaps here the ethic of a call to sustainability as Radford Ruether describes it finds a ground; divine creativity permeates the "unruly multiple" and orders it—makes it into a something. It is not chaotic, endless proliferation, but multiplying finitudes. What might a theology that uses this image as the starting point for discussion of the *imago Dei* look like in practice?

Historically, the question of determining humanity's relation to the rest of creation within a Christian paradigm has turned around this concept of the *imago Dei*, with a traditional view—often rooted in Pauline texts—that wholly applies it to men but only partially applies it to women, such that only women's (spiritual) souls qualify as *imago Dei*, while their bodies are debased. The devaluation of both materiality, and by association, women, feeds a corrupt view of the *imago Dei* in terms of domination and entitlement. In other words, what accompanies this corrupted *imago Dei* is a hierarchy based on one's position in relation to the Divine. In turn, it leads not only to a theology that systematically justifies and spiritualizes oppression of women and destruction of nature, but also to a sense of entitlement that displaces any responsibility toward or interrelationality with the rest of creation. This entitlement has reformulated, repackaged, and re-economized itself throughout historical epochs. In the modern United States it presents itself in terms of Lockean individual human rights based on a Western, separatist "self." It is only within this type of culture of individual rights that a discourse of a zygote's rights can emerge. Here I might pose a few questions: what role can ecofeminist theology play in reclaiming an *imago Dei* that is not based on entitlement—that is, what rights, powers, and privileges one "gets" with it—but rather on what responsibility is bestowed on humanity as bearers of the image of God? How can we be conduits and representatives of divine creativity and love in the immanent world? How might this avoid the pitfalls of women's (disproportionate) self-sacrifice recognized and critiqued by feminist theology, particularly in terms of Radford Ruether's call for limiting humanity's species proliferation?

Indeed, one of the major themes through Radford Ruether's text is her return to the notion of limit, highlighting Western theology's tendency toward privileging transcendence of limitations and exercise of mastery and control over a recognition of humanity's inherent limitations. Her call toward responsibility reverberates with the idea that limits are not inherently deleterious, something to be overcome, but rather something to be celebrated—and the foundation of the ethics she outlines. Both the ethic of the preferential option for the poor and the ethic of sustainability call for responsibility, and Radford Ruether acknowledges the inherent tension between them. This tension is not relegated to the theological realm but is reflected in the socioeconomic, political, and legal realms as well, and it is framed in terms of individual versus collective rights. I have already pointed to some events that highlight the ways in which this tension has surfaced. There is no simple answer to this tension, especially as it becomes a struggle for power. Radford Ruether argues that these two must not "be allowed to fall into irreconcilable dualism," but she does not offer a satisfactorily concrete picture of what this might look like.

In light of this, I propose what is perhaps an impossible but necessary question: how can ecofeminist theology maintain an immanent sense of hope? As someone for whom poststructuralism and critical theory often resonate more than the goddess thealogy attributed to some strands of ecofeminism, I find Donna Haraway a useful source here. In "A Cyborg Manifesto" she presents the concept of a cyborg—a human-machine hybrid—as the best metaphor for the permeability of boundaries in three distinctions: between humans and other living organisms; between humans/animals and machines; and between the physical and nonphysical. A cyborg world neither justifies continued degradation of natural processes nor requires asceticism from technology, because we are intricately connected with both. She asserts:

> A cyborg world might be about lived social and bodily realities in which people are not afraid of their joint kinship with animals and machines, not afraid of permanently partial identities and contradictory standpoints. The political struggle is to see from both perspectives at once because each reveals both dominations and possibilities unimaginable from the other vantage point.[4]

---

[4] Donna Haraway, "A Cyborg Manifesto," *Transgender Studies Reader*, ed. Susan Stryker and Stephen White, 103–18 (New York: Routledge, 2006), 107.

The cyborg is the way through what she refers to as the "maze of dualisms," not as a means to a common language, but rather a heteroglossia.[5] She emphasizes situated knowledges and the necessity of seeing from multiple perspectives. I submit that this must be the starting point for hope—the willingness and ability to see multiple perspectives, not to hold them as equally valid, but to be able with empathy to hold each other and our communities accountable, as well as with humility to *be* accountable to others, both as individuals and collectives.

This accountability should include ecofeminists, particularly in terms of how ecofeminism as a movement can seek to address more critically the intersection of oppressions as they play out against the oppressed. A few prominent ethicists and feminist theologians address this complex issue, pointing out the ways not only gender, but also race and class, play into cultures of domination that lead to ecological destruction. James H. Cone has written about the connection between white world supremacy and the degradation of nature. He asserts that there is a "connection between the struggle against racism and other struggles for life" and names the womanist theologians who have begun to make this critique.[6] He calls out white ecological ethicists and theologians for being unwilling to cede any claims to ecological knowledge to people of color, who are the communities typically most affected by the degradation of creation.[7]

Likewise, in "The Integrity of Creation and Earth Community: An Ecumenical Response to Environmental Racism," ecofeminist theologian Aruna Gnanadason spotlights the ways in which corporate globalization under the guise of "sustainable development" enacts environmental racism.[8] She argues, "In my analysis, what seems to be missing in the writings of many environmentalists . . . is the need to stress the integral relation between social and environmental justice."[9] As an example, she recounts the testimony from a Dalit Indian doctoral student at Union Theological Seminary speaking about ecological issues: "Please do not ask us to be less anthropocentric, when it is only now that we Dalits are 'becoming a people' who can

---

[5] Ibid., 116.

[6] James H. Cone, "Whose Earth Is It Anyway?" *Cross Currents* 50/1–2 (2000): 39.

[7] Ibid., 42.

[8] Aruna Gnanadason, "The Integrity of Creation and Earth Community: An Ecumenical Response to Environmental Racism," *Union Seminary Quarterly Review* 58/1–2 (2004): 100.

[9] Ibid., 114.

speak of our lives and dignity as human beings."[10] Such an example underscores the complicity ecologists and ethicists from the Global North have had in ignoring or perpetuating systems of oppression.

Most recently, Grace Y. Kao has investigated two critiques of ecofeminism in her article "The Universal Versus the Particular in Ecofeminist Ethics."[11] The first critique claims that ecofeminism erroneously universalizes the association of women and nature, arguing that there are cultures in which the absence of such an association does not reduce instances of either patriarchy or ecological crises. Within this analysis is layered a critique against the essentializing of the category woman. The second overall critique of ecofeminism questions the appropriation of cultures or religious practices deemed eco-friendly by people nonnative to those cultures or faiths. This critique asserts that even well-intentioned praise for communities that practice ecologically sustainable living can erase difference and "reify colonizing discourses by 'naturalizing' this undifferentiated and racialized *Other* over against a white, modern industrialized (read 'cultured') Western society."[12] Kao's response is simultaneously to recognize the concern underlying each of the critiques and the usefulness of some aspects of the ways of thinking critiqued.[13] In so doing, she allows the space for such theoretical constructs to be changed when they are no longer useful, emphasizing the importance of engaging the ecological crisis in ways that are both responsible and effective.

As Kao argues, and as Radford Ruether has so aptly demonstrated, a critical role remains for ecofeminism to play, not only in addressing the harmful personal practices, corporate development, and laws that undergird the ecological crisis we face, but also in exposing beliefs that warrant and perpetuate oppression, whether those beliefs are held within the movement or outside of it. The challenge of ecofeminism to theology should be the challenge of ecofeminism to itself: there must be a willingness to face the deficiencies that have historically inhibited and blinded us as global communities from combating the deeply entrenched paradigms in our collective unconscious. Echoing Radford Ruether's call for holding the ethics of sustainability and the preferential option for

---

[10] Cited in ibid.

[11] Grace Y. Kao, "The Universal Versus the Particular in Ecofeminist Ethics," *Journal of Religious Ethics* 38/4 (2010).

[12] Ibid., 628. Kao quotes here from Noel Sturgeon, *Ecofeminist Natures: Race, Gender, Feminist Theory, and Political Action* (London: Routledge, 1997), 113.

[13] Kao, "The Universal Versus the Particular in Ecofeminist Ethics," 632.

the poor in tension, Keller's recognition of both creation and the divine's plurisingularity, and Haraway's desire for a heteroglossia, I contend that we cannot recoil from or cover over difference but must begin to understand it as the grounds of a creativity that holds the possibility of hope. Theology and ecofeminism, particularly, should be hope-*full* endeavors; at rhizomatic root, they have the ability to expand, extend, and cultivate transformation.

8

The Song of the Thrush

Christian Animism and the Global Crisis Today

Mark I. Wallace

The thrush alone declares the immortal wealth and vigor that is in the forest. . . . Whenever a man hears it he is young, and Nature is in her spring; wherever he hears it, it is a new world and a free country, and the gates of Heaven are not shut against him.

— Henry David Thoreau

The Song of the Thrush

Through a set of fortuitous circumstances last year, I moved to the edge of a three-hundred-acre forest adjacent to Swarthmore College, where I teach. At the time of my move, I was startled early one morning by what I later learned from a friend to be the call of the wood thrush. I have since grown accustomed to this wonder. The song of the thrush is a melody unlike anything I have ever heard. Liquid, flute-like, perfectly pitched—the thrush sings a kind of ethereal duet with itself in which it simultaneously produces two independent melody lines that reverberate with one another back and forth, back and forth. The thrush lives in the interior of the forest and refuses the lure of my feeder; like God's Spirit, its effects are

Much of the material in this essay is drawn from the following two works: Mark I. Wallace, *Finding God in the Singing River: Christianity, Spirit, Nature* (Minneapolis, MN: Fortress Press, 2005); idem, *Green Christianity: Five Ways to a Sustainable Future* (Minneapolis, MN: Fortress Press, 2010).

felt and heard by me even though I have never seen it. In the spring and summer I wake up, and often go to sleep, to the otherworldly harmonics of a bird that I cannot see but whose delicate polyphony now pleasantly haunts my dreams. Thoreau says whoever hears the song of the thrush enters a "new world" where the "gates of Heaven are not shut against" the listener. The airy trills of the thrush open up to me the beauty and mystery of the natural world whenever I am graced by its invisible presence. Sight unseen, awash in the deep of this sweet counterpoint, the thrush for me is a moving synecdoche of the beauty of creation. In the refrain of a Native American prayer,

> Beauty is before me
> And beauty is behind me
> Above and below me hovers the beautiful
> I am surrounded by it
> I am immersed in it
> In my youth I am aware of it
> And in old age I shall walk quietly
> The beautiful trail.[1]

For me, "the beautiful trail" — the natural world — serves as the primary site for the sort of spiritual encounters listening to the wood thrush provides. "I enter a swamp as a sacred place — a *sanctum sanctorum*," wrote Henry David Thoreau.[2] The whoosh of a strong wind, the taste of the sea on my tongue, the delicate movement of a monarch butterfly, the arch of the bright sky on a cold winter night, the screech of a red-tailed hawk — these events are preternatural overtures that greet me from another plane of existence. It is not that this other plane stands over and against everyday reality, but rather that commonplace existence is a window into another world that is *this* world but now experienced in its pregnant depths and deeper possibilities. Like the disciples on the road to Emmaus in Luke's Gospel who walked and talked with Jesus but did not recognize him until their understanding was changed — like the gift of bread and wine that is not experienced as God's body and blood apart from its ritual transformation — the natural world stands mute until it is spiritually encountered as saturated with grace and meaning.

---

[1] "Now Talking God," in *Earth Prayers: From Around the World, 365 Prayers, Poems, and Invocations for Honoring the Earth*, ed. Elizabeth Roberts and Elias Amidon (San Francisco: HarperSanFrancisco, 1991), 32.

[2] Henry David Thoreau, "Walking," in *The Norton Book of American Nature Writing*, ed. John Elder and Robert Finch (New York: W. W. Norton, 1990), 183.

In secular parlance, to be human is to dwell poetically on the Earth; in religious terms, to be human is to dwell mythically on the Earth.[3] How to experience Earth mythico-poetically—how to find God as Eco-Spirit through the daily miracle of ordinary existence—is the thrust of this essay.

The orientation that drives my appreciation of nature as sacred ground is what I call Christian animism—the biblically inflected conviction that all of creation is infused with and animated by God's presence. The term *animism* has its origins in the early academic study of the vernacular belief systems of indigenous peoples in Africa and the Americas. Sharing resonances with the Latin word *animus*, which means "soul" or "spirit," it originated with nineteenth-century British anthropologist E. B. Tylor who used it to analyze how primordial people attributed "life" or "soul" to all things, living and nonliving. Animism was central to an evolutionary, occidental vocabulary that described the unusual folkways of so-called primitive peoples. In spite of its colonial and pejorative origins, the term today carries a certain analytical clarity by illuminating how indigenous communities envision nonhuman nature as "ensouled" or "inspirited" with sacred presence and power. As Graham Harvey writes:

> [Animism] is typically applied to religions that engage with a wide community of living beings with whom humans share this world or particular locations within it. It might be summed up by the phrase "all that exists lives" and, sometimes, the additional understanding that "all that lives is holy." As such the term animism is sometimes applied to particular indigenous religions in comparison to Christianity or Islam, for example.[4]

What intrigues me about Harvey's definition is his assumption that monotheistic traditions such as Christianity should be regarded

---

[3] The sensibility here is borrowed from Friedrich Hölderlin who writes: "Full of merit, and yet poetically, dwells man on this Earth" (Friedrich Hoelderlin, *Samtliche Werke*, ed. Gotthold Friedrich Staudlin [Berlin: Cotta, 1846], 372; English translation by Stefan Schmanski from *Martin Heidegger, Existence and Being* [South Bend, IN: Regnery, 1949], 282). Poetry is a meaning-making activity that invests life with a measure of coherence and purpose. Language is a world-creating exercise that converts existence in empty space into habitation or "dwelling," in Hölderlin's parlance, in a world charged with rich possibilities.

[4] Graham Harvey, "Animism—A Contemporary Perspective," in *The Encyclopedia of Religion and Nature*, ed. Bron R. Taylor et al., 2 vols. (New York: Continuum, 2005), 1:81.

as distinct from animism. Initially, this makes sense in light of the historic Christian proclivity to cast aspersions on the material world as dead matter and the flesh as inferior to the concerns of the soul. Pseudo-Titus, for example, an extra-canonical exhortation to Christian asceticism from late antiquity, urges its readers to cleanse themselves of worldly pollution by overcoming fleshly temptations: "Blessed are those who have not polluted their flesh by craving for this world, but are dead to the world that they may live for God!"[5] At first glance Christianity's emphasis on making room for God by denying the world and the flesh is at odds with the classical animist belief in the living goodness of all inhabitants of sacred Earth.

In the main, however, Christian faith offers its practitioners a profound vision of God's "this-worldly" identity. Harvey's presumption that Christianity and animism are distinct is at odds with the biblical worldview that all things are bearers of divinity—the whole biosphere is filled with God's animating power—insofar as God signaled God's love for creation by incarnating Godself in Jesus and giving the Holy Spirit to indwell everything that exists on the planet. The miracle of Jesus as the living enfleshment of God in our midst—a miracle that is alongside the gift of the Spirit to the world since time immemorial—signals the ongoing vitality of God's sustaining presence within the natural order. God is not a sky-god divorced from the material world. As once God became earthly at the beginning of creation, and as once God became human in the body of Jesus, so now God continually enfleshes Godself through the Spirit in the embodied reality of life on Earth.

In this essay I analyze the biblical promise of Christian animism: that human beings are obligated to care for creation because everything God made is a bearer of the Holy Spirit. In this formulation, however, I do not mean that nature is dull and inert and only becomes sacred and alive with the infusion of Spirit into all things. Nature, rather, is always-already aflame with movement, weight, color, voice, light, texture—and spiritual presence. Nature's capacity for *relatedness*, its proclivity to encounter us, as we encounter it, in constantly new and ever-changing patterns of self-maintenance and skillful organization is the ground tone of its sacred, vibrant power. Recent work in anthropology, ethnology, and comparative religious studies highlights how indigenous peoples celebrated, and continue to celebrate, relations with other-than-human communities

---

[5] "Pseudo-Titus," in Bart D. Ehrman, *Lost Christianities: Books That Did Not Make It into the New Testament* (Oxford: Oxford University Press, 2003), 239.

of beings that are alive with spirit, emotion, desire, and personhood. The ascription of personhood to all things locates humans in a wider fraternity of relationships that includes "bear persons" and "rock persons" along with "human persons."[6] In other words, all things are persons, only some of whom are human. As David Abram argues, nature or matter is not a dead and lesser thing that stands in a lower relationship to animate spirit but is a self-organizing field of living, dynamic relationships.

> Yet as soon as we question the assumed distinction between spirit and matter, then this neatly ordered hierarchy begins to tremble and disintegrate. If we allow that matter is *not* inert, but is rather animate (or self-organizing) from the get-go, then the hierarchy collapses, and we are left with a diversely differentiated field of animate beings, each of which has its own gifts relative to the others. And we find ourselves not above, but in the very midst of this living field, our own sentience part and parcel of the sensuous landscape.[7]

The insight that nature is a living web of gifted relationships is not, however, equivalent to other similar-sounding perspectives that are often equated or used interchangeably with the term *animism* in daily discourse. *Paganism* and *heathenism*, Latin and Old English terms, respectively, stand for the *paganus* or country-dwelling people, and the "heathen" or people of the heath, both of which developed agricultural spiritualities of sacrifice and planting-and-harvest rituals prior to the arrival of Christianity in Western cultures. The term *pantheism*, on the other hand, emphasizes that God and the cosmos are one and the same equivalent reality without remainder. Animism—now refracted though biblical optics—shares affinities with these viewpoints but emphasizes with more force the indwelling of Spirit in all things—echoing its Latin root's notion of "soul" or "spirit"—so that the great expanse of the natural world can be reenvisioned as alive and sacred and thereby deserving of our nurture and love.

---

[6] See "new animism" studies of human-nature intersubjectivity in Patrick Curry, "Grizzly Man and the Spiritual Life," *Journal for the Study of Religion, Nature, and Culture* 4 (2010): 206–19; and Priscilla Stuckey, "Being Known by a Birch Tree: Animist Refigurations of Western Epistemology," in *Journal for the Study of Religion, Nature, and Culture* 4 (2010): 182–205.

[7] David Abram, *Becoming Animal: An Earthly Cosmology* (New York: Vintage, 2010), 47.

Of the current models of the interconnected relation between God and Earth, *pan-en-theism* is closest to Christian animism. Panentheist theologian Sallie McFague argues for the mutual, internal related- ness of God and creation but notes that God is not fully realized in the material world; God is in the world, indeed, but God is not "totally" embodied within everyday existence. She writes:

> Pantheism says that God is embodied, necessarily and totally; traditional theism claims that God is disembodied, necessarily and totally; panentheism suggests that God is embodied but not necessarily or totally. Rather, God is sacramentally embod- ied: God is mediated, expressed, in and through embodiment, but not necessarily or totally.[8]

While my sensibility and McFague's are deeply aligned, Christian animism pushes further her initial point by suggesting that God is fully and completely embodied within the natural world.[9] Here the emphasis does not fall on the limited relatedness of God and world such that God, finally, can escape the world, but rather the focus falls on the world as thoroughly embodying God's presence. Unlike many Christian theologies that emphasize God's transcendence, my position, akin to McFague's, champions divine *subscendence*: God flowing out into the Earth, God becoming one of us in Jesus, God gifting to all creation the Spirit to infuse all things with divine energy and love. Or to phrase this point differently, as God's Spirit *ensouls* all things with sacred purpose so also are all things the *en- fleshment* of divine power and compassion on Earth. This dialectic of ensoulment—Earth is blessed as the living realization of divine grace—and enfleshment—God pours out Godself into the carnal reality of lived existence—is the mainspring of my Christian animist vision of reality. Now nothing is held back as God overflows Godself into the bounty of the natural world. Now all things are bearers of the sacred; each and every creature is a portrait of God; everything that is, is holy.

---

[8] Sallie McFague, *The Body of God: An Ecological Theology* (Minneapolis, MN: Fortress Press, 1993), 149–50.

[9] For wider discussion, see Mark I. Wallace, "Crum Creek Spirituality: Earth as a Living Sacrament," in *Theology That Matters: Ecology, Economy, and God*, ed. Darby Kathleen Ray (Minneapolis, MN: Fortress Press, 2006), 121–37; and Ric Hudgens, "On Christian Animism" (July 29, 2011), available on the www. jesusradicals.com website.

Carnal Spirit

Christian animism takes flight when the ancient Earth wisdom of the biblical witness is recovered afresh.[10] A nature-based retrieval of the person and work of the Spirit as the green face of God in the world is an especially potent exercise in ecological biblical hermeneutics. Recovering biblical texts through environmental optics opens up the Spirit's ministry as a celebration of the good creation God has made for the joy and sustenance of all beings. Thich Nhat Hanh, the Vietnamese Buddhist monk and Christian discussion partner, writes that when "we touch the Holy Spirit, we touch God not as a concept but as a living reality."[11] A retrieval of the Spirit's disclosure of herself in the biblical literatures as one with the four cardinal elements — earth, air, water, and fire — is a principal means by which Christianity's carnal identity can be established — not as a concept, but as a living reality, or better, as a living being.[12] (Incidentally, I will use

---

[10] For this perspective, see Norman C. Habel, "Introducing the Earth Bible," in *Readings from the Perspective of Earth*, ed. Norman C. Habel, vol. 1 of *The Earth Bible* (Sheffield, England: Sheffield, 2000), 25–37. The five volumes of *The Earth Bible*, edited variously by Norman C. Habel, Shirley Wurst, and Vicky Balabanski from 2000 to 2002 set the standard for systematic eco-exegesis of the Bible. Similarly, see Norman C. Habel and Peter Trudinger, eds., *Exploring Ecological Hermeneutics* (Atlanta: Society of Biblical Literature, 2008); and Richard Bauckham, *The Bible and Ecology: Rediscovering the Community of Creation* (Waco, TX: Baylor University Press, 2010).

[11] Thich Nhat Hanh, *Living Buddha, Living Christ* (New York: Riverhead, 1995), 21.

[12] The emerging field of eco-pneumatology — nature-based reconstructions of the doctrine of the Holy Spirit — is represented by the work of Sharon V. Betcher, *Spirit and the Politics of Disablement* (Minneapolis, MN: Fortress Press, 2007); Chung Hyun-Kyung, "Welcome the Spirit; Hear Her Cries: The Holy Spirit, Creation, and the Culture of Life," *Christianity and Crisis* 51 (July 15, 1991): 220–23; Catherine Keller, *Face of the Deep: A Theology of Becoming* (London: Routledge, 2003); Anselm Kyongsuk Min, "Solidarity of Others in the Power of the Holy Spirit: Pneumatology in a Divided World," in *Advents of the Spirit: An Introduction to the Current Study of Pneumatology*, ed. Bradford E. Hinze and D. Lyle Dabney (Marquette, WI: Marquette University Press, 2001), 416–43; Jürgen Moltmann, *God in Creation: A New Theology of Creation and the Spirit of God*, trans. Margaret Kohl (Minneapolis, MN: Fortress Press, 1993); idem, *The Source of Life: The Holy Spirit and the Theology of Life*, trans. Margaret Kohl (Minneapolis, MN: Fortress Press, 1997); Geiko Müller-Fahrenholz, *God's Spirit: Transforming a World in Crisis*, trans. John Cumming (New York: Continuum, 1995); Nancy Victorin-Vangerud, *The Raging Hearth: Spirit in the Household of God* (St. Louis: Chalice, 2000); Wallace, *Finding God in the Singing River;* Wallace, *Green Christianity;* and Michael Welker, *God the Spirit*, trans. John F. Hoffmeyer (Minneapolis, MN: Fortress Press, 1994).

the female pronoun throughout this essay to name the Spirit based on some compelling scriptural precedents.)[13] As Jesus' ministry was undergirded by his intimate communion with the natural world, so also is the work of the Spirit biblically understood according to the primal elements that constitute biological existence.

As *Earth*, the Spirit is a fleshy, avian life form — a dove — who is God's helping, nurturing, inspiring, and birthing presence in creation. The mother Spirit Bird in the opening creation song of Genesis, like a giant hen sitting on her cosmic nest egg, broods over the planet and brings all things into life and fruition. In turn, this same hovering Spirit Bird, as a dove that alights on Jesus as he comes up through the waters of his baptism, appears in all four of the Gospels to signal God's approval of Jesus' public work. At Jesus' baptism, Luke's Gospel says the Spirit appeared in "bodily form" — the Greek term is *somatikos* — as a dove. This winged, feathered God actualizes an Earth-based communion in which all beings are filled with divine presence, heaven and Earth are unified, and God and nature are one. In the Bible, God is human flesh in the person of Jesus, to be sure, but God is also animal flesh in the person of the Spirit, the bird God of the scriptural witness (Gn 1:1–2; Mt 3:13–17; Mk 1:9–11; Lk 3:21–22; Jn 1:29–34).

As *Air*, the Spirit is both the animating divine breath who brings into existence all living things (Gn 2:7; Psalms 104:29–30), and the wind of prophecy and judgment who renews and transforms those she possesses and indwells (Jdg 6:34; Jn 3:6–8; Acts 2:1–4). *Rûach* (Hebrew) and *pneuma* (Greek) are the biblical terms for *spirit*; they mean "breath," "air," or "wind." The breathy God is closer to us than we are to ourselves. In meditation when we say, "Focus on your breath," in essence we are saying "focus on God." Our lives are framed and made possible by the perennial gift of divine wind. We enter consciousness drawing our first breath — we inhale God at the moment of our birth — and we exhale God with our last breath — we pass into death by evacuating the aerial Spirit from our mortal bodies. The Holy Spirit is God's invigorating, life-giving presence

---

[13] On the biblical and theological history of feminine language and imagery for the Spirit, see Susan Ashbrook Harvey, "Feminine Imagery for the Divine: The Holy Spirit, the Odes of Solomon, and Early Syriac Tradition," *Saint Vladimir's Theological Quarterly* 37 (1993): 111–40; Gary Steven Kinkel, *Our Dear Mother the Spirit: An Investigation of Count Zinzendorf's Theology and Praxis* (Lanham, MD: University Press of America, 1990); and Elizabeth A. Johnson, *She Who Is: The Mystery of God in Feminist Theological Discourse* (New York: Crossroad, 1992), esp. 128–31.

within the atmosphere who sustains our need-for-air existence and the existence of all creatures on the planet.

As *Water*, the Spirit brings life and healing to all who are baptized and drink from her eternal springs (Jn 3:1–15, 4:1–30, 7:37–38; Acts 8:26–40, 11:1–18). True thirst, true desire, true need is satiated by drinking the liquid God who soaks all beings with a deep sense of wholeness and joy. In the Eucharist we eat God in the bread and drink God in the wine. In this act we are reminded that all of Earth's vital fluids that make planetary existence possible—blood, mucus, tears, milk, semen, sweat, urine—are infused with sacred energy. Again, as with Earth and air, life is a primordial gift in which God graces all things with the necessary elements for survival and full fruition. The Water God entertains us with torrential rains, seeping mudholes, rushing rivers, and cascading waterfalls so that life on this juicy, liquid planet can be hydrated and refreshed.

As *Fire*, the Spirit is the blaze of God that prophetically condemns the wealthy and unjust who exploit others, and the divine spark that ignites the multilingual and interracial mission of the early church (Mt 3:11–12; Acts 2:1–4). On the one hand, fire is a harsh metaphor for God's judgment against human arrogance and overly inflated sense of self; on the other, it is an expression of God's unifying presence in the fledgling church, as happened at Pentecost with the Spirit's incandescent announcement of herself in tongues of fire to a diverse collection of disciples. This sacred fire erased false differences and consumed the ethnic and cultural divisions that marked the early Christians apart from one another. In the wider biosphere the Fire God continues as a unifying, vivifying power necessary for the well-being of planetary life; fire cooks our food, heats our homes, powers our transportation systems, and maintains our planet's temperate climate. Without the gift of fire we would all perish, but with our dumping of carbon dioxide into the atmosphere, we have unleashed the sun's lethal potential, and perverted nature's balance by producing a superheated weather system that will endanger the survival of future generations.

To be human is to live in spiritual harmony with the primary elements. A full life consists of everyday gratitude and care for the elemental gifts of natural existence. In part, this elemental sensibility is recoverable by a return to historic belief and practice. Ancient Christian belief teaches that God is present to us "under the elements" of bread and wine. Putting to work the Christian animist model, this belief is deemed ever so true and now expanded as well: beyond bread and wind, God's Spirit continues to be real under *all* of the cardinal elements—earth, air, water, fire—that constitute the building blocks of life. While the Holy Spirit is sometimes regarded as a vague and disembodied phantom irrelevant to religious belief or planetary existence, the Bible tells a different story of a radically embodied God who incarnates Godself as Spirit in the four elements. Correspondingly, and using language borrowed from French philosopher Luce Irigaray, Ellen Armour develops an "elemental theology" in which God is known and loved through the primal elements. By reimagining core liturgical practices in accord with the elemental dynamics of bodily existence, Armour injects new life—new elemental life—into the ritual heart of Christian faith:

> The central Christian rituals, baptism and eucharist, connect immediately with water and earth. The waters of baptism signify the move from sin to redemption, death to rebirth. The grain and grapes that become bread and wine (and ultimately body and blood) are products of earth and water. The Feast of Pentecost celebrates the descent of the Holy Spirit—in the form of "divided tongues, as of fire" (Acts 2:3)—on Christ's apostles, endowing their ministry with new authority as each listener heard the gospel message in his or her own native tongue. The Feast of the Ascension calls attention to air as the medium through which Christ ascends, thus linking the heavens and the earth, human and the divine. . . . We are quite literally sustained by air, water, and earth—physically and, if we adopt this way of thinking, spiritually. We have, then, religious and moral obligations to the natural world. Elemental theology repositions the relationship between divinity, humanity and the natural world. . . . The elements bind all three together in a fragile network of interdependency rather than domination.[14]

Earthen Spirit

This elemental model of the Spirit's real and ongoing union with Earth is resonant with the fifth-century vocabulary used in Christianity's early doctrine of Jesus Christ's "two natures." In 451 CE the ecumenical churches met in Chalcedon, in what is today Western Turkey, to formulate a more refined understanding of how the divine and the human relate in Jesus of Nazareth. The historic

---

[14] Ellen Armour, "Toward an Elemental Theology," in *Theology That Matters*, ed. Darby Kathleen Ray (Minneapolis, MN: Fortress Press, 2006), 54.

churches decided that in the one person of Jesus, divinity and humanity are fully realized in an organic and permanent unity that admits no separation or confusion. The Chalcedonian Creed asks all Christians to confess to the

> one and the same Christ, Son, Lord, Only-begotten, to be acknowledged in two natures without confusion, alteration, division, separation; the distinction of natures being by no means taken away by the union, but rather the property of each nature being preserved.[15]

Jesus, then, is an integrated, complete, and whole person, fully divine and fully human, and his two natures are understood as being neither confused with nor internally divided from one another.

The Chalcedonian formula is an instance of a productive contradiction. Such a contradiction imaginatively juxtaposes two apparently opposing ideas—the ideas of divinity and humanity in one person—in order to articulate a new vision of reality—in this case, the idea that this one person, Jesus, is a divine human being. Another way to refer to this type of tensive thinking is to speak of a "coincidence of opposites," an instance of "semantic impertinence," or a "non-oppositional dualism."[16] When dialectical thought is stretched to its limits, there is the possibility of discovering, paradoxically, a previously undisclosed unity, a blinding flash of new insight, that was not possible prior to an isolated inventory of the oppositions in question.

Employing, then, the dialectical grammar of Chalcedon, we can say that the Spirit indwells the Earth and the Earth enfleshes the Spirit. This formulation of the relationship between Spirit and Earth signals an inseparable unity between the two realities without a consequent absorption of the one into the other. Another way to put this is to say that Spirit and Earth are one and that Spirit and Earth are not one. To be sure, Spirit and Earth enjoy a permanent

---

[15] "The Creed of Chalcedon," in *The Creeds of Christendom*, 3 vols., ed. Philip Schaff (Grand Rapids, MI: Baker Book House, 1983), 2:62.

[16] These phrases, which speak to the reconciliation of apparently opposing positions to form a burst of new insight into reality, are used, respectively, by Karl Barth, *The Epistle to the Romans*, trans. Edwyn C. Hoskins, 6th German ed. (Oxford: Oxford University Press, 1933); Paul Ricoeur, *The Rule of Metaphor: Multidisciplinary Studies of the Creation of Meaning in Language*, trans. Robert Czerny with Kathleen McLaughlin and John Costello, SJ (Toronto: University of Toronto Press, 1977); and Walter Lowe, *Theology and Difference: The Wound of Reason* (Bloomington: Indiana University Press, 1993).

and living unity one with the other; each reality internally conditions and permeates the other in a cosmic festival of love and harmony. Erotically charged, Spirit and Earth dwell in oneness and fellowship with one another. But both modes of being live through and with one another without collapsing into confusion with, or separation from, one another. The reciprocal indwelling of Spirit and Earth is neither an absorption of the one into the other nor an admixture of the two. By the same token, the mutual indwelling of Spirit and Earth does not signify merely an outward and transitory connection between the two realities.

The Spirit is the "soul" of the Earth — the wild, life-giving breath of creation — empowering all life forms to enter into a dynamic relationship with the greater whole. In turn, the Earth is the "flesh" of the Spirit — the living landscapes of divine presence — making God palpable and viscous in nature's ever-widening circles of evolutionary and seasonal changes. Whether manifesting herself as a living, breathing organism like a dove, or an active life-force, such as wind or fire, Spirit indwells nature as its interanimating power in order to bring all of creation into a harmonious relationship with itself. Spirit is the vital *rûach* — God's breath — that gives life to all beings. All things — rocks, trees, plants, rivers, animals, and humans — are made of Spirit and are part of the continuous biological flow patterns that constitute life on our planet. As Denis Edwards writes, "The Creator Spirit is present in every flower, bird, and human being, in every quasar and in every atomic particle, closer to them than they are to themselves, enabling them to be and to become."[17] The Spirit ensouls the Earth as its life-giving breath, and the Earth embodies the Spirit's mysterious interanimation of the whole creation. To experience, then, the full range of nature's birthing cycles, periods of growth, and seasons of death and decay — to know the joy and sadness of living in harmony with nature's cyclical processes and flow patterns — is to be empowered by Spirit and nurtured by nature's

---

[17] Denis Edwards, "For Your Immortal Spirit Is in All Things," in *Faith Revealing — Earth Healing: Ecology and Christian Theology*, ed. Dennis Edwards (Collegeville, MN: Liturgical Press, 2001), 56. For Amos Yong's Pentecostal theology of Spirit-filled creation, see his "A Spirit-filled Creation? Toward a Pneumatological Cosmology," in *The Spirit of Creation: Modern Science and Divine Action in the Pentecostal-Charismatic Imagination*, 173–228 (Grand Rapids, MI: Eerdmans, 2011); for her ecofeminist pneumatology, see Sharon Betcher, "Grounding the Spirit: An Ecofeminist Pneumatology," in *Ecospirit: Religions and Philosophies for the Earth*, ed. Laurel Kearns and Catherine Keller, 315–66 (New York: Fordham University Press, 2007).

bounty. The Spirit is the hidden, inner life of the world, and the Earth is the outward manifestation of the Spirit's sustaining energies.

Deploying Chalcedonian grammar to model the interrelationship between Spirit and Earth challenges the classical, philosophical idea of God in Christian thought. In the metaphysical model God is an immovable heavenly being insulated from this-worldly concerns. God is divorced from the passions and vagaries of transient existence. In the classical paradigm God is unfeeling, self-subsistent, and independent from the ebb and flow of life and death that make up our earthly habitations. Metaphysical doctrines about "divine apathy" and "divine impassibility" — the standard, philosophically influenced belief that God is a stolid, dispassionate being not susceptible to the whims and fancies of human emotions — achieved the status of obvious truth in early Christian thought as a reaction to the fire-and-fury characteristic of the gods and goddesses of pre-Christian pagan mythology.[18] In the face of the malevolent and capricious actions of pagan divinities, Christians envisioned their God as pure goodness and impassive to change and circumstance. Beyond life and death, the supreme God of Christianity was seen as quintessentially self-possessed and far removed from the tumult and impermanence of mortal existence. All flesh is mortal; "their days are like grass" (Ps 103:15). But God, according to classical Christianity, is not mortal, God is not fleshly being. God is the All-Powerful, who is uniquely immortal, invisible, and unchangeable. God, in a word, is Being itself — eternal and immovable.

The Chalcedonian logic of the Spirit — that Spirit and Earth, interactively conceived, are one — opposes this metaphysical idea of God as unchangeable and apathetic in the face of the suffering and turmoil within the creation that God has spun into existence. The earthen God of biblical witness is not a distant abstraction but a living being who subsists in and through the natural world. Because God as Earth Spirit lives in the ground and circulates in water and wind, God suffers deeply the loss and abuse of our biological heritage through our continued assaults on our planet home. God as Spirit is pained by ongoing ecological squalor; God as Spirit undergoes deprivation and trauma through the stripping away of Earth's bounty. As the Earth heats up and melting polar ice fields flood shore communities and indigenous habitats, God suffers; as

---

[18] See Jaroslav Pelikan, *The Christian Tradition: A History of the Development of Doctrine*, vol. 1, *The Emergence of the Catholic Tradition (100–600)* (Chicago: University of Chicago Press, 1971), 172–277.

global economic imbalance imperils family stability and intensifies the quest for arable land in native forests, God suffers; as coral reefs bleach into decay and ecosystems of fish and marine life die off, God suffers; and as our planet endures what appears to be the era of the Sixth Great Extinction, like the great extinctions of the Ice Age and other mass death events, God suffers. When we plunder and lay waste to the Earth, God suffers.

Because God and Earth mutually indwell, God is vulnerable to the same loss and degradation the Earth undergoes at the greedy hands of its human caretakers. This means that God as Spirit, Earth God, lives on "this side of eternity," as it were. Earth God lives on "this side" of the ecological squalor our global greed has spawned. God is not an inert, metaphysical concept but a living, suffering co-participant in the pain of the world. The God of Christian animism has cast her lot with a depredated planet and has entered into the fullness of the tragic history of humankind's abuse of our planet home. God has become, then, in our time, a tragic figure. God is a tragic figure not in the sense that God evokes our pity because God is weak and inadequate in the face of environmental terror—fated for destruction along with the destruction of the Earth—but rather in the sense that the tragedy of human rapaciousness is now God's own environmental tragedy as well. Who can say what profound torment is felt in the depths of the divine life when God surveys the devastation human avarice and stupidity has wrought? The sorry spectacle of Earth under siege and God's longing for a renewed biosphere are one. In union of heart, in agony of spirit, God and Earth are one.

In Jesus, God enfleshed Godself at one time in one human being; in the Spirit, God enfleshes Godself continually in the Earth. In both instances God decides in freedom and love for all beings, not by any internal necessity, to enter into the fullness of human tragedy. In making this decision regarding our sad eco-drama, Spirit puts herself in harm's way by becoming fully a part of a planet ravaged by human arrogance. *God is at risk in the world today.* It is not an extreme statement to say, then, that the threat of ecocide brings in its wake the specter of deicide: to wreak environmental havoc in the biosphere is to run the risk that we will inflict lasting injury to the source and ground of our common life together, Earth God. Spirit and Earth are one. Spirit and Earth are one in suffering. Spirit and Earth are one in the tragedy of ecocide. Spirit and Earth's common unity and life-centered identity raise the frightening possibility that despoiling our planet and chronically unsustainable living may result in permanent trauma to the divine life itself.

The Reformed Tradition and the Eco-Crisis

The biblical ideas of creation, incarnation, and Spirit are the fountainhead of a Christian animist vision of the sacred character of the natural order. But Christian animism does not sit well with some Christian thinkers. One reviewer of my earlier work writes:

> Beware! Under the inspirational title, *Finding God in the Singing River*, Mark I. Wallace proposes that Christianity needs to return to its roots in paganism, animism, and deep ecology. . . . The author uses a lofty tone and densely constructed sentences that disguise his warping of truth and to present his beliefs. . . . This book is alarming in that it teaches the worldview of deep ecology, and that the religions of paganism and animism are biblical. . . . It might work as a textbook for training students to spot propaganda, educational hogwash, faulty logic, and false teachings.[19]

My response is to suggest, to paraphrase Graham Harvey's earlier comment, that all that exists is alive, all that exists is good, all that exists is holy. We will not save what we do not love, and unless, as a culture, we learn to love and care for the gift of the created order again, the prospects of saving the planet, and thereby ourselves as well, are terrifyingly bleak. But insofar as God is in everything and all things are inter-animated by divine power and concern, we can affirm that God is carnal, God is earthen, God is flesh. And with this animist affirmation the will is empowered and the imagination ignited to fight against the specters of global warming and the loss of biodiversity as the great threats of our time.

Hungry for eruptions of the animist sacred, personally speaking, I mourn in our time the continued loss of the wider community of nature as the seedbed for full fruitions of God in my life. This terrible loss signifies, in the language of Reformed theology, that we are living in a time of *status confessionis*.[20] In historic Reformation theology a *status confessionis*, or "state of confession," existed whenever

---

[19] Elece Hollis, review of *Finding God in the Singing River: Christianity, Spirit, Nature*, by Mark I. Wallace, available at christianbookpreviews.com.

[20] See Eberhard Busch's discussion of *status confessionis* in the Reformed tradition in Darrell Guder, "Reformed Confessions and Confessing Church—Interview with Eberhard Busch," in *The Presbyterian Outlook* (May 14, 2002), 22–28.

the heart of the biblical message, the gospel, was fundamentally threatened by ecclesiastical and political authorities. In recent times such periods of *status confessionis* included the Nazi period in the 1930s, when German churches were charged with expelling non-Aryan pastors and members, and the apartheid period in the 1980s, when white churches and the governing South African authorities enforced rigid social, educational, and housing divisions based on ethnic backgrounds.

Today marks a similar crisis, a *status confessionis*, because the church and world leaders have stood by while major oil and gas companies have wrought havoc with the global climate system. The natural systems that support life on Earth are under attack — a direct consequence of anthropogenic climate change — because no one has the moral courage to rise up and challenge the dominant economic culture. The most important issue that confronts Christianity in our time is the fate of creation. Without a biologically robust planet, Christian community, and all other forms of community, human and otherwise, will wither and die. The climate crisis is a knife to the heart of church life — as it is to all forms of life. Without clean air, fresh water, and biodiverse land masses, the prospects of a healthy future for humankind and otherkind are increasingly bleak. Correspondingly, the Christian message will lose its relevance in an eco-dystopian tomorrow where populations of humans and other beings shrink and mass die-offs are a common occurrence.

This, then, is the most compelling theological issue of our time: the prospect that God's Spirit will no longer be able to renew the face of the Earth (Ps 104:30) because Earth itself will be no more, at least not for human habitation. Can the Spirit renew creation when creation itself, to paraphrase Paul in Romans 8, suffers and groans to the point that it can no longer bear the weight of human sin — the sin of massive global degradation? In a coming world that is dangerously hot and unstable, we face the prospect, to paraphrase Bill McKibben, of the death of life *and* the death of death itself; that is, we face the specter of the realities of life and death losing their existential meaning in a future when the despoilment is now complete of the a/biotic systems that make human and all other existence possible.[21] Our and other species' fate is doomed until we find solutions to the release of heat-trapping emissions into the atmosphere,

---

[21] See this analysis in Bill McKibben, *The End of Nature* (New York: Random, 1989). See also Dieter Gerten and Sigurd Bergmann, eds., *Religion in Environmental and Climate Change: Suffering, Values, Lifestyle* (New York: Continuum, 2012).

the primary driver of global warming. Climate change destroys the very ecosystems that make life possible in the first place—and, in theological parlance, such change destroys the vision of a healed and restored creation that is central to Christian hope. Without hope, Christian faith is doomed. If billions of people and other life forms are at risk, the Christian message of promise and purpose will ring hollow. Christianity may not survive the global collapse of nature—the apocalyptic destruction of God's handiwork, creation itself, which God promised in Genesis never to destroy again. Unless ecosystemic life and well-being is secured, therefore, the Christian church, adrift and rudderless, has no future. This is the *status confessionis* of our time.

In every respect, therefore, the Earth crisis is a spiritual crisis because without a vital, fertile planet it will be difficult to find traces of divine wonder and providence in the everyday order of things. Personally speaking, when the final Arctic habitat for the polar bear melts into the sea due to human-induced climate change, I will lose something of God's beauty and power in my life. When the teeming swell of equatorial amphibians can no longer adapt to deforestation and rising global temperatures, something of God will disappear as well, I fear. I am like the First Peoples of the Americas, who experienced the sacred within the Black Hills of what is now South Dakota, or on top of Mount Graham in southern Arizona, and then found that when these places were degraded, something of God was missing as well. Without these and other places charged with sacred power, I am lost on Earth. Without still-preserved landed sites saturated with divine presence, I am a wanderer with no direction, a person without hope, a believer experiencing the death of God on a planet suffering daily from human greed and avarice.

"We are on the precipice of climate system tipping points beyond which there is no redemption," wrote Jim Hansen, director of the NASA Goddard Institute for Space Studies, in 2003. As we reach these catastrophic tipping points, what will human existence on Earth look like in ten to twenty years? Chronic heat waves will provoke mega-droughts and render daily life unbearable at times; Arctic permafrost and sea ice will crack and disappear, causing islands and shorelines to shrink and vanish; continued carbon dumping will render the world's oceans more acidic and ultimately lethal to coral reefs and fish stocks; melting permafrost in Siberia and elsewhere will release huge amounts of methane into the atmosphere, resulting in killer hurricanes and tsunamis; biodiverse ecosystems will collapse and produce dead monocultures of invasive species where the basic dynamic of plant pollination itself is undermined; and a hotter and less forgiving planet will cause crop failures and large stretches of arable land to become desert, mosquito-borne diseases such as dengue fever and malaria to reach epidemic proportions, and mass migrations of tens of millions of people as rising sea levels destroy homes and communities. In the near future we will look back at greenhouse gas–induced events such as the European heat wave of 2003 that killed thirty thousand people—or Hurricane Katrina in 2005, the costliest natural disaster in U.S. history that killed eighteen hundred people—as telltale portents of the coming storm. We will remember other positive environmental changes—the banning of DDT in the United States in the 1960s, the general eradication of ozone-depleting CFCs (chlorofluorocarbons) in the 1980s—and then wonder why we were not able to extricate ourselves from the "Big Oil" economy that was even then destroying the planet. In 2015, 2020, or 2025 we will rue the day we allowed those who denied global warming to confuse the public into thinking that current climate change is a natural cycle for which we have no responsibility. We will recall the definitive reports by the Millennium Ecosystem Assessment in 2005 and the Intergovernmental Panel on Climate Change in 2007, based on tens of thousands of studies by hundreds of climate researchers over many years of investigation, that made clear to us that our fossil-fuel economy is the most important anthropogenic factor driving the dangerous climate changes we now see all around us.

With an alarming sense of urgency, we will know then, even as we know now, that it is time to act. In my life, the song of the wood thrush calls me to action.

Every generation, to borrow Thomas Berry's phrase, has its "Great Work." Every generation has an overarching sense of responsibility for the welfare of the whole that gathers together people and societies across their cultural and ideological differences. In this generation our Great Work is to fight global warming by reenvisioning our relationship to Earth not as exploiters but as biotic kinspeople with the myriad life forms that populate our common home. This is the mandate of our time. As Berry writes:

> The Great Work before us, the task of moving modern industrial civilization from its present devastating influence on the Earth to a more benign mode of presence, is not a role that we have chosen. It is a role given to us, beyond any consultation with ourselves. We did not choose. We were chosen by some power beyond ourselves for this historical task. We did not choose the

moment of our birth, who our parents will be, our particular culture or the historical moment when we will be born. . . . The nobility of our lives, however, depends upon the manner in which we come to understand and fulfill our assigned roles.[22]

Every generation has a sacred calling to seize the moment and battle the forces of oppression and degradation so that future generations can live richer and more meaningful lives. The Great Work of our generation is to develop inspired models of sustainable development that promote ecological and climate justice for all of God's children. Sustainability is a forward-looking category that asks how institutions today can secure and manage the labor and environmental resources necessary for achieving their economic goals while also preserving the capacity of future human communities and ecosystems to survive and flourish. Native American folklore often speaks of animal and related resource-management practices done with an eye toward their impact on the seventh generation to come. Seventh-generation full-cost business and accounting practices relocate the goal of financial profitability within the context of fair labor performance, responsible consumption of energy, and careful management of waste.[23] Sustainable development, then, articulates policies that address this generation's vital needs without sacrificing the ability of future generations to meet their own vital needs. For highly industrialized economies like our own, sustainability will be predicated on kicking our habit of dependence on fossil fuels, the primary source of global climate change. My hope is that Christian animism can provide the theological and moral foundations necessary for practical responses to weaning ourselves off unsustainable

---

[22] Thomas Berry, *The Great Work: Our Way into the Future* (New York: Bell Tower, 1999), 7.

[23] The seventh-generation ideal is also identified today as the *triple bottom line business model* (people, planet, profit). In this model financial profits depend upon carefully managed environmental and social performance. Here corporate, societal, and ecological interests dynamically interact and mutually support one another. This model is analyzed as the "new bottom line" in Michael Lerner, *The Left Hand of God: Taking Back Our Country from the Religious Right* (San Francisco: HarperSanFrancisco, 2006), 227–40; as "oikonomia economics" in Herman E. Daly and John B. Cobb, Jr., *For the Common Good: Redirecting the Economy Toward Community, the Environment, and a Sustainable Future*, 2d ed. (Boston: Beacon, 1989, 1994), 138–75; and as "ecologically reformed capitalism" in Roger S. Gottlieb, *A Greener Faith: Religious Environmentalism and Our Planet's Future* (Oxford: Oxford University Press, 2006), 81–110.

coal, oil, and natural gas supplies in order to save the planet for future generations.

Religious faith is uniquely suited to fire the imagination and empower the will to make the necessary changes that can break the cycle of addiction to nonrenewable energy. Many of the great social movements in the history of the United States—the abolitionist groundswell of the nineteenth century, the suffragist associations of the early twentieth century, the civil rights movement in the 1950s and 1960s, and today, the Occupy movement—were and are energized by prophetic religious leaders who brought together their spiritual values and passion for justice to animate a moral force for change more powerful than any force to stop them. To paraphrase William James, religion today, in the face of cataclysmic climate change, must become the moral equivalent of war by becoming more disciplined, more resourceful, and more visionary in fighting the causes of global ecological depredation. The hope of Christian animism—the vision of a verdant and beautiful Earth saturated with divine presence—can religiously charge practical responses to the crisis of unsustainable living today. The supreme calling of our time will be for all of us to find a spiritually grounded, aesthetically resonant, and morally compelling approach to engaging the problem of climate change—and to do so now, before it is too late.

A Response to Mark I. Wallace

Divining Boundaries

Fabrizio D'Ambrosio

Two summers ago, while I was visiting relatives in central Italy with my parents and my brother, a cousin drove us to a Franciscan convent in the process of restoration. For the first time since the Napoleonic Wars and the consequent suppression of religious orders, the friars had at long last come around to restoring their little neck of the woods. And when I say "woods," I mean it literally. Nestled high in the green mountains that form a ring about the ancient city of Fabriano, access to the convent is virtually blocked during the winter, and only enough trees have been felled around the edifice to make it noticeable during the more clement seasons. In this respect it is a typical forest hermitage, one amenable to finding God beyond the constraints of life in town. Now the friars and their helpers had not expected visitors from abroad that day, but they nonetheless gamely demonstrated the ethic of hospitality and treated us to a tour of the grounds as well as to a snack. For me, the most conspicuous feature of that late-afternoon *merenda* was the sweet water they poured for us in earthenware cups, water that they proudly announced had come from their own well, pure from the source and untreated.

But the conversation on the drive to the convent was just as memorable, for from my cousin and my mother I heard a recurrent theme: *Dio e la natura*, "God and nature," the two terms deployed in such a way that the latter somehow gave access to the former. There was talk of monks and hermits coming close to God by removing themselves to the desert (read: wilderness); the clear inference was that if people drew near to the realm of "otherkind," they would more vividly know themselves and therefore God. Nature in this discourse was thus a mirror that reflected spiritual, human, and

235

animal dimensions. The human recapitulates all the "lower" orders, even as these bear the impress of the divine footprint; in turn, the human order dimly reflects the angelic hierarchies, even though, precisely by virtue of our embodiment, we men and women more strikingly resemble God than do the angels.[1] All of us, however, whether spirit, human, or animal, lie on the nearer side of the God/cosmos dichotomy, and thus we are, in our sundry ways, part of a single creation.

Probing one aspect of this sensibility, Thomas Merton writes that the authentic saint enjoys all things in God by virtue of detachment, here understood not as life-denying self-absorption but rather as liberation from a false consciousness that would reduce the world and its inhabitants to mere objects in relation to the ego.[2] Even more startling, this new vision of things discloses that precisely by being themselves — in their concreteness and "individuality" — nonhuman creatures "imitate God"; they do so quite spontaneously, for they cannot but exist according to the way divine wisdom intended. Thus it is that a certain tree "glorifies" the Creator by growing in a unique and irreplaceable manner, that is, by being none other than *this* tree. Moreover, *this* particular flower or stream, mountain or animal, becomes, so to speak, a "saint" in disguise, if we understand sanctity as unconstrained living in accordance with God's will.[3] For us human beings, however, gifted with the ambiguous freedom to be something other than our authentic selves, the path to sainthood involves a painful struggle to uncover our true "identity" in God. Only then — and then perhaps only fitfully — do we love and enjoy creation as we ought.[4]

I mention Thomas Merton and the orientation he embodies because, despite the obvious difference in tradition, several of his concerns resonate with the perspective Mark Wallace has outlined in his essay. Both authors insist on a conversion of ordinary human modes of relating to "otherkind," both try to recover a sense of nature's sacredness, and both affirm that a shift in human comportment toward the natural will yield at least some measure of intersubjectivity between ourselves and the life forms that share this world with us.

---

[1] Cf. Thomas Aquinas, who argues in the *Summa Theologiae* (I, q. 93, a. 3) that certain features of our materiality give us an "accidental" advantage over the angels in regards to the *imago Dei*.

[2] Thomas Merton, *New Seeds of Contemplation* (New York: New Directions, 1961), 21–24.

[3] Ibid., 29–31, 24.

[4] Ibid., 31–36, 25–26.

On the other hand, Merton parts company with Wallace in stress-
ing the renewal of consciousness through engagement with God as
transcendent, whereas Wallace proposes that we encounter God as
fleshing forth in the matrix of life. Furthermore, Merton regards the
world as a source of both joy and sorrow for those of us who have
not learned to "love God perfectly." He writes:

> The fulfillment we find in creatures belongs to the reality of the
> created being, a reality that is from God and belongs to God
> and reflects God. The anguish we find in them belongs to the
> disorder of our desire which looks for a greater reality in the
> object of our desire than is actually there: a greater fulfillment
> than any created thing is capable of giving.[5]

Responding to environmental degradation, however, the burden of
Wallace's discourse shifts to nature as a fragile good; his goal is not
to detail the ambiguity of the human soul in regard to other created
beings but to unleash imaginative resources for overcoming the
present crisis. We might venture to say, then, that Wallace directs
contemplation of the world toward action on the world's behalf,
while his Cistercian counterpart—though himself no stranger to
politics—regards such action (traditionally enough) as an element
within an overarching contemplative framework.

Wallace names his theological project Christian animism, a stance
that has as its basic "conviction" the intimate, vivifying "presence"
of God in the world. This conviction, in turn, drives a retrieval of
earth-centered imagery for God from the Christian Bible, particularly
those images and metaphors used of the Holy Spirit. Distinguish-
ing his approach from the related standpoints of paganism and
pantheism, Wallace avers greater kinship with panentheism in its
metaphorical register, especially as practiced by Sallie McFague.
Maintaining, however, that the latter's formulation suggests God
might evade the consequences of ecocide, Wallace affirms that God
"thoroughly" embodies Godself in the world. Later in his essay he
states that the Spirit willingly unites herself to the earth in all its
tragedy, even at the cost of divine well-being.

At this point a question arises for me. In what sense are we to
understand the thoroughness of God's bodying forth in the cosmos?
If creation instantiates God without any divine "remainder," then
pantheism seems hard to avoid; if, on the other hand, the Spirit

---

[5] Ibid., 26.

chooses without internal compulsion to become one with us, then it is difficult to see how Wallace's position differs substantially from McFague's. The language here oscillates uncomfortably between pantheism and panentheism, and I am left wondering whether our author wants to have it both ways, or whether he is simply proposing complementary models. Wallace avers that the image of thorough embodiment stresses the intrinsic holiness of the earth, and I admit that this can be grasped with the help of William Blake's "eternity in an hour." But the latter would appear to require a notion of divine simplicity, such that, for example, the whole of God could be conceived to dwell in each of the world's parts without being divided in Godself.

In the second phase of his essay Wallace recovers, to ecological effect, the biblical images linking the Spirit to the traditional four elements — earth, air, water, and fire. Such a move, he tells us, "is a principal means by which Christianity's carnal identity can be established — not as a concept, but as a living reality, or better, as a living being." Employing a dialectic between the particular economy of the incarnation and the broader economy of the Spirit — a movement that structures the whole essay — here Wallace underscores Irigaray's "material transcendental" that makes possible not only the Christ-event but biological existence as such. Earth, then, limns the Spirit as the bird who both warmed creation to life and confirmed Jesus' ministry, while air, water, and fire evoke, respectively, the intimacy of breath and the dynamism of prophecy; the vivifying power of rain and the sacredness of bodily fluids; and the unpredictability of flame poured out at Pentecost and singeing our hubris, yet lighting our domestic fires.

These elemental passages display Wallace's obvious delight in, and gratitude for, the physical energies that sustain embodied beings; in the case of fire particularly, his writing underscores the fact that nature always exceeds our objectifying grasp, that it has worth and agency apart from human interest. Moreover, when *we* exceed ourselves toward otherkind in arrogance and rapacity, the life-matrix responds, as it were, with evident and at times deadly rage — and not only does this apply to fire, of course, but to the tornados, landslides, and floods produced by one or a combination of the other forces. Insofar as the tropes of "carnal Spirit" evoke respect for natural agency, they would seem to cohere well with Wallace's proposal, but these very images also point to the ambiguity of the four elements and hence raise the problem of natural evil or of what we sometimes refer to as acts of God. This, in turn, leads to the further question of whether divine metaphors taken from unpredictable processes can sustain our reverence. Of course, in Christian tradition God — Spirit especially — has often been imagined in non-anthropomorphic terms, the better, no doubt, to convey a sense of the labile and mysterious character of the divine Third. However, must we stop at the image? Doesn't the sheer multiplicity of divine images call for their partial negation and, eventually, call *forth* an affirmation of Spirit's radical, unambiguous goodness?[6]

In his final pneumatological offering Wallace transposes the logic of Chalcedon to the relation between Spirit and world. Here, once again, he broadens language applied to Christ in order to focus our attention on divine earthiness. Thus, the human nature assumed by the Logos in the incarnation becomes the biosphere as whole, and the oneness of the person, despite the difference of natures is now understood by analogy with the hypostatic union, so that Spirit and earth inhabit each other with neither division nor confusion. Distancing himself from classical Christology, however, Wallace makes what appear to be three moves. First, he deploys the panentheistic metaphor of Spirit as animating force and earth as its embodiment, to the point where they can be compared to "soul" and "flesh," respectively; second, he posits internal relations between Spirit and earth, thereby making the two terms capable of changing each other; and third, reprising the *communicatio idiomatum*, he can now ascribe the suffering of the biosphere to God, such that when earth is degraded by human callousness, God experiences real tragedy (just as when Christ died on the cross, the human death could be predicated of God).

Unfortunately Wallace's use of Chalcedonian grammar breaks down at several points. First, the Spirit/flesh metaphor limits the world to the body, but the intent of Chalcedon was to affirm that the Logos assumed a full human nature, not simply its physical component.[7] Therefore, unless Wallace unfolds the relation between Spirit and spirit in more detail, he risks a haunting by the ghost of Apollinaris, who replaced Jesus' rational soul with the divine Logos. Nor need such an unfolding amount to a reinscription of dualism, for Wallace has already given us some crucial hints in the direction

---

[6] For a discussion of Aquinas on divine incomprehensibility, see Elizabeth Johnson, *She Who Is: The Mystery of God in Feminist Theological Discourse* (New York: Crossroad, 1992), esp. 109.

[7] For the unfolding of the inclusive and emancipatory potential of Chalcedonian Christology, see ibid., 164–67.

of intersubjectivity.[8] Perhaps what would be needed, then, is a meta-phorical treatment of spirit/breath/soul as the depth-dimension of physicality. Second, and in spite of the intimate, reciprocally conditioned union of earth and Spirit, it stands to reason that these two would function at least somewhat autonomously; for if they affect each other, then they might also at times refuse or even thwart each other. But this raises the possibility of Nestorianism, the very teaching that occasioned Chalcedon. Third, it is an integral part of Chalcedonian logic that God's assumption of a finite nature involves no change *in divinis*. On the other hand, if we alter the divine referent such that it becomes an object as well as a subject—and traditional Christology insists that the Logos is the subject of Jesus' human-ity—then we have to change the grammar also.

In spite of the difficulties mentioned above, Wallace's Christian animism presents an eloquent case for the resacralization of the world. Additionally, by focusing on the bodily resonances of scrip-tural imagery for the Spirit, this project has the advantage of stand-ing in a tensive, and therefore creative, continuity with the tradition. To my mind, however, the most evocative feature of Wallace's ap-proach is its courage in letting otherkind reveal itself as a prelude to right action on our part, for only a contemplative reordering of our way of being in the world can enable a just response to the crisis in which we now find ourselves.

---

[8] For instance, he gives us a powerful notion of the world's relationality. Re-garding spirit as the depth dimension of the physical, a good hint can be found in the disclosure of the world's sacredness as a consequence of our transformed "understanding."

Contributors

Susan Abraham, assistant professor of ministry studies at Harvard Divinity School at the time of this conference, is now assistant professor of theological studies at Loyola Marymount University, Los Angeles, California. She received her ThD from Harvard Divinity School and holds MA degrees from Catholic Theological Union and the University of Mumbai. She has been on the faculty at Harvard Divinity School since 2007 and has served as associate director of the Center for the Study of World Religions since 2010. She is author of *Identity, Ethics and Nonviolence in Postcolonial Theory: A Rahnerian Theological Assessment* (2007) and *Shoulder to Shoulder: Frontiers in Catholic Feminist Theology* (2009). She has also published numerous journal articles and book contributions.

John Behr is dean and professor of patristics at St. Vladimir's Orthodox Theological Seminary and distinguished lecturer at Fordham University. He received his DPhil degree in theology and an MPhil in Eastern Christian studies from Oxford University, and an MTh from St. Vladimir's Orthodox Theological Seminary. One of the most outstanding patristics scholars writing today, he is the author of, among others, *The Way to Nicaea* (2001), *The Nicene Faith* (2004), *The Mystery of Christ: Life in Death* (2006), *The Case Against Diodore and Theodore: Texts and Their Contexts* (2011), and *Irenaeus of Lyons: Identifying Christianity* (2013), in addition to editing numerous patristic texts.

Marlene Block is a PhD candidate in religion at Claremont Graduate University.

Fabrizio D'Ambrosio is a PhD candidate in religion at Claremont Graduate University.

James Fredericks is professor of theological studies at Loyola Marymount University in Los Angeles, California. He holds the PhD from the University of Chicago; an STL from the Jesuit School of Theology, Berkeley, California; and an MA from St. Patrick's Seminary in Menlo Park, California. He has lectured internationally, has been a Senior Fulbright Research Scholar in Kyoto, Japan, and held the Numata Chair in Buddhism and Culture at Ryukoku University in Kyoto. A specialist in interreligious dialogue, he is the author of *Faith Among Faiths: Christian Theology and the Non-Christian Religions* (1999) and *Buddhists and Christians: Through Comparative Theology to a New Solidarity* (2004), as well as numerous journal articles.

Kirsten Gerdes is a PhD candidate in religion at Claremont Graduate University.

Rhys Kuzmic is a PhD candidate in religion at Claremont Graduate University.

Paul Miller is a PhD candidate in religion at Claremont Graduate University.

Anselm Min is Maguire Distinguished Professor of Religion, Claremont Graduate University, Claremont, California. He received the PhD in philosophy from Fordham University and the PhD in religion from Vanderbilt University. He has been teaching in the area of philosophy of religion and theology at Claremont since 1992. He is the author of *Korean Catholicism in the 1970s* (co-authored, 1975), *Dialectic of Salvation: Issues in Theology of Liberation* (1989), *The Solidarity of Others in a Divided World: A Postmodern Theology After Postmodernism* (2004), and *Paths to the Triune God: An Encounter Between Aquinas and Recent Theologies* (2005). He has also published numerous articles on a wide range of topics from Hegel and Aquinas to Christology and trinitarian theology to issues of liberation, interreligious dialogue, pluralism, and globalization, to postmodern and Asian theologies.

Joseph Prabhu is professor of philosophy at California State University, Los Angeles. He has held visiting professorships at the University of Chicago; University of California, Berkeley; Graduate Theological Union; and Harvard University, among others. He has served as president of the Society of Asian and Comparative Philosophy and program chair of the Philosophy of Religion section of the American Academy of Religion. He now serves on the board of trustees for the Council for the Parliament of the World's Religions.

He is editor of *The Intercultural Challenge of Raimon Panikkar* (1996), and *Indian Ethics: Classical Traditions and Contemporary Challenges*, volume 1 (co-edited with P. Bilimoria, 2007). He has published numerous journal articles and book contributions on Panikkar, Gandhi, Indian and comparative philosophy, and Hegel studies.

Rosemary Radford Ruether is visiting professor of religion at Claremont Graduate University and Claremont School of Theology. She is the Carpenter Emerita Professor of Feminist Theology at the Pacific School of Religion and the Graduate Theological Union as well as the Georgia Harkness Emerita Professor of Applied Theology at Garrett Evangelical Theological Seminary. She received the MA and PhD from the Claremont Graduate School. One of the most prolific feminist thinkers of our time, she has published, among others, *Sexism and God-Talk* (1984), *Faith and Fratricide* (1996), *Women and Redemption* (1998), *The Wrath of Jonah: The Crisis of Religious Nationalism in the Israeli-Palestinian Conflict* (1998, 2002), *Goddess and the Divine Feminine* (2005), *Integrating Ecofeminism, Globalization, and World Religions* (2005), and *Christianity and Social Systems* (2009), not to speak of countless journal articles and book contributions.

Robert Schreiter is Vatican II Professor of Theology at Catholic Theological Union, Chicago. He holds a TheolDr from the University of Nijmegen. He has held guest professorships at universities in Germany and the Netherlands and is past president of the American Society of Missiology and the Catholic Theological Society of America. Among his numerous books are *Constructing Local Theologies* (1985), *Reconciliation: Mission and Ministry in a Changing Social Order* (1992), *The New Catholicity: Theology Between the Global and the Local* (1997), *The Ministry of Reconciliation: Spirituality and Strategies* (1998), *In Water and in Blood: A Spirituality of Solidarity and Hope* (2007), and *Mission as Ministry of Reconciliation* (ed., 2013). He has also published numerous journal articles and book chapters. His publications have appeared in twenty languages.

Francis Schüssler Fiorenza is Charles Chauncey Stillman Professor of Roman Catholic Theological Studies at Harvard Divinity School. He holds a DTheol from the University of Münster, an MDiv from St. Mary's University and Seminary, and a DD, *honoris causa*, from St. Mary's University and Seminary. In addition to more than 150 essays in the areas of fundamental theology, hermeneutics, and political theology, his publications include *Foundational Theology: Jesus and the Church* (1992), *Systematic Theology: Roman Catholic Perspectives* (edited with John Galvin, 2011), *Habermas, Modernity, and Public Theology* (edited with Don Browning, 1992), and *Modern Christian Thought*, volume 2, *The Twentieth Century* (written with James Livingston, 2006).

Mark Lewis Taylor is Maxwell M. Upson Professor of Theology and Culture at Princeton Theological Seminary. He holds the PhD from the University of Chicago and an MDiv from Union Theological Seminary in Virginia. In addition to numerous articles his works include *Remembering Esperanza: A Cultural Political Theology for North American Praxis* (1990), *The Executed God: The Way of the Cross in Lockdown America* (2001), *Religion, Politics, and the Christian Right: Post-9/11 Politics and American Empire* (2005), and *The Theological and the Political: On the Weight of the World* (2011). He is a frequent teacher and lecturer in the Presbyterian Church, supporting efforts to organize around justice and peace issues. He is also involved in studies in Guatemala and Mexico, and is coordinator for Educators for Mumia Abu-Jamal.

William A. Walker III is a PhD candidate in religion at Claremont Graduate University.

Mark I. Wallace is professor of religion at Swarthmore College. He holds the PhD from the University of Chicago, where he studied under Paul Ricoeur. His books include *The Second Naïveté: Barth, Ricoeur, and the New Yale Theology* (1990), *Fragments of the Spirit: Nature, Violence, and the Renewal of Creation* (1996), *Finding God in the Singing River: Christianity, Spirit, Nature* (2005), and *Green Christianity* (2010). He is also editor of Paul Ricoeur's *Figuring the Sacred: Religion, Narrative, and Imagination* (1995) and co-editor of *Curing Violence: Essays on René Girard* (1994). He has published numerous journal articles and book chapters and recently received an Andrew W. Mellon New Directions Fellowship for a research sabbatical in Costa Rica.

Selected Bibliography

Abraham, Susan. *Identity, Ethics, and Nonviolence in Postcolonial Theory: A Rahnerian Theological Assessment.* New York: Palgrave, 2007.

Abram, David. *Becoming Animal: An Earthly Cosmology.* New York: Vintage, 2010.

Adorno, Theodor. *The Culture Industry.* New York: Routledge, 1991.

Alexander, Michelle. *The New Jim Crow: Mass Incarceration in the Age of Colorblindness.* New York: The New Press, 2010.

Arbuckle, Gerald. *Culture, Inculturation, and Theologians: A Postmodern Critique.* Collegeville, MN: Liturgical Press, 2010.

Armour, Ellen. "Toward an Elemental Theology." In *Theology That Matters,* edited by Darby Kathleen Ray. Minneapolis, MN: Fortress Press, 2006.

Ashcroft, Bill, Gareth Griffiths, and Helen Tiffin. *The Empire Writes Back: Theory and Practice in Postcolonial Literatures.* London: Routledge, 1989.

Audi, Robert. *Democratic Authority and the Separation of Church and State.* New York: Oxford University Press, 2011.

———. "Liberal Democracy and Religion in Politics." In *Religion in the Public Square: The Place of Religious Convictions in Political Debate,* edited by Robert Audi and Nicholas Wolterstorff. New York: Rowman and Littlefield, 1997.

———. *Religious Commitment and Secular Reason.* Cambridge: Cambridge University Press, 2000.

Auerbach, Eric. *Mimesis: The Representation of Reality in Western Literature* Princeton, NJ: Princeton University Press, 1953.

Baldwin, James. *The Fire Next Time.* New York: Modern Library, 1962, 1995.

Balthasar, Hans Urs von. *Cordula. Oder: Der Ernstfall.* Einsiedeln: Johannes Verlag, 1966.

Barth, Karl. *Church Dogmatics I.1: The Doctrine of the Word of God.* New York: T & T Clark 2004 <1936>.

———. *Church Dogmatics III.4: The Doctrine of Creation.* New York: T & T Clark, 1978 <1961>.

———. *The Epistle to the Romans.* Trans. Edwyn C. Hoskins from the 6th German ed. Oxford: Oxford University Press, 1933.

Bauckham, Richard. *The Bible and Ecology: Rediscovering the Community of Creation.* Waco, TX: Baylor University Press, 2010.

Bauer, Walter. *Orthodoxy and Heresy in Earliest Christianity*. Edited by Robert A. Kraft and Gerhard Knodel. Philadelphia: Fortress Press, 1971.

Behr, John. *Irenaeus of Lyons: Identifying Christianity*. Oxford: Oxford University Press, 2013.

———. *The Way to Nicaea*, Formation of Christian Theology, vol. 1. Crestwood, NY: SVS Press, 2001.

———. "What Are We Doing Speaking About God: The Discipline of Theology." In *Thinking Through Faith: New Perspectives from Orthodox Christian Scholars*, edited by Aristotle Papanikolaou and Elizabeth H. Prodromou. Crestwood, NY: SVS Press, 2008.

Benestad, J. Brian. "Doctrinal Perspectives on the Church in the Modern World." In *Vatican II: Renewal Within Tradition*, edited by Matthew Levering and Matthew Lamb. New York: Oxford University Press, 2008.

Bergmann, Sigurd, and Dieter Gerten, eds. *Religion in Environmental and Climate Change: Suffering, Values, Lifestyles*. New York: Continuum, 2012.

Berry, Thomas. *The Great Work: Our Way into the Future*. New York: Bell Tower, 1999.

Betcher, Sharon. "Grounding the Spirit: An Ecofeminist Pneumatology." In *Ecospirit: Religions and Philosophies for the Earth*, edited by Laurel Kearns and Catherine Keller. New York: Fordham University Press, 2007.

———. *Spirit and the Politics of Disablement*. Minneapolis, MN: Fortress Press, 2007.

Bhabha, Homi. *The Location of Culture*. London: Routledge, 1994.

Bird, Phyllis. "'Male and Female He Created Them': Gen 1:27b in the Context of the Priestly Account of Creation." In *Image of God and Gender Models in the Judaeo-Christian Tradition*, edited by Kari Borresen. Minneapolis, MN: Fortress Press, l994.

Boff, Leonardo. *Church: Charism and Power: Liberation Theology and the Institutional Church*. New York: Crossroad, 1985.

Bonilla-Silva, Eduardo. *Racism Without Racists: Color-Blind Racism and Racial Inequality in Contemporary America*. 3rd ed. Lanham, MD: Rowman and Littlefield, 2010.

Bonino, José Míguez. *Doing Theology in a Revolutionary Situation*. Philadelphia: Fortress Press, 1975.

———. "Reading Jürgen Moltmann from Latin American." *The Asbury Theological Journal* 55 (Spring 200): 105–14.

Borg, Marcus, and John Dominic Crossan. *The Last Week: What the Gospels Really Teach About Jesus' Final Days in Jerusalem*. New York: HarperOne, 2007.

Bourdieu, Pierre. *The Logic of Practice*. Stanford, CA: Stanford University Press, 1990.

———. *Masculine Domination.* Translated by Richard Nice. Stanford, CA: Stanford University Press, 2001.

Brakke, David. *The Gnostics: Myth, Ritual, and Diversity in Early Christianity.* Cambridge, MA: Harvard University Press, 2010.

Brockman, John, ed. *Is the Internet Changing the Way You Think?* New York: Harper, 2011.

Brown, Candy Gunther, ed. *Global Pentecostal and Charismatic Healing.* New York: Oxford University Press, 2011.

Butler, Judith. *Frames of War: When Is Life Grievable?* New York: Verso, 2009.

———, Jürgen Habermas, Charles Taylor, and Cornel West. *The Power of Religion in the Public Sphere.* New York: Columbia University Press, 2011.

Calhoun, Craig, Mark Juergensmeyer, and Jonathan van Antwerpen, eds. *Rethinking Secularism.* New York: Oxford University Press, 2011.

Caputo, John D. *St. Paul Among the Philosophers.* Indianapolis: University of Indiana Press, 2009.

Casey, Shaun A. *The Making of a Catholic President: Kennedy vs. Nixon 1960.* New York: Oxford University Press, 2009.

Castells, Manuel. *Communication Power.* New York: Oxford University Press, 2009.

Cavanaugh, William T. "'A Fire Strong Enough to Consume the House': The Wars of Religion and the Rise of the State," *Modern Theology* 11/4 (October 1995): 397–420.

———. *Theopolitical Imagination: Discovering the Liturgy as a Political Act in an Age of Global Consumerism.* London: Continuum, 2002.

Césaire, Aimé. *Discourse on Colonialism.* Translated by Joan Pinkham. New York: Monthly Review Press, 1955, 2000.

Chaput, Charles J. *A Heart of Fire.* New York: Image, 2012.

———. *Render unto Caesar: Serving the Nation by Living Our Catholic Beliefs in Political Life.* New York: Doubleday, 2008.

Chenu, M.-D. "Les signes des temps." *Nouvelle Revue Théologique* 87 (1965): 29–39.

Chestnut, R. Andrew. *Born Again in Brazil.* New Brunswick, NJ: Rutgers University Press, 1997.

Chow, Rey. *The Age of the World Target: Self-Referentiality in War, Theory, and Comparative Work.* Durham, NC: Duke University Press, 2006.

Clanton, J. Caleb. *The Ethics of Citizenship: Liberal Democracy and Religious Convictions.* Waco, TX: Baylor University, 2009.

Cone, James H. "Whose Earth Is It Anyway?" *Cross Currents* 50/1–2 (2000).

Congar, Yves. *Lay People in the Church.* London: Geoffrey, 1959.

———. *The Meaning of Tradition.* San Francisco: Ignatius, 2004 <1964>.

———. Consiglio Pontificio de la Cultura. *Fede e cultura.* Vatican City: Libreria Editrice Vaticana, 2003.

Cornille, Catherine. *Many Mansions? Multiple Religious Belonging and Christian Identity.* Eugene, OR: Wipf and Stock, 2002.

Corten, André. *Pentecostalism in Brazil: Emotion of the Poor and Theological Romanticism.* New York: MacMillan Press, 1999.

Cox, Harvey. *Fire from Heaven: The Rise of Pentecostal Spirituality and the Reshaping of Religion in the Twenty-first Century.* New York: Da Capo Press, 1995.

Cummings, Bruce. *The Origins of the Korean War: Liberation and the Emergence of Separate Regimes, 1945–1947.* Princeton, NJ: Princeton University Press, 1981.

Cunningham, David S. *Faithful Persuasion: In Aid of a Rhetoric of Christian Theology.* Notre Dame, IN: University of Notre Dame Press, 1991.

Cuomo, Mario. *More Than Words: The Speeches of Mario Cuomo.* New York: St. Martin's Press, 1993.

Curry, Patrick. "Grizzly Man and the Spiritual Life." *Journal for the Study of Religion, Nature, and Culture* 4 (2010).

Daly, Herman E., and John B. Cobb, Jr. *For the Common Good: Redirecting the Economy toward Community, the Environment, and a Sustainable Future.* 2d. ed. Boston: Beacon, 1994 <1989>.

Derrida, Jacques. *Specters of Marx: The State of the Debt, the Work of Mourning, and the New International.* Translated by Peggy Kamuf. New York: Routledge, 1994.

Di Stasi, Lawrence. *Una Storia Segreta: The Secret History of Italian American Evacuation and Internment During World War II.* Berkeley, CA: Heyday Books, 2004.

Donziger, Steven R., ed. *The Real War on Crime.* The National Report of the National Criminal Justice Commission. New York: HarperPerennial, 1996.

Doyle, Michael. *Empires.* Ithaca, NY: Cornell University Press, 1986.

Du Bois, W. E. B. *Darkwater: Voices from Within the Veil.* New York: Dover, 1999 <1920>.

Dulin, Rachel Zohar. *Old Age in the Hebrew Scriptures.* PhD thesis, Northwestern University, 1982.

Dussel, Enrique. *Beyond Philosophy: Ethics, History, Marxism, and Liberation Theology.* Edited by Eduardo Mendieta. New York: Rowan and Littlefield, 2003.

Eagleton, Terry. *The Illusions of Postmodernism.* Cambridge, MA: Blackwell, 1996.

Easwaran, Eknath. *Nonviolent Soldier of Islam: Badshah Khan, A Man to Match His Mountains.* Tomales, CA: Nilgiri Press, 1999.

Edwards, Denis. "For Your Immortal Spirit Is in All Things." In *Faith Revealing – Earth Healing: Ecology and Christian Theology,* edited by Denis Edwards. Collegeville, MN: Liturgical Press, 2001.

Ehrman, Bart D. *Lost Christianities: The Battles for Scripture and the Faiths We Never Knew.* Oxford: Oxford University Press, 2003.

Escobar, Arturo. *Encountering Development: The Making and Unmaking of the Third World.* Princeton, NJ: Princeton University Press, 1995.

Fanon, Frantz. *Black Skin, White Masks.* New edition. Translated by Richard Philcox. New York: Grove Press, 2008 <1952>.

———. *The Wretched of the Earth.* New edition. Translated by Richard Philcox. New York: Grove Press, 2004 <1964>.

Farley, Edward. *Theologia: The Fragmentation and Unity of Theological Education.* Philadelphia: Fortress Press, 1983.

Feldman, Noah. *Divided by God: America's Church-State Problem and What We Should Do About It.* New York: Farrar, Straus, and Giroux, 2005.

Fiorenza, Elisabeth Schüssler. *Jesus: Miriam's Child, Sophia's Prophet.* New York: Continuum, 1994.

———. *The Power of the Word: Scripture and the Rhetoric of Empire.* Minneapolis, MN: Fortress Press, 2007.

Fiorenza, Francis Schüssler. "Christian Redemption Between Colonialism and Pluralism." In *Reconstructing Christian Theology,* edited by Rebecca Chopp and Mark Taylor. Minneapolis, MN: Fortress Press, 1994.

———. "The Church as a Community of Interpretation: Political Theology Between Discourse Ethics and Hermeneutical Reconstruction." In *Habermas, Modernity, and Public Theology,* edited by Don S. Browning and Francis Schüssler Fiorenza. New York: Crossroad, 1992.

———. "Marriage." In *Systematic Theology: Roman Catholic Perspectives,* edited by Francis Schüssler Fiorenza and John Galvin. Minneapolis, MN: Fortress Press, 2011.

———. "Political Theology and Modernity: Facing the Challenges of the Present." In *Distinktion* 10 (2005): 87–105.

———. "Politische Theologie und liberale Gerechtigkeits-Konzeption." In *Mystik und Politik: Johann Baptist Metz zu Ehren,* edited by Eduard Schillebeeckx. Mainz: Matthias Grünewald, 1988.

———. "Prospects for Political Theology in the Face of Contemporary Challenges." In *Politische Theologie: Neuere Geschichte und Potenziale,* edited by Michael Welker. Neukirchen-Vluyn: Neukirchener, 2011.

Fisher, Eran. *Media and New Capitalism in the Digital Age: The Spirit of Networks.* New York: Palgrave, 2010.

Fletcher, Jeannine Hill. *Monopoly on Salvation? A Feminist Approach to Religious Pluralism.* New York: Continuum, 2005.

Fredricksen, Paula. *Jesus of Nazareth, King of the Jews: A Jewish Life and the Emergence of Christianity.* New York: Knopf, 1999.

Garman, Bryan K. *A Race of Singers: Whitman's Working Class Hero from Guthrie to Springsteen.* Greensboro: University of North Carolina Press, 2000.

Gebara, Ivone. *Teología a Ritmo de Mujer.* Madrid: San Pablo, 1995.

———. "The Trinity and Human Experience." In *Women Healing Earth: Third World Women on Ecology, Feminism, and Religion,* edited by Rosemary Radford Ruether. Maryknoll, NY: Orbis Books, 1996.

Gilkey, Langdon. "Plurality and Its Theological Implications." In *The Myth of Christian Uniqueness: Toward a Pluralistic Theology of Religions,* edited by John Hick and Paul Knitter, 37–52. Maryknoll, NY: Orbis Books, 1987.

Gilmore, Ruth Wilson. *Golden Gulag: Prisons, Surplus, Crisis, and Opposition in Globalizing California.* Berkeley and Los Angeles: University of California Press, 2007.

Gnanadason, Aruna. "The Integrity of Creation and Earth Community: An Ecumenical Response to Environmental Racism." *Union Seminary Quarterly Review* 58/1–2 (2004).

Gordon, Avery F. *Ghostly Matters: Haunting and the Sociological Imagination.* Minneapolis: University of Minnesota Press, 1997.

Gordon, Linda, and Gary Okihiro, eds. *Impounded: Dorothea Lange and the Censored Images of Japanese-American Internment.* New York: W. W. Gordon, 2008.

Gottlieb, Roger S. *A Greener Faith: Religious Environmentalism and Our Planet's Future.* Oxford: Oxford University Press, 2006.

Grau, Marion. *Rethinking Mission in the Postcolony: Salvation, Society, and Subversion.* New York: T & T Clark, 2011.

Grimke, Sarah. "Letters on the Equality of the Sexes and the Condition of Women" (1837). In *Feminism: The Essential Historical Writings,* edited by Miriam Schneir. New York: Vintage, 1992.

Grudem, Wayne. *Evangelical Feminism and Biblical Truth: An Analysis of More than 100 Disputed Questions.* Colorado Springs, CO: Multnomah, 2004.

Guder, Darrell. "Reformed Confessions and Confessing Church—Interview with Eberhard Busch." In *The Presbyterian Outlook* (May 14, 2002), 22–28.

Habel, Norman C. "Introducing the Earth Bible." In *Readings from the Perspective of Earth,* edited by Norman C. Habel. Vol. 1 of *The Earth Bible.* Sheffield, England: Sheffield, 2000.

——, and Peter Trudinger, eds. *Exploring Ecological Hermeneutics.* Atlanta: Society of Biblical Literature, 2008.

Habermas, Jürgen. *An Awareness of What Is Missing: Faith and Reason in a Post-Secular Age.* Malden, MA: Polity, 2010.

——. *Between Naturalism and Religion.* Malden, MA: Polity, 2008.

——. *The Inclusion of the Other.* Edited by Ciaran Cronin and Pablo De Greiff. Cambridge, MA: MIT, 1998.

——. *Postmetaphysical Thinking. Philosophical Essays.* Cambridge, MA: MIT, 1993.

——. "Replik auf Einwände, Reaktion auf Anregungen." In *Symposium mit Jürgen Habermas,* edited by Rudolf Langthaler and Herta Nagl-Docekal. Glauben und Wissen. Oldenbourg: Akademie, 2007.

——, and Joseph Ratzinger. *The Dialectics of Secularization: On Reason and Religion.* San Francisco: Ignatius, 2006.

Haidt, Jonathan. *The Righteous Mind: Why Good People Are Divided by Politics and Religion.* New York: Free Press, 2012.

Hanh, Thich Nhat. *Living Buddha, Living Christ.* New York: Riverhead, 1995.

Hanson, R. P. C. "Achievement of Orthodoxy." In *The Making of Orthodoxy: Essays in Honour of Henry Chadwick,* edited by R. Williams. Cambridge, MA: Cambridge University Press, 1989.

———. *The Search for the Christian Doctrine of God: The Arian Controversy, 318–381.* Edinburgh: T & T Clark, 1988.

Haraway, Donna. "A Cyborg Manifesto." In *Transgender Studies Reader,* edited by Susan Stryker and Stephen White. New York: Routledge, 2006.

Hardt, Michael, and Antonio Negri. *Empire.* Cambridge, MA: Harvard University Press, 2000.

Harper, Graeme. *Colonial and Postcolonial Incarceration.* New York: Continuum, 2001.

Harvey, David. *The New Imperialism.* New York: Oxford University Press, 2003.

Harvey, Graham. "Animism—A Contemporary Perspective." In *The Encyclopedia of Religion and Nature,* edited by Bron Taylor. 2 vols. New York: Continuum, 2005.

Harvey, Susan Ashbrook. "Feminine Imagery for the Divine: The Holy Spirit, the Odes of Solomon, and Early Syriac Tradition." *Saint Vladimir's Theological Quarterly* 37 (1993): 111–40.

Hedges, Chris. *Empire of Illusion: The End of Literacy and the Triumph of Spectacle.* New York: Nation Books, 2009.

Hehir, Bryan. "The Idea of a Political Theology." *Worldview* 14 (January 1971): 5–7 and (February 1971): 5–7, 31.

Heidegger, Martin. *Martin Heidegger: Basic Writings.* Revised and expanded edition. Edited by David Farrell Krell. San Francisco: HarperCollins, 1993.

Hick, John. *The Myth of God Incarnate.* London: SCM, 1977.

Horkheimer, Max, and Theodore Adorno. *Dialectic of Enlightenment.* Revised translation. Stanford, CA: Stanford University Press, 2007.

Hyun-Kyung, Chung. "Welcome the Spirit; Hear Her Cries: The Holy Spirit, Creation, and the Culture of Life." *Christianity and Crisis* 51 (July 15, 1991): 220–23.

Ignatieff, Michael. *American Exceptionalism and Human Rights.* Princeton, NJ: Princeton University Press, 2005.

Isichei, Elizabeth. *A History of Christianity in Africa.* Grand Rapids, MI: Eerdmanns, 1995.

Jenkins, Philip. *The Next Christendom: The Coming of Global Christianity.* New York: Oxford University Press, 2002.

Joas, Hans. *Glaube als Option: Zukunftsmöglichkeiten des Christentums.* Freiburg: Herder, 2012.

Johnson, Elizabeth A. *She Who Is: The Mystery of God in Feminist Theological Discourse.* New York: Crossroad, 1992.

Kaiser, David, and Lovisa Stannow. "Prison Rape and the Government." *The New York Review of Books.* March 24, 2011.

Kao, Grace Y. *Grounding Human Rights in a Pluralist World.* Washington, DC: Georgetown University Press, 2011.

———. "The Universal Versus the Particular in Ecofeminist Ethics." *Journal of Religious Ethics* 38/4 (2010).

Keller, Catherine. *Face of the Deep: A Theology of Becoming.* London: Routledge, 2003.

King, Karen. *What Is Gnosticism?* Cambridge, MA: Belknap Press of Harvard University Press, 2003.

———. "Which Early Christianity?" In *The Oxford Handbook of Early Christian Studies,* edited by Susan Ashbrook Harvey and David G. Hunters. Oxford: Oxford University Press, 2008.

King, Martin Luther, Jr. *Testament of Hope: The Essential Writings and Speeches of Martin Luther King, Jr.* Edited by James M. Washington. New York: HarperSanFrancisco, 1986.

Kinkel, Gary Steven. *Our Dear Mother the Spirit: An Investigation of Count Zinzendorf's Theology and Praxis.* Lanham, MD: University Press of America, 1990.

Kugel, J. L. *Traditions of the Bible: A Guide to the Bible as It Was at the Start of the Common Era.* Cambridge, MA: Harvard University Press, 1998.

Küng, Hans. "A Vatican Spring?" *The New York Times.* February 27, 2013.

Lampe, Peter. *From Paul to Valentinus: Christians at Rome in the First Two Centuries.* Minneapolis, MN: Fortress Press, 2003.

Lasch, Christopher. *The Culture of Narcissism: American Life in an Age of Diminishing Expectations.* New York: W. W. Norton, 1979.

Layton, Bentley. "Prolegomena to the Study of Ancient Gnosticism." In *The Social World of the First Christians: Essays in Honor of Wayne A. Meeks,* edited by L. Michael White and O. Larry Yarbrough. Minneapolis, MN: Fortress Press, 1995.

Lederach, John Paul. *The Moral Imagination: The Art and Soul of Building Peace.* New York: Oxford University Press, 2005.

Lerner, Michael. *The Left Hand of God: Taking Back Our Country from the Religious Right.* San Francisco: HarperSanFrancisco, 2006.

Lessing, Gotthold. *Lessing: Philosophical and Theological Writings,* edited by H. B. Nisbet. Cambridge Texts in the History of Philosophy. Cambridge, MA: Cambridge University Press, 2005.

Lieu, Judith M. *Christian Identity in the Jewish and Graeco-Roman World.* Oxford: Oxford University Press, 2004.

Lind, Michael. *The Next American Nation: The New Nationalism and the Fourth American Revolution.* New York: Free Press, 1995.

Linebaugh, Peter, and Marcus Rediker. *The Many-Headed Hydra: Sailors, Slaves, Commoners, and the Hidden History of the Revolutionary Atlantic.* Boston: Beacon, 2000.

Lipsitz, George. *The Possessive Investment in Whiteness: How White People Profit from Identity Politics.* Philadelphia: Temple University Press, 1998.

Logan, James Samuel. *Good Punishment? Christian Moral Practice and US Imprisonment.* Grand Rapids, MI: Eerdmans, 2008.

Lopez, Davina C. *Apostle to the Conquered: Reimagining Paul's Mission.* Minneapolis, MN: Fortress Press, 2010.

Lorentzen, Lois Ann. "Indigenous Feet: Ecofeminism, Globalization, and the Case of Chiapas." In *Ecofeminism and Globalization: Exploring Culture, Context, and Religion,* edited by Heather Eaton and Lois Ann Lorentzen. Lanham, MD: Rowman and Littlefield, 2003.

Lowe, Walter. *Theology and Difference: The Wound of Reason.* Bloomington: Indiana University Press, 1993.

Lubac, Henri de. *Christian Resistance to Anti-Semitism: Memories from 1940–1944.* San Francisco: Ignatius, 1990.

Lübbe, Hermann. *Säkularisierung: Geschichte eines ideenpolitischen Begriffs.* Freiburg: K. Alber, 1965.

Lyman, Rebecca. "Hellenism and Heresy." *Journal of Early Christian Studies* 11 (2003): 209–22.

MacDonald, Dennis R. *The Legend and the Apostle: The Battle for Paul in Story and Canon.* Philadelphia: Westminister Press, 1983.

Maier, Hans. *Kritik der politischen Theologie.* Einsiedeln: Johannes-Verlag, 1970.

Maritain, Jacques. *Man and State.* Chicago: University of Chicago, 1951.

Massa, Mark S. "A Catholic for President? John F. Kennedy and the 'Secular' Theology of the Houston Speech, 1960." *Journal of Church and State* (Spring 1997): 297–318.

Mauer, Marc. *Invisible Punishment: The Collateral Consequences of Mass Imprisonment.* New York: The New Press, 2003.

McChesney, Robert W. *Digital Disconnect: How Capitalism Is Turning the Internet Against Democracy.* New York: The New Press, 2013.

McCoy, Alfred W. *A Question of Torture: CIA Interrogation, from the Cold War to the War on Terror.* New York: Metropolitan Books, 2006.

McDaniel, Jay. *Of God and Pelicans: A Theology of Reverence for Life.* Louisville, KY: Westminister/John Knox Press, 1989.

McFague, Sallie. *The Body of God: An Ecological Theology.* Minneapolis, MN: Fortress Press, 1993.

McGowan, William. *Coloring the News: How Political Correctness Has Corrupted American Journalism.* San Francisco: Encounter, 2002.

———. *Gray Lady Down: What the Decline and Fall of the New York Times Means for America.* New York: Encounter, 2010.

McGraw, Bryan T. *Faith in Politics: Religion and Liberal Democracy.* Cambridge, MA: Cambridge University Press, 2010.

McKibben, Bill. *The End of Nature.* New York: Random, 1989.

Megivern, James J. *The Death Penalty: An Historical and Theological Survey.* New York: Paulist Press, 1997.

Mendelson, Isaac, ed. *Religion in the Ancient Near East.* New York: Liberal Arts Press, 1955.

Merton, Thomas. *New Seeds of Contemplation.* New York: New Directions, 1961.

Metz, Johann Baptist. *Faith in History and Society.* New York: Seabury, 1980.

———. *Memoria Passionis.* Freiburg: Herder, 2006.

———. *Theology of the World.* New York: Herder and Herder, 1969.

Min, Anselm K. *The Solidarity of Others in a Divided World: A Postmodern Theology after Postmodernism.* New York: T & T Clark, 2004.

———. "Solidarity of Others in the Power of the Holy Spirit: Pneumatology in a Divided World." In *Advents of the Spirit: An Introduction to the Current Study of Pneumatology,* edited by Bradford E. Hinze and D. Lyle Dabney. Marquette, WI: Marquette University Press, 2001.

———. "Towards a Theology of Citizenship as the Central Challenge in Asia." *East Asian Pastoral Review* 41/2 (2004): 136–59.

Minh-Ha, Trinh T. *Woman, Native, Other: Writing Postcoloniality and Feminism.* Bloomington: Indiana University Press, 1989.

Mitchell, Margaret M. *Paul, the Corinthians, and the Birth of Christian Hermeneutics.* Cambridge, MA: Cambridge University Press, 2010.

Moltmann, Jürgen. *God in Creation: A New Theology of Creation and the Spirit of God.* Translated by Margaret Kohl. Minneapolis, MN: Fortress Press, 1993.

———. "An Open Letter to José Míguez Bonino." In *Liberation Theology: A Documentary History,* edited by Alfred Hennelly. Maryknoll, NY: Orbis Books, 1990.

———. *The Source of Life: The Holy Spirit and the Theology of Life.* Translated by Margaret Kohl. Minneapolis, MN: Fortress Press, 1997.

———. *Theology of Hope.* New York: Harper, 1967.

Moore, R. Laurence. *Selling God. American Religion in the Marketplace of Culture.* New York: Oxford University Press, 1994.

Müller-Fahrenholz, Geiko. *God's Spirit: Transforming a World in Crisis.* Translated by John Cumming. New York: Continuum, 1995.

Myers, Ched. *Binding the Strong Man: A Political Reading of Mark's Story of Jesus.* Maryknoll, NY: Orbis Books, 1997.

Newman, John Henry. *An Essay in Aid of a Grammar of Assent.* Oxford: Oxford University Press, 1985.

Niebuhr, Rienhold. *Children of Light and Children of Darkness: A Vindication of Democracy and a Critique of Its Traditional Defense.* Chicago: University of Chicago Press, 1944, 2011.

Nielsen, Marianne O., and Robert Silverman, eds. *American Indians in Prison.* Boulder, CO: Westview Press, 1996.

O'Malley, John W. *What Happened at Vatican II.* Cambridge, MA: Harvard University Press, 2008.

Okin, Susan Moller. *Justice, Gender, and Family.* New York: Basic Books, 1989.

Osborn, Eric. "Reason and the Rule of Faith in the Second Century." In *The Making of Orthodoxy: Essays in Honour of Henry Chadwick,* edited by R. Williams. Cambridge, MA: Cambridge University Press, 1989.

Oshinsky, David M. *"Worse Than Slavery": Parchman Farm and the Ordeal of Jim Crow Justice.* New York: The Free Press, 1997.

Park, Andrew Sung. *The Wounded Heart of God: The Asian Concept of Han and the Christian Doctrine of Sin.* Nashville, TN: Abingdon Press, 1993.

Pateman, Carole. *The Sexual Contract.* Stanford, CA: Stanford University Press, 1988.

———, and Charles Mills. *Contract and Domination.* Malden, MA: Polity, 2007.

Pelikan, Jaroslav. *The Christian Tradition: A History of the Development of Doctrine,* vol. 1: *The Emergence of the Catholic Tradition (100–600).* Chicago: University of Chicago Press, 1971.

Perreau-Saissome, Émile. *Catholicisme et démocratie.* Paris: Éditions du Cerf, 2011.

Petrella, Ivan. *The Future of Liberation Theology: An Argument and Manifesto.* Burlington, VT: Ashgate, 2004.

———. *Latin American Liberation Theology: The Next Generation.* Maryknoll, NY: Orbis Books, 2005.

Peukert, Helmut. *Diskussion zur Politischen Theologie.* Mainz: Matthias-Grünewald, 1969.

Pew Center. *One in 100: Behind Bars in America 2008.* Report of The Pew Center on the States. Washington, DC: The Pew Charitable Trusts, 2009.

Phan, Peter C. *Being Religious Interreligiously: Asian Perspectives on Interfaith Dialogue.* Maryknoll, NY: Orbis Books, 2004.

Pierce, Ronald W., and Rebecca Merrill Groothuis, eds. *Discovering Biblical Equality: Complementarity Without Hierarchy.* Grand Rapids, MI: Eerdmans, 2004.

Pieterse, Jan Nederveen. *Globalization and Culture: Global Melange.* Lanham, MD: Rowan and Littlefield, 2004.

Polio, Laura. *Black, Brown, Yellow, and Left: Radical Activism in Los Angeles.* Berkeley and Los Angeles: University of California Press, 2006.

Postman, Neil. *Amusing Ourselves to Death: Public Discourse in the Age of Show Business.* New York: Penguin, 1985.

Prashad, Vijay. "Bandung Is Done: Passages in AfroAsian Epistemology." In *AfroAsian Encounters: Culture, History, Politics,* edited by Heike Raphael-Hernandez and Shannon Steen. New York: New York University Press, 2006.

Putnam, Robert D. *Bowling Alone: The Collapse and Revival of American Community.* New York: Simon and Schuster, 2000.

———, and David E. Campbell. *American Grace: How Religion Divides and Unites Us.* New York: Simon and Schuster, 2010.

————, Robert Leonardi, and Raffaella Nanetti. *Making Democracy Work: Civic Traditions in Modern Italy*. Princeton, NJ: Princeton University Press, 1993.

Quarles, Chester L. *Christian Identity: The Aryan American Bloodline Religion*. Jefferson, NC: McFarland, 2004.

Quijano, Aníbal. "Coloniality of Power, Eurocentrism, and Latin America." *Napantla: Views from the South* 1/3 (2000): 533–78.

Rahner, Karl. *Politische Dimensionen des Christentums*. Edited by Herbert Vorgrimler. Munich: Kösel, 1986.

————. *Theological Investigations*. Volume 21, *Science and Christian Faith*. New York: Crossroad, 1983.

Rashid, Ahmed. *Descent into Chaos: The United States and the Failure of Nation Building in Pakistan, Afghanistan, and Central Asia*. New York: Viking, 2008.

Ratzinger, Joseph. *Theological Highlights of Vatican II*. New York: Paulist, 1966.

————. "Zur Theologie der Ehe." *Theologische Quartalschrift* (1969): 53–74.

————, and Hans Maier. *Demokratie in der Kirche: Möglicheiten, Grenzen, Gefahren*. Limburg: Lahn, 1970.

————, and Jürgen Habermas. *Dialectics of Secularization: On Reason and Religion*. San Francisco: Ignatius, 2006.

Rawls, John. *Political Liberalism*. New York: Columbia University, 1996.

Read, John Rupert. "Religion as Sedition: On Liberalism's Intolerance of Real Religion." *Ars Disputandi* 11 (2011): 83–100.

Reimarus, Hermann Samuel. *Reimarus: Fragments*. Edited by Charles H. Talbert. Translated by Ralph S. Fraser. Eugene, OR: Wipf and Stock, 2009.

Ricoeur, Paul. *The Conflict of Interpretations*. Evanston, IL: Northwestern University Press, 1974.

————. *The Rule of Metaphor: Multidisciplinary Studies of the Creation of Meaning in Language*. Translated by Robert Czerny with Kathleen McLaughlin and John Costello, SJ. Toronto: University of Toronto Press, 1977.

Rieff, Philip. *The Triumph of the Therapeutic: Uses of Faith After Freud*. Chicago: University of Chicago Press, 1987 <1966>.

Roberts, Elizabeth, and Elias Amidon, eds. "Now Talking God." In *Earth Prayers: From Around the World: 365 Prayers, Poems, and Invocations for Honoring the Earth*. San Francisco: HarperSanFrancisco, 1991.

Robinson, James M., and Helmut Koester. *Trajectories Through Early Christianity*. Philadelphia: Fortress Press, 1971.

Rousseau, Philip. *Pachomius: The Making of a Community in Fourth Century Egypt*. The Transformations of the Classical Heritage. Berkeley and Los Angeles: University of California Press, 1985.

Ruether, Rosemary Radford. *Gaia and God: An Ecofeminist Theology of Earth Healing*. San Francisco: HarperSanFrancisco, 1992.

————. *Women and Redemption: A Theological History*. Minneapolis, MN: Fortress Press, 1998.

————, and Dieter Hessel, eds. *Christianity and Ecology: Seeking the Well-Being of Earth and Humans*. Religions of the World and Ecology. Cambridge, MA: Harvard University Press, 2000.

Ruggieri, Giuseppe. "Zeichen der Zeit: Herkunft und Bedeutung einer christlichen-hermeneutischen Chiffre der Geschichte." In *Das Zweite Vatikanum und die Zeichen der Zeit heute*, edited by Peter Hünermann. Freiburg: Herder, 2006.

Rynne, Xavier. *Vatican Council II*. Maryknoll, NY: Orbis Books, 1999.

Sander, Hans-Joachim. "Theologischer Commentar zur Pastoralen Konstitution zur Kirche in der Welt von heute *Gaudium et spes*." In *Herders Theologischer Kommentar zum Zweiten Vaticanischen Konzil*, edited by Peter Hünermann and Bernd Joachim Hilberath. Freiburg: Herder Verlag, 2006.

Sanneh, Lamin O. *West African Christianity*. Maryknoll, NY: Orbis Books, 1983.

Schiller, Dan. *Digital Capitalism: Networking the Global Market System*. Cambrdige, MA: MIT Press, 2000.

Schreiter, Robert. *The New Catholicity: Theology Between the Global and the Local*. Maryknoll, NY: Orbis Books, 1997.

————. "Two Forms of Catholicity in a Time of Globalization." *Himig Ugnayan* 8 (2007): 1–17.

Schutz, Alfred. *On Phenomenology and Social Relations*. Chicago: University of Chicago Press, 1999.

Snyder, T. Richard. *The Protestant Ethic and the Spirit of Punishment*. Grand Rapids, MI: Eerdmans, 2001.

Spitale, Lennie. *Prison Ministry: Understanding Prison Culture Inside and Out*. Nashville, TN: Broadman and Holman, 2002.

Stark, Rodney. *The Rise of Christianity: A Sociologist Reconsiders History*. Princeton, NJ: Princeton University Press, 1996.

Steinfels, Peter. *A People Adrift: The Crisis of the Roman Catholic Church in America*. New York: Simon and Schuster, 2003.

Stout, Jeffrey. *Democracy and Tradition*. Princeton, NJ: Princeton University Press, 2005.

Stuckey, Priscilla. "Being Known by a Birch Tree: Animist Refigurations of Western Epistemology." *Journal for the Study of Religion, Nature, and Culture* 4 (2010).

Sturgeon, Noel. *Ecofeminist Natures: Race, Gender, Feminist Theory, and Political Action*. London: Routledge, 1997.

Sugirtharajah, R. S. *Postcolonial Reconfigurations: An Alternative Way of Reading the Bible and Doing Theology*. London: SCM Press, 2003.

Sung, Jung Mo. *Desire, Market, and Religion*. London: SCM Press, 2007.

Sykes, Stephen. *The Identity of Christianity: Theologians and the Essence of Christianity from Schleiermacher to Barth*. Philadelphia: Fortress Press, 1984.

Tanner, Kathryn. *Theories of Culture: A New Agenda for Theology*. Minneapolis, MN: Augsburg Fortress Press, 1997.

Taylor, Charles. *Dilemmas and Connections*. Cambridge, MA: Harvard University Press, 2010.

———. *A Secular Age*. Cambridge, MA: The Belknap Press of Harvard University Press, 2007.

Taylor, Mark Lewis. *The Executed God: The Way of the Cross in Lockdown America*. Minneapolis, MN: University of Minnesota Press, 2001.

———. *Religion, Politics, and the Christian Right: Post-9/11 Powers and American Empire*. Minneapolis, MN: Fortress Press, 2005.

———. *The Theological and the Political: On the Weight of the World*. Minneapolis, MN: Fortress Press, 2011.

Thiemann, Ron. *Religion in Public Life: A Dilemma for Democracy*. Washington, DC: Georgetown University Press, 1996.

Thoreau, Henry David. *The Heart of Thoreau's Journals*. Edited by Odell Shepard. New York: Dover, 1961.

———. "Walking." In *The Norton Book of American Nature Writing*, edited by John Elder and Robert Finch. New York: W. W. Norton, 1990.

Tilley, Terrence W. *Inventing Catholic Tradition*. Maryknoll, NY: Orbis Books, 2000.

Tillich, Paul. *Systematic Theology*. Three volumes in one. Chicago: University of Chicago Press, 1951.

Tracy, David. *The Analogical Imagination: Christian Theology and the Culture of Pluralism*. New York: Crossroad, 1998.

———. "Writing." In *Critical Terms for Religious Studies*, edited by Mark C. Taylor. Chicago: The University of Chicago Press, 1998.

———, Hans Küng, and Johann Metz, *Toward Vatican III: The Work That Needs to Be Done*. New York: Seabury, 1978.

Trang, Chim. "The Rising Song." In *Hauling Up the Morning/Izando la Mañana: Writings and Art by Political Prisoners of War in the United States*, edited by Tim Blunk and Raymond Luc Levasseur. Trenton, NJ: Red Sea Press, 1990.

Trible, Phyllis. "Depatriarchalizing in Biblical Interpretation." *Journal of the American Academy of Religion* 41/1 (March 1973): 30–48.

Turkle, Sherry. *Alone Together: Why We Expect More from Technology and Less from Each Other*. New York: Basic Books, 2011.

———. *Life on the Screen: Identity in the Age of the Internet*. New York: Simon and Schuster, 1995.

Twomey, Gerald S. *The "Preferential Option for the Poor" in Catholic Social Thought from John XXIII to John Paul II*. Lewiston, NY: Edwin Mellen, 2005.

Uelmen, Amelia. "'It's Hard Work': Reflections on Conscience and Citizenship in the Catholic Tradition." *Journal of Catholic Legal Studies* 47 (2008): 317–42.

Utz, Arthur Fridolin. *Glaube und demokratischer Pluralismus im wissenschaftlichen Werk von Joseph Kardinal Ratzinger.* Bonn: Scientia Humana Institut; Bonn: WBV, 1989.

Vattimo, Gianni. "Nihilism as Postmodern Christianity." In *Transcendence and Beyond: A Postmodern Inquiry,* edited by John D. Caputo and Michael J. Scanlon. Bloomington: Indiana University Press, 2007.

Verba, Sidney, Kay Lehman Schlozman, and Henry E. Brady. *Voice and Equality: Civic Voluntarism in American Politics.* Cambridge, MA: Harvard University Press, 1995.

Victorin-Vangerud, Nancy. *The Raging Hearth: Spirit in the Household of God.* St. Louis: Chalice, 2000.

Volf, Miroslav. *A Public Faith: How Followers of Christ Should Serve the Common Good.* Grand Rapids, MI: Brazos, 2011.

Wacquant, Loïc. *Prisons of Poverty.* Expanded edition. Minneapolis: University of Minnesota Press, 2009.

———. *Punishing the Poor: The Neoliberal Government of Social Insecurity.* Durham, NC: Duke University Press, 2009.

Wallace, Mark I. "Crum Creek Spirituality: Earth as a Living Sacrament." In *Theology That Matters: Ecology, Economy, and God,* edited by Darby Kathleen Ray. Minneapolis, MN: Fortress Press, 2006.

———. *Finding God in the Singing River: Christianity, Spirit, Nature.* Minneapolis, MN: Fortress Press, 2005.

———. *Green Christianity: Five Ways to a Sustainable Future.* Minneapolis, MN: Fortress Press, 2010.

Weithman, Paul. *Religion and the Obligations of Citizenship.* Cambridge, MA: Cambridge University Press, 2002.

———. *Why Political Liberalism? On John Rawls's Political Turn.* New York: Oxford University Press, 2011.

Welker, Michael. *God the Spirit.* Translated by John F. Hoffmeyer. Minneapolis, MN: Fortress Press, 1994.

Western, Bruce. *Punishment and Inequality in America.* New York: Russell Sage, 2006.

Whitman, James Q. *Harsh Justice: Criminal Punishment and the Widening Divide Between American and Europe.* New York: Oxford University Press, 2003.

Williams, Rowan. *On Christian Theology.* Oxford: Blackwell, 2000.

Wills, Charles. *The Racial Contract.* Ithaca, NY: Cornell University Press, 1997.

Wills, Garry. *Why Priests? A Failed Tradition.* New York: Viking Press, 2013.

Wingeier-Rayo, Philip D. *Where Are the Poor? A Comparison of the Ecclesial Base Communities and Pentecostalism — a Case Study in Cuernavaca, Mexico.* Eugene, OR: Pickwick Publications, 2011.

Wolterstorff, Nicholas. "The Role of Religion in Decision and Discussion of Political Issues." In *Religion in the Public Square: The Place of Religious*

Convictions in Political Debate, edited by Robert Audi and Nicholas Wolterstorff. New York: Rowman and Littlefield, 1997.

Wuthnow, Robert. *Christianity in the Twenty-first Century: Reflections on the Challenges Ahead.* New York: Oxford University Press, 1993.

Yong, Amos. *The Spirit of Creation: Modern Science and Divine Action in the Pentecostal-Charismatic Imagination.* Grand Rapids, MI: Eerdmans, 2011.

Young, Richard J. C. *Postcolonialism: An Historical Introduction.* New York: Blackwell. 2001.

Žižek, Slavoj. *The Fragile Absolute: Or, Why Is the Christian Legacy Worth Fighting For?* The Essential Zizek. New York: Verso, 2001.